Contemporary Perspectives on Revelation and Qur'ānic Hermeneutics

Contemporary Perspectives on Revelation and Qurʾānic Hermeneutics

An Analysis of Four Discourses

Ali Akbar

EDINBURGH
University Press

Edinburgh University Press is one of the leading university presses in the UK. We publish academic books and journals in our selected subject areas across the humanities and social sciences, combining cutting-edge scholarship with high editorial and production values to produce academic works of lasting importance. For more information visit our website: edinburghuniversitypress.com

Edinburgh University Press Ltd
The Tun – Holyrood Road
12 (2f) Jackson's Entry
Edinburgh EH8 8PJ

First published in hardback by Edinburgh University Press 2020

Typeset in 10.5/12.5 Times New Roman by
IDSUK (DataConnection) Ltd, and
printed and bound by CPI Group (UK) Ltd,
Croydon, CR0 4YY

A CIP record for this book is available from the British Library

ISBN 978 1 4744 5616 6 (hardback)
ISBN 978 1 4744 5617 3 (paperback)
ISBN 978 1 4744 5618 0 (webready PDF)
ISBN 978 1 4744 5619 7 (epub)

Contents

Acknowledgements

This book is a revised version of my PhD thesis, which I completed at the University of Melbourne in 2017. I am indebted to a number of people who assisted me throughout the process of writing my thesis. First and foremost, I would like to thank Professor Abdullah Saeed, my supervisor, who guided me through this project with patience, understanding and his invaluable advice. This book could not have been written without his endless support and help. With my deepest appreciation, I thank him. I would also like to express my gratitude to my committee members, Dr Muhammad Kamal and Dr Abdul-Samad Abdullah, for their support throughout this project. I am thankful to them for their insightful feedback and invaluable comments.

Some parts of this book have already been published in scholarly journals of Islamic and Middle Eastern studies. An earlier version of Chapter 4 was published in *Islam and Christian–Muslim Relations* (Vol. 28, No. 3, 2017) entitled ‘ʿAbdolkarim Soroush's Approach to "Experience" as a Basis for His Reform Project'. A shorter version of Chapter 5, except for the section ‘The sources of Shabestari's theory of revelation', was published in *Arabica* (Vol. 63, No. 6, 2016) under the title ‘A Contemporary Muslim Scholar's Approach to Revelation: Moḥammad Moǧtahed Šabestarī's Reform Project'. An earlier version of Chapter 6, except for the section ‘The sources of Abu Zayd's ideas about revelation', was published in *Islamic Quarterly* (Vol. 60, No. 2, 2016) entitled ‘From Revelation to Interpretation: Abu Zayd's Approach'. A few parts of the arguments presented in this book related to the political discourses of Abdolkarim Soroush, Muhammad Mujtahed Shabestari and Nasr Hamid Abu Zayd have been published in *Digest of Middle East Studies* (Vol. 25, No. 2, 2016) under the title ‘The Political Discourses of three Contemporary Muslim Scholars: Secular, Nonsecular, or Pseudosecular?'. And finally, some parts of the book related to the theories of revelation presented by Fazlur Rahman, Soroush, Shabestari and Abu Zayd have been published in *Culture and Religion* (Vol. 20, No. 1, 2019) under the title ‘Towards a Humanistic Approach to the Quran: New Direction in Contemporary Islamic Thought'. I would like to thank the editors of the aforementioned journals for giving me the permission to reproduce parts of my articles in this book.

I am also grateful to the anonymous external reviewers of Edinburgh University Press (EUP), whose comments significantly improved the manuscript. The staff at EUP deserve special thanks for their kind support for publishing this book. In particular, I am grateful to Nicola Ramsey, the publisher for EUP's Islamic & Middle Eastern Studies list, and Adela Rauchova, EUP's Commissioning Editor on modern Middle East and Arabic literature. Finally, I thank my family members, whose support and patience were essential to finish this work. Words cannot express my debt of gratitude to them.

Notes on Transliteration and Other Conventions

All Arabic and Persian words except personal names are transliterated according to the following table:

dh	(only Arabic words)	ذ
ṣ		ص
ṭ		ط
th		ث
gh		غ
kh		خ
ḥ		ح
ʾ		ء
ʿ		ع
q		ق
ā	Long vowel	ا
ī	Long vowel	ي
ū	Long vowel	و

Names are not transliterated but ʾ and ʿ are used to distinguish between the hamza and ʿayn respectively. All fully transliterated words from Arabic and Farsi, with the exception of the words Qurʾān and Sharīʿa, are italicised. All dates of pre-modern Muslim scholars' deaths are given both in Common Era and Islamic (AH) calendars, but the dates of modern Muslim scholars' deaths are only indicated in the Common Era.

1

Introduction

During the nineteenth century, the Muslim world came heavily under the influence of Western European ideas which had emerged during the Enlightenment. It was in this context that most Muslim reformists of the late nineteenth and early twentieth centuries turned to reinterpreting the primary sources of Islam, especially the Qurʾān, in light of 'the concern and needs of a modern society'.[1] A number of Muslim thinkers of this period, such as Jamal al-Din Afghani (d. 1897), Muhammad Abduh (d. 1905) and Rashid Rida (d. 1935), sought to bridge the gap between Islamic teachings and modern ideas, norms and institutions. As an example, Rashid Rida considered 'democratic civility' a reproduction of the institutions of *shūrā* (consultation) and *ijmāʿ* (consensus), and concluded that Western-style democracy has its equivalent in *shūrā*.[2] This line of thought is often identified as 'liberal Islam' in the sense that it is 'concerned with the reconstruction of belief in response to contemporary culture'.[3]

During the second half of the twentieth century and up to the early twenty-first century, a number of innovative hermeneutical approaches, often situated under the umbrella of contextualisation, emerged in Muslim exegetical discourse. These approaches often emerged in response to the exegetical discourses of literalism/textualism. Without going into extensive detail at this stage, literalism/textualism refers generally to the idea that the literal meaning of the text is privileged over other forms of meaning in the process of interpretation.[4] As Abdullah Saeed notes, textualist scholars 'consider the literal meaning to be the basis for the exploration of the meaning of the text', and interpret the Qurʾān by relying mainly on the linguistic sources and 'observable features of language' rather than referring to the historical context in which the text emerged. Indeed, textual literalism often diminishes the relevance of historical context for understanding the meaning of the Qurʾān.[5] The result of this approach is an emphasis on the immutability of the Qurʾān's teachings on socio-legal issues, which means that the majority of such teachings should be applied for all times and places.[6]

The focus of many reformist discourses in the past few decades was to establish principles for reform based upon new hermeneutical approaches or ways of interpreting the Qurʾān. These approaches are often derived from various fields of modern social sciences, including literary criticism and historical-critical approaches to interpretation of holy scriptures. In this respect, one may specifically point to the exegetical discourses proposed by a number of female Muslim scholars such as

Amina Wadud (b. 1952) and Asma Barlas (b. 1950). Their discourses are marked by a questioning of inherited hermeneutical models, and aim to re-examine traditionally patriarchal or misogynistic readings of the Qur'ān. In this hermeneutical approach, specific Qur'ānic legislations such as those relating to polygamy or unequal distribution of inheritance have undergone substantial revision.[7] In general, as Kurzman argues, the interpretive corpus of the liberal or contextualist scholars aims to highlight certain norms such as 'opposition to theocracy, support for democracy, guarantees of the rights of women and non-Muslims in Islamic countries [and] defense of freedom of thought'.[8] Such ideas directly challenge the assertions of textualist or literalist approaches, which do not assign significant roles to the socio-historical and cultural contexts of the text in the process of generating or uncovering meaning.

This book does not aim to examine the general concerns of a 'contextualist' reading of the Qur'ān. Nor does it aim to propose a comprehensive method that dictates how one should interpret those Qur'ānic passages dealing with socio-legal issues in a way that addresses the changing needs and circumstances of Muslims in the present context. Such topics have been explored at length by a number of scholars.[9] Rather, the purpose of this book is to explore a particular trend within contemporary 'contextualist' Islamic scholarship that aims to re-examine the traditional theory of revelation – a theory that, in general, regards the Qur'ān as God's words dictated to the Prophet Muhammad through the mediation of the Angel Gabriel, and thus maintains that the Prophet played no participatory role in shaping the content of revelation. In particular, this book examines how certain Muslim scholars of the last decades of the twentieth century and the early twenty-first century, namely Fazlur Rahman (from Pakistan), Abdolkarim Soroush and Muhammad Mujtahed Shabestari (from Iran) and Nasr Hamid Abu Zayd (from Egypt), challenge the widely accepted idea about the Qur'ān being the literal Word of God. The book also discusses how these scholars' theories of revelation have been applied in their writings to the practice of interpreting the Qur'ān. It demonstrates that these scholars' efforts to re-examine elements of traditional theories of revelation have important implications not only for theological debates about, for example, the relation between God and humans, but also with regard to the practice of exegesis and implementation of Islamic law in today's context.

This study refers to the project of the scholars in question – Rahman, Soroush, Shabestari and Abu Zayd – as a 'reform theology'. As will be demonstrated, what distinguishes their project from that of other Muslim reformist scholars of previous generations and today is their emphasis on the need to re-examine various features of traditional understandings of revelation. As Jahanbakhsh notes, while the main desire of most reformist Muslim scholars is oriented around 'reshuffling the furniture in the house of tradition rather than renovating the structure itself', this particular trend aims to renovate the 'entire structure'.[10] Accordingly, fundamental theological concepts, such as the dominant theories of revelation, have undergone substantial revision in the projects of Rahman, Soroush, Shabestari and Abu Zayd, as this study will demonstrate.

It is important to emphasise from the outset that in the writings of some contemporary researchers, the ideas proposed by Rahman, Soroush, Shabestari and Abu Zayd about revelation are conventionally associated with the term 'progressive revelation'.[11] Some even go further by referring to the proponents of this approach as 'progressive Muslims'.[12] However, due to the highly shifting values and meaning of the term 'progressive', this study instead refers to this line of thought as a 'humanistic approach to revelation'. I use the term 'humanistic' to refer to any approach to interpreting the Qurʾān which rests on the view that revelation is not only dependent upon its initiator (God) but also its recipient (Muhammad), in the sense that the latter is more than a mere passive recipient of the revelation. From a humanistic perspective, revelation does not involve a one-sided process in which God communicates to His prophet without the latter contributing anything to the content of revelation. That is, the content of revelation should not only be ascribed to God's authorship or influence, but also, in some important aspects, to its human recipient as well. Accordingly, for the scholars surveyed in this study, the Qurʾān is not simply a heavenly-written scripture, but also a 'human text' that is intimately connected to the Prophet's human state of mind.

My criteria when selecting Rahman, Soroush, Shabestari and Abu Zayd for examination in this book did not involve their popularity, the number of their followers, nor the number of books and articles produced by them, or even the extent of the circulation of their lectures, interviews and writings either in their homelands and Muslim-majority countries or among Western academic centres and universities. Nor were my criteria limited to their influence on other Muslim and non-Muslim scholars, or the harsh reactions they have frequently encountered from conservative theologians of their countries. Instead, my main criterion when selecting these four scholars was their contributions in shaping a new trend in contemporary Islamic thought – a trend that revolves around a humanistic approach to revelation which is in turn used as a foundation or basis for advancing a reform project. Indeed, what has driven me to choose these scholars for analysis in this book is that they have not only launched new directions in contemporary Islamic theological discourses because of their emphasis upon the human aspects of revelation, but also used such discourses in their works in a way that they serve a theoretical foundation for the practice of interpretation of the Qurʾān and certain socio-political themes of Islam.

All four scholars selected for this study share some biographical details. They are all noted scholars with numerous publications in the area of religious and Islamic studies. They all taught courses in modern theology, humanities and Islamic studies either in their homelands (Pakistan, Egypt and Iran) or overseas. As such, they became influential religious reformers of their countries and eventually gained international reputations. All four scholars also encountered harsh reactions in their homelands, either from traditional scholars of religion or clerical authorities, since their ideas posed formidable challenges to the dominant traditional understandings of revelation. It must be noted that while Shabestari has not been forced to live in exile, the other three scholars lived in exile for significant periods of time.

Fazlur Rahman taught for many years at the Islamic Research Institute in Karachi, but was forced to leave Pakistan since his ideas about revelation and the nature of the Qur'ān were considered heretical from the perspective of conservative religious scholars of Pakistan. He published an essay in August 1968 in which he defended his ideas on revelation as an extension of the ideas of a number of Muslim reformers, especially Shah Wali Allah, in order to silence his detractors. His essay, however, was unable to convince them and consequently he resigned from the Directorship of the Central Institute for Islamic Research. The reactions provoked among conservative scholars ultimately resulted in his exile from his hometown. He accepted an offer from the University of California, and later went on to work at the University of Chicago, where he became a visiting Professor of Islamic studies.

Religious authorities of Egypt raised their voices against Abu Zayd's ideas about revelation and the nature of the Qur'ān. Due to the theological views expressed in some of his works, such as *Naqd al-Khiṭāb al-Dīnī* (*The Critique of Religious Discourse*) and *Mafhūm al-naṣṣ* (*The Concept of the Text*), the Cairo Court of Appeals proclaimed Abu Zayd an apostate, as a result of which he, together with his wife, migrated to the Netherlands where he was appointed a Professor of Islamic Studies at Leiden University.[13] In this sense, Rahman and Abu Zayd had similar fates.

Along similar lines, Soroush's theory of revelation was the subject of strong criticism among traditional scholars of religion and some clerical authorities of Iran. Siding with reformist campaigns that flourished during the two-term presidency of Muhammad Khatami, Soroush's ideas were oriented around criticising aspects of the theory of the 'guardianship of the jurists' (*velāyat-e faqīh*).[14] After years of facing censorship and restrictions on public speaking, Soroush preferred to leave his homeland. From 2000 to 2004, he was a visiting scholar in the area of Islamic Studies first at Harvard and later at Princeton University. In the past decade or so, he has been living in exile and often travels within the US and Europe to deliver lectures in relation to Islam, Iran and the modern world.[15]

Within the context of post-revolutionary Iran, Shabestari has been less controversial compared to Soroush, since his writings have been less connected with political issues and challenging the theoretical background of the Islamic Republic of Iran. What is unique about Shabestari, however, is that he is the only one among the four scholars under scrutiny in this work who received a traditional seminary education in Qom from 1950 to 1968 that resulted in the degree of *ijtihād*. Shabestari's thoughts were strongly influenced by Muhammad Iqbal (d. 1938), as well as by a number of modern Christian scholars like Karl Barth (d. 1968) and Paul Tillich (d. 1965) and Western philosophers such as Hans-Georg Gadamer (d. 2002). Although Shabestari was not forced to live in exile, he has been constantly criticised by conservative Iranian theologians during the past three decades.

Therefore, what Rahman, Soroush, Shabestari and Abu Zayd share in common is the fact that there has been a significant level of resistance to their ideas about the Qur'ān and their interpretive methods from the conservative theologians of their countries.

Throughout this study, I will mainly rely on the primary sources produced by Rahman, Soroush, Shabestari and Abu Zayd in presenting their views. Rahman's books and papers are available in English. Soroush's books, however, are mainly available in Persian, and only two of his books – *Expansion of Prophetic Experience* and *Reason, Freedom and Democracy in Islam* – have been translated into English. In investigating Soroush's ideas, I will also draw on his writings in the original language. In addition, I refer to some of his public lectures and interviews in both Persian and English. Abu Zayd was bilingual in Arabic and English. Some of his books, such as *Mafhūm al-Naṣṣ* and *al-Naṣṣ, al-Sulṭa, al-Haqīqa* (*the Text, Authority and the Truth*) are originally written in Arabic, and English translations of them are not available. In presenting Abu Zayd's ideas, I rely on both his Arabic and English writings. Shabestari's books and interviews are all in Farsi, and there is no comprehensive English translation of any one of them.[16]

Some background studies

The ideas of Rahman, Soroush, Shabestari and Abu Zayd have attracted the attention of some scholars of modern Islamic thought. A number of scholars view the projects of these thinkers as a response to 'atomistic' – a term often used for reading Qur'ānic verses in isolation or in a piecemeal manner instead of reading them in light of the Qur'ān's general principles – or 'literalist' interpretation of the Qur'ān presented by traditional scholars of religion and contemporary Islamist thinkers. In this sense, some scholars present the views of the four thinkers in question as an alternative account to such interpretations.[17]

There is often a general tendency among some scholars of modern Islamic thought to depict the projects of Rahman, Soroush, Shabestari and Abu Zayd as a liberal reinterpretation of Islam – one that coheres very well with the principles of human rights, gender equality and democratic forms of government. Indeed, the projects of the four scholars examined in this book are often framed in the existing literature as attempts to reconcile Islamic values with modern Western norms and values.[18] Along similar lines, some scholars of Iranian studies view Soroush's and Shabestari's ideas as an attempt to democratise and depoliticise religion in the Islamic Republic of Iran.[19] In the works of the named scholars, Soroush's and Shabestari's theories of revelation and their theological discourses have received less attention than their political ideas.

Several scholars of modern Islamic thought, such as Massimo Campanini, Jon Armajani, Erik Ohlander and Elizabeth Kassab, are fully aware of the significance of the views of Rahman, Soroush, Shabestari and Abu Zayd on revelation, but do not make them the main focus of their work. Indeed, they have not identified these four scholars' views on revelation as a particular trend in contemporary Islamic thought.[20] Other scholars have occasionally presented the theories of revelation presented by some or all of these four thinkers in terms of being modern Islamic discourses about revelation, though without appreciating how their views on revelation could open up a more flexible space for the interpretation of the Qur'ān.[21]

A few scholars have occasionally observed the significance of such a re-examination of traditional theories of revelation in connection with methods of interpretation of the Qur'ān only in the writings of Rahman and Abu Zayd. Ebrahim Moosa asserts that Rahman's theory of revelation and prophecy 'is a fundamental assumption in his hermeneutics and ignoring it can result in misreading his contribution to modern Qur'ānic studies'.[22] Likewise, Yusuf Rahman asserts that Fazlur Rahman's and Abu Zayd's theories of revelation are a central theme in, and a foundation for, their theories of Qur'ānic interpretation.[23] Finally, in her PhD thesis, Katharina Völker examines how 'accounts of the nature of the Qur'ān and its interpretation' proposed by scholars such as Rahman, Abu Zayd and Muhammad Arkoun are used for what she refers to as 'reform schemes'.[24] This thesis had its merits, but Völker does not extensively examine how Rahman's and Abu Zayd's theories of revelation were inspired by the earlier theories of revelation presented by some pre-modern and modern Muslim scholars and philosophers.[25] Further, she does not extensively explore how each scholar's account of revelation contributes to his interpretation of some Qur'ānic themes such as gender issues and religious pluralism.[26] And finally, she does not examine how the views of contemporary Shi'i Muslim scholars like Soroush and Shabestari have contributed to their understanding of the nature of the Qur'ān and its exegesis.

The study

Viewed in the light of the existing literature dealing with the ideas of Rahman, Soroush, Shabestari and Abu Zayd reviewed above, the contributions and outstanding features of this study become clearer. Although some work has been done towards understanding aspects of the reform projects of these scholars, this study is the first of its kind to lay out their theories of revelation in a systematic way to explore how they have approached the interpretation of the Qur'ān within the concerns of present-day context. The importance and contribution of this study is fourfold. First, it seeks not only to highlight the projects of the scholars in question as emblematic of a liberal turn among modern Muslim scholars, but also views them as part of a trend of systematic 'reform theology' within contemporary Islamic thought. Second, it demonstrates that Rahman, Soroush, Shabestari and Abu Zayd provide a model for reform that aims at re-examining traditional understandings of revelation rather than merely reinterpreting traditional socio-political discourses of Islam. That is, the present work goes beyond studying the socio-political discourses of the four scholars in isolation, instead demonstrating the extent to which such discourses represent a rethinking of traditional theories of revelation. Third, by analysing the four scholars' methods of interpretation and their applications in practice, this book engages not only with their methodological innovations from a comparative perspective, but also examines some of their limitations. And last but not least, this book examines the extent to which the accounts of revelation proposed by Rahman, Soroush, Shabestari and Abu Zayd are rooted in either pre-modern

Muslim philosophical teachings or in modern Western religious discourses. Towards this end, this study discovers the sources that each scholar has used in formulating his theory of revelation.

The importance of examining the ideas of these four scholars in light of a discourse of 'reform theology' lies also in the fact those scholars who are critical of applying modern hermeneutic approaches to the realm of the Qur᾿ān's interpretation often argue that since the Qur᾿ān represents the verbatim Word of God revealed to Muhammad through the Angel Gabriel, certain hermeneutical principles developed in the West for the interpretation of the Bible or other non-religious texts should not be employed in the task of interpreting the Qur᾿ān. Anzaruddin Ahmad, for example, criticises the use of hermeneutics when applied to the Qur᾿ān, stating that 'analysis on the psycho-social aspects of the Biblical author is possible since . . . [the] Bible has a human author; the Qur᾿ān, however, does not. The Prophet Muhammad was just a passive receiver and conveyer of the Qur᾿ānic texts.'[27] For Ahmad, Muslims 'need only Qur᾿ānic commentary (*tafsīr*) . . . and not hermeneutics, since they accept the Qur᾿ān as the word of Allah'.[28] Along similar lines, Managheb and Mehrabi assert that the Qur᾿ān is the Word of God and is 'author-oriented, consisting of real and objective meaning . . . the interpreter [should therefore follow] . . . the intention of the text's speaker'.[29] The teachings of the Qur᾿ān are, they continue, 'consistent and changeless. [The Qur᾿ān's] realities are not subject to the author's mental conditions and presuppositions but they have their meaning . . . independent of the interpreter and his conditions'.[30] Managheb and Mehrabi conclude that 'there is a significant conflict between principles of philosophical hermeneutic and principles of [the] Qur᾿ān. Their integration is impossible.'[31] Similar to the aforementioned scholars, Muhammad Jafar Elmi argues against employing modern hermeneutics to Qur᾿ānic exegesis, since he considers the Qur᾿ān as God's Word directly revealed to the Prophet Muhammad. For Elmi, the interpreter has to discover an objective meaning of the Qur᾿ān by putting 'all his or her own ideas and views aside'.[32] With the aim of bringing forth a 'reform theology' discourse that stands in contrast with the traditional Islamic theories of revelation, this study challenges the arguments of scholars such as Ahmad, Elmi, Managheb and Mehrabi, arguing that despite its divine origination, the Qur᾿ān, like any other texts, can be approached by means of modern hermeneutic methods. Further, leaning on the works of Soroush, Shabestari and Abu Zayd, this study suggests that interpreters naturally bring certain preconceived ideas or prior knowledge into their interpretation of the Qur᾿ān, and thus one's preconceived knowledge inevitably plays a significant role in one's interpretation of the text.

In addition, this book stands in contrast with the literalist/textualist approach to the interpretation of the Qur᾿ān which has gained a high degree of popularity and prominence among Muslims today.[33] Muslim scholarship in general has been reluctant to relate God's Word to the context in which the Qur᾿ān emerged. As Farid Esack noted, this reluctance 'is a direct consequence of the passionate commitment to the preservation of the Otherness of the Qur᾿ān as God's speech. The reasoning seems to be that if this-worldly events "caused" revelation then somehow revelation is not entirely "other-worldly"'.[34] Leaning on the works of Soroush, Shabestari and Abu Zayd, this book, however, argues that a humanistic approach to revelation considers that the broader social, cultural, political and economic conditions of the seventh-century Arabian society played a significant role in shaping the content of the Qur'ān. It follows from this that most legal precepts of the Qur'ān should not be literally applied in all times and contexts.

The content

This study includes four levels of analysis. First, I extract and distil the main features of each scholar's account of revelation from his work, attempting to piece together his ideas to propose a coherent picture. I analyse each scholar's views on several aspects of revelation, namely the nature of revelation as well as the Prophet's role in the process of revelation and in wording his revelatory experience. I show how their ideas about the nature of the Qur'ān have their origins in their 'humanistic' approach towards understanding the process of revelation. This level of analysis shows how each scholar emphasises the human aspect of the Qur'ān by considering revelation as an event rooted in either the Prophet's human state of mind (one that is historically situated), or in humanistic features of the society (the historical context) he lived in.

The second level of analysis in this book involves examining the extent to which each scholar's account of revelation is rooted in either pre-modern Muslim philosophical ideas or in modern Western theological discourses. The criteria that I have used when seeking to discover the sources of these figures' theories of revelation among pre-modern Muslim ideas or contemporary theological discourses are not limited to pinpointing the explicit references they often mention in their writings, but also include my own judgement concerning the similarities that can be found between these scholars' theories of revelation and the latter's ideas and discourses. This level of analysis provides an insight into how the theory of revelation presented by each scholar has been shaped. It also illustrates how their projects have broken, in a number of significant aspects, with the mainstream Islamic beliefs on revelation. It is in this sense that this study demonstrates some of the ways in which a rethinking of the dominant methods, ideas and approaches with regard to theological discourses can take place within Islamic tradition today.

The third level of analysis concerns the practice of exegesis, and here I shall examine each scholar's views and arguments, attempting to identify whether there exist any larger hermeneutical tendencies that characterise his interpretive methods. I often explain the hermeneutic approach of each scholar in two or three sections. This will give a clearer picture of how each scholar approaches the task of interpretation of the Qur'ān. Then, I will reconstruct how each scholar's theory of revelation influences his interpretive methods. Indeed, this level of analysis involves deeper discussions about how the theories of revelation proposed by the scholars in question have been applied to the practice of interpretation of the Qur᾿ān. Throughout this level of analysis, I also present the works of the named scholars in light of wider hermeneutical discourses that have appeared in the West.

Contrary to classical Qur᾿ānic hermeneutics, which tended to favour a linear and verse-by-verse approach to interpreting the text, the hermeneutic discourses presented by the scholars discussed in this book have not been used by these figures to produce a detailed exegesis of the Qur᾿ān (*tafsīr*). Therefore, in the fourth and last level of analysis, I shall select certain Qur᾿ānic passages that are found in the works of each scholar to show whether or not their hermeneutic approaches have been applied in practice. I provide occasional examples of specific themes raised by each scholar to show whether or not they fit with their larger hermeneutical principles and their theories of revelation. In this respect, I focus mainly on three themes that appear in their works, namely (1) Qur᾿ānic socio-legal provisions (*aḥkām*), especially in relation to discourses of women's rights and gender equality; (2) religious pluralism; and (3) political discourses, especially the concepts of governance, *shūrā* (consultation) and democracy.

This book is comprised of five chapters. Chapter 1 explores the main features of traditional theories of revelation to establish a proper basis for the discussion about the specific views concerning revelation held by the scholars examined in this book. This chapter examines how traditional accounts of revelation in the Islamic tradition have consistently emphasised the externality of revelation vis-à-vis the Prophet Muhammad – the idea that Muhammad was only a passive transmitter of the divine message to his audiences, and played no role whatsoever in shaping the content of revelation. Chapters 2–5 argue that the main thread connecting the work of Rahman, Soroush, Shabestari and Abu Zayd is that, in the course of their own research, they developed theories about revelation that challenged various aspects of traditional theories of revelation. Each chapter is devoted to one scholar's ideas in the four levels of analysis mentioned above. That is, each chapter first of all examines how each scholar explores the process of revelation and the Prophet's role in it. Second, it examines how various aspects of each scholar's theory correspond to pre-modern and modern Muslim and non-Muslim scholars' views on revelation. Third, it explores how each scholar's theory of revelation relates to his understanding of the Qur᾿ān and the practice of exegesis. Fourth, it provides a number of examples that illustrate how his interpretive methods function in practice.

Notes

1. Saeed, *Reading the Qur᾿an in the Twenty-First Century*, p. 20.
2. For details of this line of thinking, see Ana Belen Soage, 'Shūra and Democracy: Two Sides of the Same Coin?', p. 97.
3. This general definition of the term 'liberal', which seems to be a common theme among 'liberal' interpretations of all sacred scriptures, is presented by McGrath in his *Historical Theology*, p. 234.
4. For definition of literalism, see Ruthven, *Fundamentalism*, p. 61; Robert Gleave, *Islam and Literalism*, p. 1.

5. Saeed, *Reading the Qur'an in the Twenty-First Century*, p. 20.
6. According to Hanafi, the result of this method of interpretation is the partial and even contradictory understandings of the Qur'ān. See Wahyudi, 'Hasan Hanafi on Salafism and Secularism', p. 260.
7. See Ohlander, 'Modern Qur'anic Hermeneutics', pp. 630–1; Barlas, 'Amina Wadud's hermeneutics of the Qur'an', p. 97; pp. 106–12.
8. Kurzman, 'Introduction: Liberal Islam and Its Islamic Context', p. 4.
9. Saeed, *Reading the Qur'an in the Twenty-First Century*; Saeed, 'Some Reflections on the Contextualist Approach to ethico-legal texts of the Qur'ān'; Saeed, 'Reading the Qur'an', pp. 55–85.
10. Jahanbakhsh, 'Introduction: Abdolkarim Soroush's Neo-Rationalist Approach to Islam', pp. xxii–xxiii.
11. Esack, *Qur'an, Liberation and Pluralism*, pp. 54–73; Leirvik, 'Waḥy and Tanzīl'.
12. Duderija, *Constructing a Religiously Ideal "Believer" and "Woman" in Islam*, pp. 139–67; Ahmed, 'Progressive Islam and Qur'anic Hermeneutics'; Safi, 'Between Ijtihad of the Presupposition and Gender Equality', p. 79.
13. Abu Zayd and Nelson, *The Voice of an Exile*, p. ix.
14. According to this theory, in the absence of Mahdi (the twelfth imam of the Shī'ī Muslims), jurists have the same privileges as the Prophet and imams in governing socio-political matters of society.
15. Tavassoli, *Christian Encounters with Iran*, p. 136.
16. To my knowledge, Goldberg is the only scholar who has translated some passages from Shabestari's writings into English in his *Shi'i Theology in Iran*. For translations of these interviews, see *Shi'i Theology in Iran*, pp. 134–6; pp. 143–56.
17. For example, see Ahmad, 'Progressive Islam and Qur'anic Hermeneutics', p. 81; Ebrahim Moosa, 'Introduction', pp. 16–17.
18. For example, see Bennett, *Muslims and Modernity*; Sonn, 'Fazlur Rahman and Islamic Feminism'.
19. For example, see Foody, 'Interiorizing Islam: Religious experience and state oversight in the Islamic Republic of Iran'; Ghobadzadeh, *Religious Secularity*; Kamrava, *Iran's Intellectual Revolution*, pp. 155–72; Bayat, *Making Islam Democratic*, pp. 91–6; Ghamari-Tabrizi, *Islam and Dissent in Post-revolutionary Iran*, pp. 223–42.
20. Campanini has explored various aspects of Rahman's, Abu Zayd's and Shabestari's ideas, but only places them within the context of other Muslim thinkers of the modern period from various Schools of thought (Campanini, *The Qur'an*, pp. 55–6; pp. 58–9; pp. 68–9). See also Armajani, *Dynamic Islam*, pp. 81–2. Kassab views Abu Zayd's project as an attempt to historicise the notion of revelation (Kassab, *Contemporary Arab Thought*, p. 174) but does not make Abu Zayd's ideas the main focus of her work and has not recognised his views or those of scholars such as Soroush and Shabestari as a particular emerging trend within modern Islamic thought. Along similar lines, Ohlander refers to the hermeneutics of Abu Zayd and Rahman as 'Revisionist Hermeneutics', discussing briefly their 'literary-historical methodology' in the study of the Qur'ān, but does not discuss their theories of revelation and how their hermeneutic approaches have their roots in their insights about revelation. Ohlander, 'Modern Qur'ānic Hermeneutics', pp. 629–30.
21. For some studies, see Leirvik, 'Waḥy and Tanzīl', pp. 101–25; Saeed, *Reading the Qur'an in the Twenty-First Century*, pp. 53–6; Jahanbakhsh, 'Introduction', pp. xv–xlix; Sukidi, 'Naṣr Hāmid Abū Zayd', pp. 181–211; Duderija, *Constructing a Religiously Ideal "Believer" and "Woman" in Islam*, pp. 141–2.
22. Moosa, 'Introduction', p. 11; see also Ibid., p. 15.
23. Yusuf Rahman, 'The Qur'ān in Egypt', p. 250. In his PhD thesis, Yusuf Rahman deals with Abu Zayd's theory of interpretation, exploring how it functions in practice, but has mainly limited himself to examining how it is applied to the realm of gender issues. Yusuf Rahman, 'The Hermeneutical Theory of Nasr Hamid Abu Zayd', pp. 180–9.
24. Völker, 'Qur'an and Reform: Rahman, Arkoun, Abu Zayd', p. i.
25. For a brief examination of such issues in her work, see Ibid., pp. 274–6.
26. For some brief explanations of the notion of gender equality in Abu Zayd's work, see Ibid, pp. 172–7.
27. Anzaruddin Ahmad, 'Applying Hermeneutics to the Qur'an', p. 94.
28. Ibid., p. 95.
29. Managheb and Mehrabi, 'Philosophical hermeneutic and its interaction with principles of Qur'ān apprehension', p. 239.

30. Ibid.
31. Ibid., p. 242.
32. Elmi, 'Word of God and Revelation', p. 287.
33. A number of contemporary scholars have identified a shift towards so-called 'literalism' in modern Islamic thought. For example, see Saeed, *Reading the Qur'an in the Twenty-First Century*, p. 3, pp. 180–2; Moosa, 'The Debts and Burdens of Critical Islam', p. 124. Robert Gleave has examined the manner in which a focus on the literal meaning of the text has played out in two modern Muslim intellectual movements: Salafism and Twelver Shiʿism (Gleave, *Islam and Literalism*, pp. 175–96).
34. Esack, *Qur'an, Liberation and Pluralism*, p. 53.

2

Traditional Understanding of Revelation

The concept of revelation is fundamental to any discussion about the Qurʾān. In the course of Islamic history, Muslim theologians, scholars and philosophers could hardly avoid engaging with the question about how God communicated to His Prophet through revelation. The purpose of this chapter is twofold. First, it explores how the Qurʾān and some prophetic hadiths describe the event of revelation, including the means by which God's message was delivered to the Prophet Muhammad. Second, it discusses what the majority of Muslim scholars in the course of Islamic history have understood to be the nature of what the Qurʾān refers to as 'God's speech' and the process by which it was conveyed to the Prophet. In this respect, this chapter will outline the main characteristics of what I identify as a 'traditional theory of revelation', or what is often recognised as the dominant Muslim view on revelation. I argue that although certain Muslim scholars have challenged various aspects of traditional theories of revelation, the fundamental features that these accounts have in common have been accepted by most Muslim scholars even during the modern period.

Revelation in the Qurʾān

According to the Qurʾān, prophets have been recipients of divine revelation, the content of which does not contradict any other: 'We have revealed to thee as We revealed to Noah, and the Prophet after him, and We revealed to Abraham, Ishmael, Isaac, Jacob, and the Tribes, Jesus and Job, Jonah and Aaron and Solomon, and We gave to David Psalms' (Q 4:163).[1] This verse suggests that prophets have not been sent with a radically new message, but rather carry a renewal of God's essential message in order to re-establish the relation between the Divine and humanity. The Qurʾān sees itself as confirming (*muṣaddiq*) the revelations given to God's prophets before Muhammad.[2] The means by which God's message was transmitted to His prophets are not described in great detail in the Qurʾān, but there is a key Qurʾānic passage which describes three different ways that divine communication can occur between God and humanity: by direct inspiration, from behind a veil, or through a messenger:

> It is not given to any human being that God should speak to him except by inspiration (*waḥyan*), or from behind a veil, or by sending a Messenger who with God's permission is inspired and transmits what God wills. He is Most High, Most Wise. (Q 42:51)

This verse considers the possibility that the process of revelation did not necessarily involve a mediatory figure. God is said in another Qur'ānic verse (Q 7:117) to have directly 'put into Moses' mind by inspiration' the command to throw his rod on the ground. Stefan Wild indicates, 'In some Medinan passages of the Qur'an, the notion of a mediator between God and the Prophet seems to recede or to disappear.'[3] According to Wansbrough, 'That *waḥy* may signify communication, without recourse to an emissary is confirmed not only by Q 42:51, but also by the use of *awḥā* in' other Qur'ānic verses.[4] Q 6:119, for example, states that 'Allah is witness between me and you. And this Qur'ān was revealed (*awḥā*) to me that I may warn you thereby and whomever it reaches.' And Q 18:27 reads, 'recite, (O Muhammad) what has been revealed (*awḥā*) to you of the Book of your God (*kitāb-e rabbika*)'. However, the idea that a mediating figure was involved in transmitting God's message to the Prophet is hinted at in some Qur'ānic passages, though this figure's name is not mentioned (Q 53:1–8; 81:22–3). There are also some Qur'ānic verses which indicate that revelation took place through the mediation of a figure, identified as *rūḥ al-qudus* (the Holy Spirit) (Q 16:102) or *rūḥ al-amīn* (the Trustworthy Spirit) (Q 26:192–5). The Qur'ān does not describe in detail how the mediatory figure transmitted God's message to the Prophet. Nor does it elaborate details of the Trustworthy Spirit or Holy Spirit. In some Qur'ānic verses, emphasis is placed on the Prophet's heart (*qalb*) as a locus where God's message has been brought down, either by the intervention of Gabriel (Q 2:97) or by the Trustworthy Spirit (Q 26:193), though no further details are provided.

Muslim theologians and commentators on the Qur'ān in general believe that the Angel Gabriel acted as a mediator between the human and divine worlds, and thus was responsible for delivering God's message to Muhammad.[5] In the exegetical material, the term Spirit (*rūḥ*) is often associated with Gabriel. For instance, in his *tafsīr* on Q 2:87, Muhammad b. Jarir al-Tabari (d. 310/923) argues that *rūḥ* refers to Gabriel, outlining that 'this is the position adopted in most exegeses of this verse'.[6] John Wansbrough shows how a number of early interpreters of the Qur'ān, such as Muhammad Kalbi (d. 204/819) and Muqatil b. Sulayman (d. 150/767), incorporated such phrases as 'We send Gabriel to you with it' and 'Gabriel came to him and informed him of it' when interpreting Q 42:51, although Gabriel is not mentioned by name in this verse.[7] Similarly, as Wild shows, in the reports of the *sīra* (the biography of the Prophet), the notion of Gabriel as mediator is clearly implied.[8] It is worth noting that there are a number of Qur'ānic verses, such as Q 16:2 and Q 97:4, in which the terms *rūḥ* and angels (*malā'ika*) are used together. These verses provide the strongest evidence for assuming that *rūḥ* is tantamount to the angel of revelation, though Gabriel is not named in such verses. The name Gabriel is mentioned in just three Qur'ānic verses (Q 2:97; Q 2:98; Q 66:4), of which only one explicitly identifies Gabriel as the transmitter of God's message to the Prophet: 'Gabriel . . . has brought the Qur'ān down upon your heart' (Q 2:97). Even in this verse it is not suggested that Gabriel narrated God's Words to the Prophet in an 'auditory' manner (as is dominantly believed); rather, emphasis seems to be placed on the Prophet's experience and feeling in the process of revelation – a theme highlighted in the theories of revelation presented by some of the scholars whose ideas are the focus of this book.

Two terms for revelation in the Qur'ān: *waḥy* and *tanzīl*

Waḥy and *tanzīl* are two key terms associated with the concept of revelation in the Qur'ān. Although there are significant differences between these two terms, as Leirvik notes, 'contemporary dictionaries . . . tend to blur the diverse semantic origins of *waḥy* and *tanzīl* by associating both with inspiration and revelation . . . [even] in modern translations of the Qur'ān, revelation functions as a standard rendering of both terms'.[9] The general tendency to translate both *waḥy* and *tanzīl* as revelation is problematic since there are a number of factors which distinguish the former from the latter.

In the Qur'ān, the term *tanzīl*, from the Arabic root *n-z-l*, and its derived forms such as *nuzūl* and *inzāl*, has the connotation of a movement from a higher sphere to a lower sphere – a movement downwards: 'with the truth We have sent it down (*anzalnā*) and with the truth it has come down (*nazal*)' (Q 17:105). And 'this [the Qur'ān] is a sending down (*tanzīl*) from the Lord of the worlds. The trustworthy spirit came down with it (*nazala bi-hā*) to your heart' (Q 26:192. see also Q 16:101). The medieval Arab lexicographer Ibn Manzur (d. 711/1311) defines the term *tanzīl* as a 'coming down of the compassion and the divine grace . . . to mankind'.[10] Ibn Faris mentions that the meaning of *nazala* refers to an act of *hubūṭ* (the descent).[11] Along similar lines, the contemporary scholar Wild asserts that the term *tanzīl* and its derivatives only make sense when 'there is an above and a below'.[12] It is worth noting that the term *nuzūl* was used in pre-Islamic poetry in the connotation of a downwards movement.[13] The notion of *tanzīl* as a downwards movement is intimately associated with the Qur'ānic idea that God rules over the heavens and the earth from above. According to Wild, it is in this context that the Qur'ān uses the term *tanzīl* for sending down God's graces and punishments out of the heavens (Q 2:22; 24:43; 50:9).[14] Other uses of *n-z-l* occur in Q 9:26, where God 'sends down' his peace (*sakina*), and in Q 3:151, Q 6:81, Q 7:33 and Q 22:71, where He 'sends down' his authority (*sulṭān*).

The term *tanzīl* and its derived forms connote divine communication in the Qur'ān, and do not refer to communication between humans. As Izutsu notes, '*tanzīl* can never be used in reference to an occurrence of speech act between man and man. The basic meaning of the word . . . forbids it to be applied except to supernatural communication'.[15] In this respect, revelation, Izutsu asserts, is something essentially 'mysterious, incapable of being grasped by human analytic thought which does not allow of analysis; it is something only to be believed in'.[16] This is why revelation, at this level, is inaccessible to the human mind, and humans are incapable of recognising the mode, the code or the language used in *tanzīl*.

Waḥy, however, is used in a much broader sense in the Qur'ān. For example, some verses of the Qur'ān indicate that *waḥy*, as a form of communication, is not limited to a relationship between God and His prophets. God is said in the Qurʾān to have communicated with Moses' mother (Q 20:38) and Jesus' disciples (Q 5:111) through *waḥy*. The term *waḥy* is also used in the Qurʾān to describe God's communication with animals such as the bee (Q 16:68–9), the heavens (Q 41:12) and the earth (Q 99:5). In addition, it is used to refer to non-divine forms of communication, such as that which occurred among demons (Q 6:112; 6:121), as well as between humans such as Zakariya and his companions (Q 19:11). The term *waḥy* was even used among pre-Islamic Arab poets to describe terrestrial or non-divine communication. For example, a pre-Islamic poet used this term to describe the communication between a male ostrich and his nestling: '[T]he male ostrich is talking to her (*yuḥī*) with cracking sounds, just like the Greeks talk with each other in an incomprehensible language in their castles'.[17] Although the term *waḥy* was used here to describe a form of mysterious communication between two parties, what is of particular importance is that it is used for a communication in which there is no divine purpose.

Therefore, the difference between the terms *waḥy* and *tanzīl* is that the former is used to refer solely to super-human communications, or communications in which a divine being is somehow involved, whereas the latter is used to refer to different kinds of interaction, and not only divine communication. Closely related to the notions of *waḥy* and *tanzīl* as well is the question concerning whether the Qurʾān was sent down to the Prophet during his prophetic mission over twenty-three years, or whether it was sent down instantaneously. Two Qurʾānic verses seem to support the idea that the whole Qurʾān was revealed at once: 'The month of Ramadan is that in which the Qurʾān was sent down as guidance for people' (Q 2:185) and 'We sent down (*anzalnāhu*) the Qurʾān in the Night of Decree (*laylat al-qadr*)' (Q 97:1). The use of the root *n-z-l* in these verses is consistent with the idea that *tanzīl* indicates a super-human form of communication. Classical Muslim theologians often argued that the Qurʾān was sent down to the First Heaven instantaneously and was stored on a Preserved Tablet (*lawḥ al-maḥfūz*) during *laylat al-qadr* (night of decree), after which its revelation to the Prophet took place gradually over twenty-three years during his prophetic mission.[18] Ayatollah Tabatabaʾi (d. 1981), a contemporary Shiʿi commentator from Iran and the author of *Tafsīr al-Mizān* (*The Balance in Interpretation of the Qurʾān*), however, argues that the Qurʾān was initially sent down to the Prophet's heart instantaneously in an 'unchangeable and concrete' form on the night of decree, and was then revealed to the Prophet a second time as 'scattered, detailed and changeable' texts (that were subject to change by abrogation) throughout the twenty-three years of his mission.[19]

Tabatabaʾi's comment reminds us that understanding the differences between the terms *tanzīl* and *waḥy* is not simply a question of semantics or etymology, but instead may influence different interpretive discourses. A number of Muslim and Western scholars during the past few decades have distinguished between the terms *tanzīl* and *waḥy* to suggest another understanding of revelation that recognises the role of human agency. Leirvik distinguishes between *waḥy* and *tanzīl*, arguing that '*waḥy* – in the sense of personal inspiration – may imply a more open understanding of revelation than the term *tanzīl* which is conventionally associated with the idea of a divine message being sent down'.[20] For him, the use of the term *tanzīl* for revelation places an ultimate limitation on what he refers to as an 'open-ended reinterpretation of the sacred text' and on the connection that exists between the text and the socio-historical context of its emergence.[21] Without going much further into the details at this stage, Nasr Hamid Abu Zayd and Muhammad Arkoun introduce a shift away from the term *tanzīl* in their projects, calling for a modern hermeneutic methodology to be used in approaches to the interpretation of the Qur'ān. In particular, the use of the term *waḥy* instead of *tanzīl* can lead the interpreter to recognise the role of human agency as a significant element in the revelatory process, and can lead him/her to take the time, place and dominant culture of the revelatory era into consideration when approaching the interpretation of the Qur'ān.[22]

Strongly connected to the distinction between *waḥy* and *tanzīl* too is the idea that the former, unlike the latter, is to be understood as an 'open-ended discourse', and that it does not necessarily have any 'connection with written communication'.[23] In regards to the verb *awḥā* (to reveal), only three out of seventy-one occurrences of the term and its derived forms are connected to 'text-related words' such as *kitāb* (book).[24] Madigan argues that even the notion of *kitāb* 'is understood by the Qur'ān itself more in terms of process than that of fixed content'.[25] According to him, key connotations associated with the Qur'ān's use of the word *kitāb* (such as 'mercy, recitation, sending down, and communicating') all refer to processes of engagement between God and humanity, rather than a notion of the delivery of a pre-existing text.[26] Along similar lines, Karl Ernst argues that in a number of Qur'ānic passages, such as Q 85:21–2 and Q 56:77–8, the word *Qur'ān* refers to a 'mysterious cosmic archetype' rather than a 'physical text'. The term *Qur'ān*, especially in the Meccan chapters, has a generic sense of 'recitation' rather than a 'fixed body of materials'.[27]

Although the methods of the message's delivery from God to the Prophet, the nature of revelation and the Prophet's feelings/experiences at the moment of revelation are not stated in the Qur'ān, there exist details concerning such issues in the hadith literature and in the writings of medieval Muslim theologians.[28] The following sections examine how revelation and the Prophet's role in it have been traditionally understood in Islamic literature.

Revelation in the traditional accounts: internal and direct, or external and mediated?

As outlined above, some Qur'ānic verses consider the possibility that revelation took place in a direct way, and without the involvement of an intermediary figure; but as Madigan has aptly noted, 'the Muslim tradition . . . has privileged those parts of the Qur'ān that suggest that revelation is mediated through' an angelic figure because such verses tend to maintain 'the distance between the divine and the human'.[29] There are some indications in earlier traditions which suggest that the

Prophet received revelation either by being approached by the angel or without an intermediary. According to one of the most often quoted hadiths, when the Prophet was asked how he received revelations, he replied:

> Sometimes it is [revealed] like the ringing of a bell, this form of inspiration is the hardest of all and then this state passes off after I have grasped what is inspired. Sometimes the Angel comes in the form of a man and talks to me and I grasp what he says.[30]

The first method of transmission of *waḥy* to the Prophet, as outlined in the first part of this hadith, is more internal and direct rather than being external and mediated. In addition, the hearing of the bell in this hadith, as Watt has noted, indicates an experience in which 'there is no mention of hearing anyone speaking or of hearing words spoken' and thus refers to 'a description of an intellectual locution'.[31] Along similar lines, Tirmidhi (d. 279/892), one of the earliest collectors of hadiths, narrates a tradition that describes revelation as containing sounds like those of 'humming of bees',[32] and the theologian and jurist Ahmad b. Hanbal (d. 241/855) cites a tradition that describes it as a sound like 'metal being beaten'.[33]

Later Muslim scholars adopted the second part of the above-mentioned hadith ('sometimes the Angel comes in the form of a man and talks to me and I grasp what he says') as the standard interpretation of the manner in which the revelation was transmitted, and identified Gabriel as the angel of revelation.[34] As Madigan has noted, 'The Muslim tradition has tended to emphasize . . . that revelation is mediated through Gabriel.'[35] Similarly, Graham argues that the 'traditional Muslim theory has tended to be that Muhammad received all the Qur'ān orally from Gabriel as explicit verbal revelation given when the latter appeared to him'.[36] Accordingly, in traditional Muslim theory, 'the stress has been upon the didactic, "external" nature of Gabriel's "teaching" of specific "texts" to the Prophet' and thus there are only a few accounts that contain 'hints of a less rigid understanding of the modes of revelation'.[37] This emphasis on the 'externality' of revelation and of the figure of Gabriel vis-à-vis the Prophet is grounded in the fact that Muslim scholars have tended to maintain a distance between the divine sphere and the human realm. Some medieval Muslim scholars even emphasised that Gabriel's role was not only limited to transmitting God's Words to His prophet, but that the angel also played a role in communicating the meaning (*maʿnā*) of these Words to Muhammad as well.[38] Traditions often quoted Muhammad as saying that he received the Sunna, unrecited texts, together with the Qur'ān, the recited texts. To support this viewpoint, some scholars connected the belief in Muhammad with the belief in God, based on their interpretation of some Qur'ānic verses such as Q 3:164, 4:171 and 24:62.[39] This idea gave rise to the position according to which 'the sayings and deeds of the Prophet' were viewed as 'inspirations from God' or 'unrecited revelation' (*waḥy ghayr matlw*).[40]

Al-Shafiʿi (d. 204/820) played an important role in portraying the prophetic Sunna as a form of revelation. For him, the Qur'ān is 'recited' revelation, while the Sunna 'is revelation that one does not recite'.[41] This means that al-Shafiʿi treated the Qur'ān and Sunna as 'co-equal revelation'.[42] Al-Shafiʿi gave hadith the paramount significance, arguing that the hadith literature should be used together with the Qur'ān in the process of lawmaking. As Lowry argues, 'what underlines the *Risala* as a whole is Shafiʿi's attempt to account for all the possible ways in which the Qur'ān and the Sunna express rules of law'.[43] Indeed, this approach led to the rise of a law-oriented hermeneutical paradigm which viewed the Qur'ān and the Sunna as a means of developing laws for Muslims. In addition, the outcome of this approach, according to Saeed, is that every word in both the Qur'ān and hadith are considered God's revelation, and this results in 'less flexibility for Muslims to develop laws based on changing circumstances and needs', which is to say that it reduces the extent of human reasoning in any lawmaking process.[44] This demonstrates that certain approaches or understandings of what constitutes the content of revelation may play a significant role in shaping interpretive discourses, and even influence an interpreter's perspective towards the scope of ethico-legal instructions that religion can provide believers with.

Revelation and its link to the personality of the Prophet

The second part of the aforementioned hadith, which describes revelation as being delivered to the Prophet by the mediation of the Angel in the form of a man, also offers a less rigid understanding of the mode of revelation than was generally recognised later on, although it indicates that revelation took place by the mediation of an angelic figure. The term 'in the form of a man' implicitly indicates that 'revelation was presumably an imaginative locution . . . accompanied by either an intellectual or an imaginative vision of Gabriel'.[45] Unlike the Qur'ān, which does not emphasise the physicality of Gabriel, the Qur'ānic exegetical literature contains stories of the Angel Gabriel appearing as a physical being before the Prophet.[46] Also, unlike the second part of the aforementioned hadith, which may implicitly refer to 'an imaginative vision of Gabriel', some traditional accounts explicitly considered Gabriel as a physical being that was not only visible to the Prophet, but could also be seen by some of his companions in specific circumstances.[47] This emphasis on the physicality of Gabriel reflects an effort to maintain the externality of Qur'ānic revelations vis-à-vis the person of the Prophet, since it tends to disregard the possibility that Gabriel appeared in the Prophet's psyche or in his faculty of imagination.

Strongly related to the notion of the externality of the revelation vis-à-vis the Prophet is the idea that Muhammad was only a passive transmitter of the divine message to his audience, and played no role whatsoever in shaping the content of revelation. That is, central to traditional theories of revelation is the idea that the Prophet's personality was not of particular importance in the event of revelation, since he was only a passive channel for delivering God's message to humanity. In other words, the Prophet's personality is not normally dealt with as part of the larger discussion of the concept of revelation as traditionally understood. As Smith noted, 'To say "and Muhammad is the apostle of God" is to commit oneself to a belief, not about the person of Muhammad, but about the validity of what he brought. The personality of Muhammad is essentially irrelevant.'[48] In sum, traditional accounts of revelation emphasise that the Prophet's persona and psychological make-up or mind did not affect the content of revelation at all.

The Prophet's feelings/experiences at the moment of revelation

The theme of the Prophet's feeling at the moment of revelation appears in numerous hadiths and traditional accounts. The Prophet is often reported in such literature to have explained the revelation process as a difficult, painful and agonising experience. A hadith in the collection of Bukhari states that 'the Prophet's face was red and he kept on breathing heavily for a while [during the process of revelation] and then he was relieved'.[49] According to another hadith, the Prophet's face was often covered with sweat in the process of revelation, even during a very cold day.[50] In some instances, the Prophet 'covered his head with his shirt [since he was] suffering intensely'.[51] Along similar lines, the Prophet is reported to have asserted that 'never once did I receive a revelation without thinking that my soul had been torn away from me'.[52] In an attempt to explain why the process of revelation involved suffering for Muhammad, the medieval Muslim scholar and historiographer Abd al-Rahman Ibn Khaldun (d. 808/1406) argued that the Prophet's painful experience at the moment of revelation was intimately related to the Prophet's transformation from his own state to another, or a sudden leap from the human level of consciousness to that of a supernatural order. Although Ibn Khaldun did not go so far as to reject the idea that the Prophet's mind was a mere passive channel during the event of revelation, he stated that 'revelation means leaving one's humanity in order to attain angelic perceptions and to hear the speech of the soul. This causes pain since it means that an essence leaves its own essence and exchanges it . . . for the ultimate stage.'[53]

God's words, revelation and the Qurʾān

It has been shown so far that revelation as portrayed in most prophetic traditions and in the writings of most medieval Muslim scholars consists of a number of characteristics: (1) God revealed His message to the Prophet Muhammad through the mediation of an angelic figure, recognised as Gabriel; (2) the angelic figure did not merely appear in the Prophet's psyche, but appears as an external being before Muhammad; and (3) the Prophet was a passive recipient of revelation, and his personality did not affect the content of revelation, and thus the Qurʾān. In this sense, as Saeed notes, the Prophet in the traditional accounts is portrayed as 'much like an audio-recording instrument such as a tape-recorder',[54] having been reduced to a 'passive bystander'.[55] The medieval theologian al-Nasafi (d. 508/1114) summarises the views of the scholars of his time concerning revelation as follows:

> The Qur'ān is God's speaking . . . He caused Gabriel to hear it [His speaking] as sounds and letters . . . Gabriel, upon whom be peace, memorized it, stored it in his mind and then transmitted to the Prophet . . . by bringing down a revelation and a message. He recited it to the Prophet . . . the Prophet memorized it, storing up in his mind and then recited it to his companions.[56]

Along similar lines, the author of *Lisan al-ʿArab*, Ibn Manzur (d. 712/1312), reflects the views of most classical Muslim scholars when he defines the Qur'ān as 'the inimitable revelation, the Speech of God revealed to the Prophet Muhammad through the Angel Gabriel literally and orally in the exact wording of the purest Arabic'.[57] Indeed, in the traditional accounts, the idea that the Qur'ān was verbally revealed to the Prophet is accepted as virtually axiomatic. As such, central to the traditional theories of revelation is the idea that the words of the Qur'ān are equivalent to God's Words, and that the revelation was given verbally to the Prophet Muhammad. There were some debates among Muslim scholars about whether the letters of the Arabic Qur'ān and its sounds when recited were uncreated speech of God. The Hanbalis often believed that God's speech, which is one of His essential attributes, is identical to the letters of the Qur'ān, and thus concluded that the Arabic Qur'ān is literally the uncreated speech of God without beginning and end (*azalī* and *abadī*).[58] Abu al-Hasan al-Ashʿari (d. 324/935) and his followers accepted the idea that God's speech is one of His essential attributes and thus is uncreated, but distinguished between God's speech (which they considered God's eternal attribute) and the created sequence of sounds and letters that give expression to His speech. Therefore, they believed that the 'temporal sequence of sounds that we hear when someone recited the Qur'ān is not itself God's speech, but only an expression of the eternal meaning (*maʿnā*) that is God's attribute of speech'.[59] Despite such minor differences in their viewpoints, for both Ashʿaris and Hanbalis, the Qur'ān was considered to represent God's words, and had nothing to do with Muhammad's own words or ideas.

As shown, the traditional theories of revelation did not distinguish between God's Speech, the words given to Muhammad in the event of revelation, and the Qur'ān. All three were considered equal, or one and the same. The citations from Nasafi and Ibn Manzur clearly show how the majority of classical Muslim scholars understood revelation and its relation to the Qur'ān: the Qur'ān is God's Word; it contains neither Muhammad's own words nor his own interpretation of his revelatory experience. As Amirpur has put it, from the late second century of Islamic history onwards, the idea that 'the Qur'ān in form and content was shaped by the historical figure of the Prophet' was not thinkable for mainstream Muslim scholars.[60] Up to the present day, mainstream Muslims have adhered to this viewpoint. Indeed, as Esack notes, 'the Qur'ān as the compilation of the "Speech of God" does not refer to a book inspired or influenced by Him or written under the guidance of His spirit. Rather, it is viewed as His direct speech.'[61]

It is worth noting that the Muʿtazilis (who created a rationalist school of thought by the end of the first century of Islamic history and flourished for a few centuries) believed in the notion of the 'createdness' of the Qurʾān. This view was in line with their idea that God's attributes of essence should be distinguished from God's attributes of action (*ṣefāt-e feʿlīye*).[62] The Muʿtazilis' view often gave rise to the idea that the Qurʾān was a manifestation of divine speech in human language.[63] Some Muʿtazili figures went so far as to distinguish between God's speech and the words of the Qurʾān, arguing that 'what we have on earth is never the [literal] word of God itself but rather an account or report of what God said, a kind of indirect speech'.[64] Within this line of thinking, the Muʿtazili theologian Abd al-Jabbar (d. 415/1025) argued that 'God's speech can be neither a book – a written text is not speech, but only a sign of speech once spoken – nor a person'.[65] Despite such viewpoints, the Muʿtazilis did not in general reject the dogma that God speaks,[66] and that the Qurʾān itself is God's speech, even if it could be viewed as a kind of indirect speech. The idea that the Qurʾān contains the created speech of God recorded in a human language, too, was not often used by Muʿtazili scholars to argue for more flexibility in the interpretation of the Qurʾān. The debate between the Muʿtazilis and the Ashʿaris (or the Hanbalis) was mainly limited to theological discussions about the nature of the Qurʾān, the divine attributes, and their relation to the unity of God; and as Madigan has aptly noted, the conflict between them was not related to 'the Qurʾān's role as an authoritative source for law and theology; both were agreed on that'.[67] In addition, the Muʿtazilis did not, in general, challenge the dominant accepted view that the Qurʾān contains neither the Prophet's own words nor his own interpretation of the revelation. In this sense, any idea that the Prophet's own words were incorporated as part of the Qurʾān was alien to the Muʿtazilis in general.

Challenges to traditional theories of revelation

The idea that the Qurʾān is of a divine origin has not been a central theme in Western/non-Muslim scholarship. The Qurʾān in its very nature, according to many Western scholars of the nineteenth and twentieth centuries, is connected to a number of contextual and human elements, such as Muhammad's personality, his biography and his familiarity with earlier religious scriptures, as well as the socio-cultural norms of Arabian society and the historical events that the Prophet and the nascent Muslim community confronted.[68] In this sense, a significant number of Western scholars challenged the traditional understanding of revelation by claiming that Muhammad was not a passive recipient of revelation. Tor Andrae (d. 1947) emphasised the Prophet's human role in revelation, arguing that Muhammad's relation to the revelations became more 'stylized' and 'objectivized' in the course of his prophetic mission.[69] In a similar vein, the French scholar of Islamic studies Maxime Rodinson (d. 2004) highlighted the state of Muhammad's mind and personality in the event of revelation, stating that some features of the Qur'ān could be ascribed to the Prophet's human traits, such as his thoughts and desires.[70] Richard Bell (d. 1952) argued that '*waḥy* does not mean the verbal communication of the text of a revelation, but is a "suggestion", "prompting" or "inspiration" coming into a person's mind'.[71] Montgomery Watt (d. 2006) went so far as to argue that the notion of revelation is connected to both Muhammad's personality and the development of his prophetic career.[72] These scholars indeed paid significant attention to the active role that Muhammad may have played within the process of revelation or in wording his revelatory experiences. Accordingly, the Qur'ān, for them, has humanistic nature inherently attached to it.

Such ideas have, in general, not been welcomed by Muslim scholars. While it is not surprising for a non-Muslim scholar to question the divine nature of the Qur'ān, Muslim scholars do not generally tend to do so. Without going into extensive detail at this stage, I emphasise that there have been a few Muslim philosophers in the medieval period, such as Abu Nasr al-Farabi (d. 339/950) and Ibn Sina (d. 428/1037), who did not ignore the Prophet's role in the process of revelation.[73] In addition, the view that the Prophet played a role in shaping the content of revelation had some adherents during the early modern period among some Muslim scholars from the Indian subcontinent – in particular, Shah Wali Allah (d. 1762).[74] Another aspect of the traditional understanding of revelation, namely its emphasis on the role of the angelic figure in transmitting God's message to the Prophet, was challenged by the Indian scholar Sayyid Ahmad Khan (d. 1898).[75] During the twentieth century, there were a few Muslim scholars who presented some alternatives to the traditional view regarding Muhammad's role in revelation. One may refer, in particular, to Maruf Rusafi (d. 1945)[76] from Iraq, Ali Dashti (d. 1982)[77] from Iran and the Indian reformer Asaf Fyzee (d. 1981),[78] although none of these authors was primarily concerned with developing a systematic theory of revelation. Despite the existence of such views, the general tendency among contemporary Muslim scholars has involved a commitment to the traditional understanding of revelation. As Saeed notes:

> The standard traditional Muslim view, both Sunni and Shi'i, of the revelation attributes the composition of the Qur'ān to God alone, and denies any human role in its production. According to this view, the Prophet faithfully communicated what had been 'dictated' to him by God in the Arabic language through the angel of revelation, usually identified as Gabriel, without addition or alteration . . . to his followers. On the whole, this understanding of the revelation has been maintained throughout Islamic history and is still the basis of most Islamic exegetical work. By and large, Muslim scholars, even of the modern period, adhere to this doctrine of revelation.[79]

In this respect, even the majority of the so-called 'liberal' scholars of the late twentieth and early twenty-first centuries either considered it unnecessary to re-examine the concept of revelation in their reform project, or accepted the dominant standard view concerning revelation, even if they sought to challenge various aspects of traditional Islamic jurisprudence. For example, although Fatima Mernissi (d. 2016) was engaged in promoting gender equality and challenged patriarchal interpretations of the Qur᾽ān, she accepted various aspects of traditional theories of revelation. When dealing with the notion of the revelation, Mernissi's ideas are close to the orthodox view in that she believes in the 'externality' of revelation.[80] Another scholar, Asma Barlas, who reads the Qur᾽ān as an anti-patriarchal and egalitarian text, does not challenge the idea that the Qur᾽ān is the verbatim Word of God. For her, 'the Qur᾽ān is inimitable, inviolate, inerrant and incontrovertible'.[81] Likewise, although the Sudanese scholar Abdullahi Ahmed an-Na῾im sought to reform the Sharī῾a in light of human rights and modern democracy, he never challenged the established traditional accounts of revelation. He accepts the general Muslim belief that revelation and the Qur᾽ān do not have any human dimensions: 'every word and letter of the Qur᾽ān is direct revelation . . . To doubt the direct and totally divine nature of any part of the text of the Qur᾽ān is to cease to be a Muslim.'[82] Along similar lines, Malik Bennabi (d. 1973), an Algerian scholar who has interpreted the Qur᾽ān in light of the changing needs of Muslims today, believes that revelation and the Qur᾽ān have nothing to do with the Prophet's personality and feelings. He is quoted as having stated that:

> As for the revelations themselves, they occurred according to definite measures and in varying time intervals in such a way that was clearly indifferent to the personal state of the person who was receiving them. In other words, those revelations were taking place irrespective of the Prophet's grief and sufferings or wishes and aspirations . . . These phenomenological characteristics of the Qur᾽ān vividly indicate its impersonality and externality with regard to the Prophet's self.[83]

It is in this context that, as Muhammad Arkoun (d. 2010) notes, for most Muslim scholars 'revelation is not questioned or analyzed'.[84] Arkoun argues that 'the received idea of Revelation has been placed in the realm of the unthinkable in Islamic tradition since the eleventh century'.[85] Therefore, 'what is received, taught, interpreted and lived as Revelation in Jewish, Christian and Muslim traditions needs to be revisited, re-read and re-interpreted'.[86] This revisiting, rethinking or reinterpreting should consider revelation 'with its immanent historical dimension and not merely as a transcendental, substantial, eternal entity above human history'.[87] The importance of this revisiting or rethinking of the traditional concept of revelation, according to Arkoun, is that it enables 'Islamic thought to share the concerns of the modern reassessment of knowledge'.[88]

A new trend of Islamic 'reform theology' emerged during the late twentieth and early twenty-first centuries which is in line with Arkoun's proposal for the necessity of rethinking various features of the traditional understanding of revelation. While some significant questions about the nature of revelation and the Prophet's human contribution to shaping the content of the Qur᾽ān remain, to a great extent, unanswered in Arkoun's writings, a number of contemporary Muslim scholars like Fazlur Rahman, Nasr Hamid Abu Zayd, Abdolkarim Soroush and Muhammad Mojtahed Shabestari have dealt with such issues in great detail. Indeed, while Arkoun's thesis itself is primarily concerned with issues of interpretation rather than examining the nature of revelation, or the way in which the Qur'ān was sent down to the Prophet, the scholars examined in the present study have sought to rethink and revise various aspects of what I referred to as traditional theories of revelation. In the following chapters, I demonstrate how the mentioned scholars' projects fall within the scope of Arkoun's proposal by rethinking various features of the traditional accounts of revelation. I argue that their theses revolve around viewing the Qur'ān in a humanistic and historical fashion. A significant effect of viewing the Qur'ān in this way, as will be argued, is that it entails the use of specific hermeneutical methods and approaches to the nature of the Qur'ān and methods of its interpretation.

Conclusion

This chapter has argued that although the Qur'ān and a few hadiths present a less 'rigid' understanding of revelation and do not explicitly support the traditional thesis regarding the externality of Gabriel vis-à-vis the Prophet during the event of revelation, the majority of Muslim scholars in the course of Islamic history, including the modern period, have attempted to separate revelation from the mundane by emphasising the 'externality' of the Qur'ānic revelations vis-à-vis the person of the Prophet. To maintain the transcendence of the divine, traditional accounts have tended to disregard any interpretation that could possibly support any human role in the process of revelation. As shown, traditional theories of revelation consider the Qur'ān the literal Word of God delivered to the Prophet through the mediation of the Angel Gabriel, and thus consider Muhammad a mere passive vessel for the message's delivery. The Prophet played no role whatsoever in guiding the content of the Qur'ān. In the last section of this chapter, I argued that there have been a few Muslim scholars in the course of Islamic intellectual history who challenged various aspects of the traditional accounts of revelation. This examination has prepared the ground for exploring the ideas of Rahman, Soroush, Abu Zayd and Shabestari, who have challenged numerous aspects of this understanding of revelation and proposed theories concerning how the Prophet Muhammad received revelation and what contributions he himself made to the event of revelation. In the following chapters, I will examine as well how their ideas concerning revelation have broader consequences in terms of their approaches to the interpretation of the Qur'ān.

Notes

1. See also: Q 2:136; 4:60; 7:117.
2. See: Q 2:41; 3:3; 6:92; 12:111; 46:12; 87:18–19.
3. Wild, 'We have Sent Down to Thee the Book with the Truth', p. 147.

4. Wansbrough, *Qur'anic Studies*, p. 35.
5. Suyuti says, 'Gabriel is responsible for the Revealed Scripture, which he brings down to the Messenger' (Burge, *Angels in Islam*, p. 118). See also Ibid., p. 92.
6. See Burge, *Angels in Islam*, p. 43.
7. Wansbrough, *Qur'anic Studies*, pp. 34–5.
8. Wild, 'We have Sent Down to Thee the Book with the Truth', p. 148.
9. Leirvik, 'Waḥy and tanzīl', p. 104.
10. Wild, 'We have Sent Down to Thee the Book with the Truth', p. 141.
11. Ahmad b. Faris, *Mu'jam Maqayis al-Lugha*. under *nazala*, available online at http://www.waqfeya.com/book.php?bid=3144 (last accessed on 21 June 2017).
12. Wild, 'We have Sent Down to Thee the Book', p. 141.
13. For instance, the well-known pre-Islamic Arab poet Hassan b. Thabit used the idea that a poem came down (*nuzūlaha*) from heaven in one of his poems. This shows that the use of this term in the pre-Islamic era was related to the speech of a poet or a soothsayer for describing poetic inspiration (see Wild, 'We have Sent Down to Thee the Book with the Truth', p. 140; Izutsu, *God and Man*, p. 184).
14. Wild, 'We have Sent Down to Thee the Book with the Truth', pp. 142–3.
15. Toshihiko Izutsu, *God and Man*, pp. 165–6.
16. Ibid., p. 166.
17. Izutsu, *God and Man*, p. 171.
18. For details and the references, see Nahidi, 'Toward a New Qur'ānic Hermeneutics', p. 158. See also Madaninejad, 'New Theology in the Islamic Republic of Iran', pp. 66–7; Madigan, *The Qur'an's self-Image*, pp. 67–8.
19. See his *Tafsīr al-Mizān* under Q 2:185, available online at http://www.shiasource.com/al-mizan (last accessed 5 May 2017). See also Nahidi, 'Toward a New Qur'ānic Hermeneutics', p. 159.
20. Leirvik, 'Waḥy and Tanzīl', p. 101.
21. Ibid., p. 120.
22. See Armajani, *Dynamic Islam*, p. 117.
23. Madigan, 'Revelation and Inspiration', p. 440.
24. Ibid.
25. Madigan, *The Qur'an's Self-Image*, p. 144.
26. Ibid.; for Madigan, *kitāb* refers to 'the exercise of divine authority and knowledge, for which writing functions as a metaphor or a symbol rather than as a simple description' (Madigan, *The Qur'an's Self-Image*, p. 123). In a similar vein, Wansbrough is inclined to interpret the term *kitāb* as decree or authority rather than book or scripture (Wansbrough, *Qur'anic Studies*, p. 75). This idea stands in sharp contrast to Western scholarship as a whole. As Madigan himself noted, 'Western scholars have, by and large, taken the use of the word *kitāb* as an indication that Muḥammad intended to provide his community with a written canon of scripture parallel to those possessed by the Christians and the Jews . . . [For example] Bell understands the *kitāb* to have been intended to be the complete record of revelation' (Madigan, 'Book', p. 248).
27. Ernst, *How to read the Qur'an*, p. 118
28. According to a number of traditions, the Prophet was initially inspired by God in the form of 'good dreams' (*ruyān*, the plural of *ruyā*) before the commencement of his prophetic mission. See Bukhari, *Sahih al-Bukhari*, Vol. 1, hadith No. 3. See also Bukhari, *Sahih al-Bukhari*, Vol. 9, hadith No. 111.
29. Madigan, *Qur'an's Self-Image*, p. 142.
30. Bukhari, *Sahih al-Bukhari*, Vol. 1, hadith No. 2.
31. Watt, *Muhammad at Mecca*, p. 56.
32. Wensinck and Rippin, 'waḥy', p. 53.
33. Ibid.
34. Graham, *Divine Word*, p. 17.
35. Madigan, 'Revelation and Inspiration', p. 445.
36. Graham, *Divine Word*, p. 26.
37. Ibid.
38. Zarkashi, *al-Burhān fī 'Ulūm al-Qur'ān* [*the Proof in the Sciences of the Qur'ān*], pp. 229–30.
39. For a discussion about this, see Abrahamov, 'Scripturalist and Traditionalist Theology', p. 271.

40. Saeed, *Interpreting the Qur'an*, p. 18.
41. Ali, *Imam Shafi'i*, p. 57.
42. Ibid.
43. Lowry, *Early Islamic Legal Theory*, p. 61.
44. Saeed, *Interpreting the Qur'an*, p. 19.
45. Watt, *Muhammad in Mecca*, p. 57.
46. Webb, 'Gabriel', pp. 278–9.
47. Bukhari says that the angel of revelation was visible on one occasion to Umm Salama, one of the Prophet's wives. Madigan, 'Revelation and Inspiration', p. 442.
48. Smith, *Islam in Modern History*, p. 27.
49. Bukhari, *Sahih al-Bukhari*, Vol. 6, hadith No. 508.
50. Bukhari, *Sahih al-Bukhari*, Vol. 1, hadith No. 2.
51. Cited in Wensinck and Rippin, 'Waḥy', p. 53.
52. Cited in Esack, *The Qur'an: A Short Introduction* (Oxford: Oneworld, 2002), p. 43.
53. Ibn Khaldun, *Muqaddimah*, p. 78.
54. Abdullah Saeed, 'Fazlur Rahman', p. 45.
55. Saeed, *Interpreting the Qur'an*, p. 37.
56. Cited in Ibid., p. 38.
57. Muhammad Ibn Mukarram Ibn Manzur, *Lisan al-'Arab*, Vol. 5 (Cairo: Dar al-Kitab al-Masri, no date), p. 3563, cited in Esack, *Qur'an, Liberation and Pluralism*, p. 53.
58. For a report on this, see Heemskerk, 'Speech', p. 112. Ahmad b. Hanbal is cited to have even said that 'the Torah and the Injil and any book that God has sent (as long as it is accepted that it is the speech of God) is uncreated' (Madigan, *The Qur'an's Self-Image*, p. 49).
59. Vishanoff, *The Formation of Islamic Hermeneutics*, p. 146; see also Ibid., p. 179; There were some scholars who went so far as to declare that even the structure of the text was 'ordained by God, who intended the Qur'ān to be a written cannon of scripture'. Madigan, *The Qur'an's Self-Image*, p. 47. For a discussion of how different theologies of divine speech among early Muslim scholars may affect hermeneutics, see Vishanoff, *The Formation of Islamic Hermeneutics*.
60. Amirpur, 'The Expansion of Prophetic Experience', p. 430.
61. Esack, *Qur'an, Liberation and Pluralism*, p. 53.
62. See Campanini, 'Mu'tazila in Islamic History and Thought', pp. 41–50.
63. Saeed, *Reading the Qur'an in the Twenty-first Century*, p. 84.
64. Madigan, 'Revelation and Inspiration', p. 446.
65. Peters, *God's Created Speech*, p. 417.
66. The medieval exegete Razi states that 'there is consensus of the *ummah* (community) on the issue that God speaks'. Cited in Saeed, *Interpreting the Qur'an*, p. 30.
67. Madigan, 'The Search for Islam's True Scholasticism', p. 45.
68. The idea that the Qur'ān should be understood in light of the Prophet's biography and in connection with Muhammad's personality and the events that the nascent Muslim community experienced was highlighted in early Western Qur'ānic scholarship, including the works of Gustav Weil (d. 1889), Aloys Sprenger (d. 1893), William Muir (d. 1905), Ignaz Goldziher (d. 1921), Friedrich Schwally (d. 1919) and Theodor Noldeke (d. 1930).
69. For details of Tor Andrae's views towards revelation, see Graham, *Divine Word*, pp. 16–17.
70. Rodinson, *Muhammad*, pp. 77–8.
71. Bell, 'Muhammad's Visions', p. 148.
72. Watt, *Islam and Christianity Today*, p. 66. I will explore Watt's theory of revelation later when I discuss Soroush's account of revelation.
73. I will explore the theories of revelation presented by these philosophers later when I discuss Fazlur Rahman's account of revelation.
74. This will be discussed in detail in Chapter 4.
75. Ahmad Khan argues that there can be no interpolated angelic figure between God and the Prophet (Troll, *Sayyid Ahmad Khan*, p. 185). See also Ibid., pp. 282–4.
76. Al-Rausafi argued that the Qur'ān was the speech of Muhammad, who possessed great intelligence and imaginative power. It was this extraordinary talent of the Prophet that enabled him to transform his *waḥy*

into what became the Qur'ānic text. Accordingly, al-Rausafi argued that Muhammad's prophetic mission was not only the result of some divine intervention, but also the product of his extraordinary mind. (For details of his work, see Khalidi, *Images of Muhammad*, pp. 292–3.)

77. The Iranian scholar Dashti argues that the Qur'ān was not literally revealed to the Prophet, but was rather installed in his heart and then spoken through Muhammad's human faculties. For Dashti, the language of the Qur'ān is Muhammad's. (For details of his work, see Rippin, *Muslims*, pp. 247–8. See also Dashti, *Twenty Three Years*.)
78. Fyzee argues that in the Qur'ān God does not speak directly, but rather it is Muhammad who speaks with divine authorisation. As such, the Qur'ān should not be considered the literal Word of God. Fyzee, *A Modern Approach to Islam*, pp. 109–10.
79. Abdullah Saeed, 'Qur'ān: Tradition of Scholarship and Interpretation', p.7561.
80. Mernisssi, *Islam and Democracy*, pp. 75–6.
81. Barlas, *Believing Women in Islam*, p. 33. Aysha Hidayatullah aptly noted that 'Muslim feminist theologians unequivocally take the entire text of the Qur'ān to be the verbatim word of God. Because the entire Qur'ān is accepted as divine and authentic, none of its parts may be attributed to human error or to be edited.' Hidayatullah, 'Inspiration and Struggle', p. 167.
82. An-Naim, *Toward an Islamic Reformation*, p. 196.
83. El-Mesawi, 'Religion, Society and Culture in Malik Bennabi's Thought', p. 223.
84. Arkoun, *The Unthought in Contemporary Islamic Thought*, p. 69.
85. Ibid., p. 67.
86. Ibid., p. 73.
87. Ibid., p. 27.
88. Ibid., p. 90.

3

Fazlur Rahman: Revelation Historicised

This chapter aims to examine the relationship between Fazlur Rahman's theory of revelation and his Qur'ānic hermeneutics. The question of whether Rahman's Qur'ānic hermeneutics have their roots in his theory of revelation should be divided from the very outset into two questions, one theoretical and the other practical. On the theoretical level, the question concerns how Rahman uses his theory of revelation to develop certain hermeneutical theories when approaching the Qur'ān. On the practical level, the question concerns how Rahman uses his hermeneutical theories in his interpretation of certain texts or themes of the Qur'ān. To address these questions, this chapter first presents the key ideas and principles associated with Rahman's theory of revelation. This involves Rahman's idea about the nature of revelation and Muhammad's role in the process of revelation, including his own role in shaping the precise wording of his revelatory experiences. Then, it examines the extent to which Rahman's account of revelation has been influenced by theories of revelation presented by specific medieval Muslim philosophers. Among Muslim philosophers, I focus mainly on al-Farabi and Ibn Sina, and occasionally on Abu Yusuf Ya'qub al-Kindi (d. 259/873). The remainder of the chapter will address the two aforementioned questions in two separate sections. I explore Rahman's hermeneutical theories and their connections to various features of his theory of revelation. Then, I choose certain examples that are crucial for understanding Rahman's methods of interpreting the Qur'ān. As examples of how his interpretive method functions in practice, I look at how it is applied to the themes of gender issues and the Qur'ānic institution of *shūrā* (consultation).

Rahman's account of revelation

The nature of revelation and the Prophet's role in it

Rahman's theory of revelation begins with the question of what shaped Muhammad's revelatory experiences. Did the revelations that Muhammad received consist of words or images, or a mixture of both? Rahman is not satisfied with the traditional view that revelation was given to the Prophet in a mere verbal form. He rejects the idea that Muhammad heard some words in 'an ordinary human sense' during the event of revelation.[1] Rahman rejects the idea that the Prophet heard God's message in the same way that his addressees heard Muhammad's words. For him, revelation included 'an actual mental sound, not a physical sound'.[2] Drawing on a number of Qur'ānic verses (such as Q 42:51–2; 12:108; 75:16–19; and 20:114), Rahman argues that what the Prophet received in the process of revelation was an 'idea-word, not a physically acoustic word'.[3] Some scholars have interpreted Rahman's notion of 'idea-words' to mean that what the Prophet received were messages in the form of images, symbols and visions.[4] In Rahman's account, revelation also consisted of 'feelings' created in the Prophet's heart; indeed, God's message came to Muhammad in this way.[5] This means that 'ideas and feelings float about in revelation', and that the Prophet's feelings, expectations and anxieties are parts of the revelations he received, as the Qur'ān states (Q 80:1–3).[6] Therefore, what shaped the revelation was the mixture or combination of feelings, ideas and non-acoustic words, and thus they were all born in the heart and mind of the Prophet during the process of revelation.[7]

Central to Rahman's theory is the idea that the Prophet was not a passive recipient of revelation. There are three main elements in Rahman's argument that are closely associated with the notion that the Prophet played an active role as participant in the act of revelation: (1) Muhammad's personality, his life experience and his moral-spiritual consciousness played a key role in the content of the revelation; (2) the Prophet's mind was actively involved in the process of revelation; and (3) the Angel Gabriel was not a physical being (existing 'outside' of the Prophet) that mechanically delivered God's message to the Prophet.

The connection between the Prophet's personality and revelation

Rahman believes that Muhammad's personality and feelings played a key role in his revelatory experiences: 'whereas on the one hand, the Revelation emanated from God, on the other, it was also intimately connected with his deeper personality'.[8] Rahman did not deny that revelation was of a transcendent origin, but argued that it was 'equally intimately related to the inmost personality of the Prophet Muhammad whose relationship to it cannot be mechanically conceived like that of a record'.[9] This emphasis on the role of the Prophet's personality in somehow shaping the revelation is strongly related to the idea that although Muhammad did not consciously seek out prophethood, he had to prepare and increase his potential to receive divine revelations from God. Indeed, revelation could not have taken place 'in a vacuum' since the Prophet, having been an orphan himself, had an acute sensitivity towards the moral problems of his society, which made him think deeply about them. Rahman asserts:

> The Prophet had certain problems on his mind that tormented him, that drove him to the cave of Hera to contemplate and pray to God for a solution, and that it is then that the *waḥy*, the divine guidance, burst upon him. How can all this happen in a vacuum?[10]

That is, the Prophet's concerns about the moral problems of his society provided the broader context in which revelation came into being, and played a key role in determining the content of the divine revelations he received in the later stages of his life. Muhammad had to possess some 'potentials' without which he could not have been able to receive revelation.[11] Muhammad's contemplation in the cave of Hera prepared his potential human intellect for the emanation of revelation from God. These potentials were acquired both by natural endowments given to him by God and by his own personal efforts, meaning that revelation had both human and divine aspects. While Muhammad did not consciously seek out prophethood, he nevertheless prepared himself for such a task,[12] since he had 'an intense, natural, inborn sensitivity for moral problems . . . [and] this sensitivity was increased by his having been orphaned so early in life'.[13] As such, in Rahman's humanistic approach, *waḥy* is the culmination of a long internal process and a deep contemplative mood, meaning that 'Muhammad's mind had to be in a receptive state in order to be illuminated through revelation'.[14] Indeed, for Rahman, the revelation was somehow conditioned by the personality of Muhammad.

Rahman further asserts that Muhammad 'was not by temperament an aggressive or obtrusive man'.[15] A close study of Muhammad's life shows that he was 'a naturally pensive, introverted, shy and withdrawn' person who 'had been impelled by an inner urge born of an acute perception of the existential human situation to enter the arena of historic action'.[16] According to Rahman, this personality of the Prophet had an influence on the revelations that he received, especially in its early stages. Closely related to his deeper personality, the Prophet's early revelations were characterised by 'a staccato-like abruptness' and consisted of 'very short expressions like sudden volcanic outbursts or the passage of a huge river through a gorge'.[17] That is, Rahman's theory implies that Muhammad's personality played a far greater role in the formation, content and style of revelation than is traditionally understood.

The role of the Prophet's heart and mind in revelation

Rahman's idea about Muhammad's role in revelation is closely related to his views on the nature of revelation. One of the main characteristics of prophets, according to Rahman, is that God's message 'fills' their heart.[18] As noted in Chapter 1, the Qur'ān in a number of verses (Q 26:193; 2:97) states that God's message has not been brought down into the Prophet's ear, but has been brought upon the Prophet's heart (*qalb*). Drawing on these verses, Rahman suggests that God's message was not simply heard by the Prophet but was installed in his heart.[19] Rahman reads the Qur'ānic verse 'if God so willed, He could seal up your heart' (Q 42:24) to mean that there will be no more revelation without the contribution of the Prophet's heart: 'the Prophet's consciousness was invaded from time to time, when the opportunity for it arose, by some force and this force definitely came from his heart'.[20] It is in light of Rahman's emphasis on the role of the Prophet's heart in revelation that his notion of 'feeling-idea-words' becomes clearer. The non-acoustic words that were born in the Prophet's mind had become intertwined with his feelings in the process of revelation. Muhammad received revelation as mental words ('idea-words') that had become closely tied with his heart ('feeling'),[21] meaning that revelation involved an internal process, integral to the heart and mind of the Prophet. Revelation, according to Rahman, 'pushed so forcefully through [the Prophet's] heart that immediately it got clothed in words'.[22]

The role of the angelic figure in revelation

The idea that revelation was sent down to Muhammad's heart and that Muhammad heard words mentally is intimately connected to Rahman's rejection of the externality of the angelic figure vis-à-vis the Prophet. For Rahman, the agent of revelation was not an angel as traditionally understood; rather, it was the Spirit. This Spirit was not external in relation to the Prophet and did not have a physical nature, meaning that it was 'spiritual and internal' to Muhammad.[23] Rahman suggests that God 'infuses a Spirit in the Prophet's mind'[24] in the actual process of revelation when required. Rahman considers Spirit as 'the highest form of angelic nature and closest to God', rather than identifying it as a mediator between God and the Prophet, or the Angel Gabriel.[25] He asserts:

> [Muslim orthodoxy] tried to portray the angel of revelation, the 'trusted spirit', as some kind of a being who came from the outside and gave to the Prophet messages from God, more or less in the same manner as the postman hands you over your mail. And . . . this mechanical sort of picture has done a lot of damage to a real understanding of the relationship between the person of the Prophet and the Qurʾān.[26]

This view is in line with my discussions in the previous chapter. Traditional accounts highlighted Gabriel's role as the transmitter of revelation in order to preserve the transcendental features of the revelation, and thus to downplay Muhammad's role in revelation. For Rahman, the idea that the Prophet received revelation via the mediation of Gabriel was invented in the eighth or ninth century of the Common Era. Although angels (*malāʾika*) are mentioned in the Qurʾān, they are never referred to as the angels of revelation.[27] It is in this context that Rahman rejects the validity of those hadiths in which the angel is depicted as a physical figure conversing with Muhammad in the presence of his companions. Orthodoxy, according to Rahman, 'made the Revelation of the Prophet entirely through the ear and external to him and regarded the angel . . . an entirely external agent'.[28]

God's role in revelation

Rahman sought to distinguish between the source of revelation and the process of revelation in his theory. Insofar as its source is concerned, the revelation was external to the Prophet, but it was internal to him in regard to its process. The words Muhammad heard in the revelation were mental, and the Spirit was internal to him, but the ultimate source of revelation was external to him: 'the divine messages broke through the consciousness of the Prophet from an agency whose source is God',[29] and thus 'the true revealing subject always remains God'.[30] That is, 'the entire process occurs in [the Prophet's] mind . . . insofar as the psychological process [of revelation] is concerned, but is Revealed Word insofar as its source lies beyond his reach'.[31] In addition, although the Prophet's mind had to go through various stages of development prior to receiving his first revelatory experiences, his extraordinary mind and personality were also God's endowment. That is, although the Prophet had to prepare himself for his prophetic career, he had 'a potential revelation in him' bestowed by God.[32] Therefore, in both stages – in the Prophet's preparation for beginning his prophetic mission and in the actual process of revelation – God was the ultimate source.

Rahman compares revelation with other forms of inspiration, attempting to distinguish the former from the latter. Psychologically speaking, divine revelation is similar to poetic and mystic inspiration, and the relation between ideas, feelings and words is the same in each event.[33] However, the prophetic revelations were 'entirely *sui generis*' and should be differentiated from any other form of inspiration in the sense that 'divine revelation forms ascending degrees of the same phenomena of creative inspiration'.[34] Rahman notes that prophets are different from philosophers, mystics and poets because they have 'sensitive and impregnable personalities', enabling them to be recipients of divine messages.[35] They are recipients of some special power, gifted by God, which enables them to 'see and know things the way others are not able to'.[36]

The Prophet's role in releasing God's Words: the Qur'ān's duality

The last key theme of Rahman's theory concerns how the Qur'ānic text emerged from the revelation. To explain this, Rahman attributes another role to the Prophet within the process of revelation. We recall that the Spirit is an agency in Rahman's theory which developed in the Prophet's heart and that the Prophet's heart represents an intermediate sphere in which God's Words were stored. The Prophet's role was then to release the Spirit as well as the mental words and visions, and to clothe them in acoustic words. For Rahman, the 'Qur'ān was first "brought down" to the lowest heaven (i.e. the Prophet's heart) . . . and then relevant verbal passages produced when needed'.[37] Drawing on Hocking's *The Meaning of God in Human Experience*, Rahman argued that the Prophet had a powerful ability that enabled him to propel his feelings 'automatically into an idea, and the idea expresses itself automatically in words'.[38] In Rahman's account, the nature of the words the Prophet heard in revelation is different from the words he used for his audiences. The former consists of 'non-acoustic' words, while the latter includes words in an 'ordinary human sense'. The Prophet uses his own words (in acoustic forms) for his audiences but these words are in conformity with the mental words received in revelation.

Therefore, in addition to the role the Prophet played in revelation, Rahman suggests that Muhammad transformed mental Words (or what he identifies as 'idea-words') into acoustic words (or what he identifies as 'sound-words'). In this way, the Qur'ān becomes a part of Muhammad's speech: 'the Qur'ān is entirely the Word of God and, in an ordinary sense, also entirely the word of Muhammad'.[39] The Qur'ān, for Rahman, 'is entirely the Word of God insofar as it is infallible and absolutely free from falsehood, but, insofar as it comes to the Prophet's heart and then his tongue, it was entirely his word'.[40]

This sense of the Qur'ān's dual nature, as both human and divine, is the result of the revelation being both external to, but also closely connected to, the Prophet's personality, including his feelings, reflections and life experiences. Rahman's theory of revelation, I suggest, justifies appropriately his view about the two-fold character of the Qur'ān – the idea which emphasises that the Qur'ān does not only have a divine nature, but also has a human aspect attached to it. In fact, Rahman utilises his theory of revelation in order to argue for this last point that opens up a flexible space for exegesis, which will be demonstrated later. The Qur'ān was not merely a product of the Prophet's subjective faculties, nor was it completely external to his personality. In Rahman's account, prophecy is considered a divine favour which cannot be acquired by sheer effort alone, but has also humanistic features since the Prophet's human faculties must be raised to their heights by his personal efforts prior to receiving the revelation.

The final issue that should be emphasised here is that although Rahman acknowledges the essential character of the Scripture as an 'Arabic Qur'ān', he does not discuss in detail how 'idea-words' received by the Prophet in the process of revelation are specifically transferred into the Arabic language. This is the main shortcoming of Rahman's theory. Rahman asserts that the Prophet had the power of transferring his revelatory experience into words, familiar for his immediate audiences, because Muhammad, like other prophets, had to do everything to 'get his message across'.[41] This power, which was endowed by God, enabled Muhammad to propel his feeling into ideas and words, which is to say that there is 'an organic relationship between feelings, ideas and words'.[42] However, it is not clear how much the Prophet was guided by God in transferring his experience into 'sound-words', or how much he himself contributed to the wording of the revelations.[43] It seems clear that Muhammad's role was more than that of a mere transmitter of 'idea-words' into the Arabic language in Rahman's theory, but the extent to which the Prophet himself contributes to this process remains somehow unclear.

The sources of Rahman's theory of revelation

As the account outlined in Chapter 2 made clear, Rahman's theory of revelation is unacceptable to those Muslim scholars who believe in what was there described as a traditional theory of revelation. Rahman's views challenge various aspects of the traditional accounts of revelation, which assert that revelation occurred verbally and Muhammad had only to repeat what he had received from the Angel Gabriel. One could ask at this stage whether Rahman's theory of revelation is rooted in any medieval Islamic sources. By way of example, we might point to the influence of the Muʿtazili idea that the Qurʾān is not the eternal speech of God and was not a book given to the Prophet at one time. Rahman himself appreciated the Muʿtazili position on the temporal nature of revelation.[44] Similar to the Muʿtazilis, Rahman believed in the *createdness* of the Qurʾān, and thus like the Muʿtazilis held a position that might be said to involve 'the humanization of the Word of God', although the Muʿtazilis, as discussed in the previous chapter, did not often go so far as to state that the Prophet played a role in articulating his revelation, such that the Qurʾān might be viewed as the Prophet's own word.[45] In addition, Rahman, in a fashion not dissimilar to the Muʿtazilis, has stressed the Qurʾānic principle of *naskh* (abrogation) in his writings to defend the idea that the Qurʾān is created.[46] I shall demonstrate this in detail later.

In addition to the Muʿtazilis, Rahman has also been heavily influenced by a number of medieval Muslim philosophers' accounts of revelation.[47] The fact that Rahman wrote his PhD thesis on Avicenna's psychology at Oxford University gives some indication that he was interested in medieval philosophical teachings.[48] Further, Rahman's teaching career, which included lecturing in Islamic philosophy at Durham University from 1950 until 1958, reveals his interest in medieval philosophical ideas.[49] His interest in philosophy continued and he later wrote a book entitled *Prophecy in Islam* in which he explained the theories of revelation and prophecy developed by medieval Muslim philosophers such as al-Farabi and Ibn Sina.[50] In terms of the influence of Islamic philosophical teachings on his ideas, Rahman himself asserted that 'from the later forties to the mid-fifties I experienced an acute skepticism brought about by the study of philosophy. It shattered my traditional beliefs.'[51] In addition, his interest in philosophical teachings is evident in the light of his reasoning about why philosophical rationalism was a necessary instrument of religion. Although philosophy had been effectively banned from the Islamic curriculum since the twelfth century of the Common Era, Rahman considered it a 'perennial intellectual need' and indispensable for instilling an analytical attitude in future generations of Muslim intellectuals.[52] As a result, given that Rahman was interested in philosophy and wrote extensively on medieval Muslim philosophers, it is not unreasonable to assume that he developed his theory of revelation under the influence of Islamic philosophical thought. This section examines how some aspects of Rahman's theory of revelation have been influenced by the accounts of revelation proposed by medieval Muslim philosophers, focusing mainly on Farabi and Ibn Sina, and occasionally on al-Kindi. Here, I do not analyse the complete oeuvre of these philosophers, but only consider salient elements of their work insofar as they reflect Rahman's ideas about revelation. In other words, it is not claimed here that Rahman's ideas about revelation are totally influenced by the aforementioned philosophers, but rather that certain features of his ideas reflect the philosophers' influence.

Farabi's and Ibn Sina's projects

Both al-Farabi and Ibn Sina developed theories related to revelation and prophecy in their works. Al-Kindi's contribution to this field, however, is not as detailed as that of Farabi and Ibn Sina, since he only points to a few issues concerning revelation in his writings. His importance, as Frank Griffel notes, lies mainly in the fact that 'with him began the tradition of adopting concepts . . . in Greek philosophy to explain processes of prophecy and revelation'.[53] In Islamic Neoplatonic ideas developed by a number of philosophers such as al-Farabi and Ibn Sina, a descending series of ten immaterial Intellects emanates or flows from God (or the First Cause) until it reaches the last. From the tenth Intellect, which is the lowest of the Intellects and governs the terrestrial world, emanates the human souls and the four basic elements of life, namely fire, air, water and earth. Therefore, Islamic Neoplatonism in general rejects the traditional Islamic belief concerning creation *ex nihilio* (creation out of nothing and in time).[54] The crucial element in this theory is the idea that the Active Intellect (*ʿaql al-faʿāl*), which is the ultimate source of knowledge and the cause of human intellection, is responsible for establishing a link between the spiritual realm and the physical world, and thus its function involves giving universal concepts to humans, enabling them to acquire knowledge.[55] The corollary of this idea, which is important to the theme of this chapter, is that the Active Intellect is considered to be the channel through which prophetic knowledge, or revelation, is sent to human beings. That is, al-Farabi and Ibn Sina believe that any form of knowledge, including the content of revelation, is brought about only through a process of emanation from the Active Intellect to human beings.

According to al-Farabi, prophets gain knowledge from the Active Intellect only through emanation, or the overflow of the divine.[56] Central to his account of prophecy is the notion that prior to the stage in which the prophet receives revelation his intellect must go through various stages of development. It is only at the end of this development that the prophet reaches the stage of conjunction with the Active Intellect (*ittiṣāl bilʿaql al-faʿāl*) and accordingly receives revelation. This is the highest stage of human perfection or the highest power of human intellection – or what al-Farabi calls the Acquired Intellect (*ʿaql al-mustafād*).[57] Al-Farabi further asserts that human beings, including prophets, also possess the faculty of imagination through which they receive abstract knowledge. This imaginative faculty (*al-quwwa al-mutakhayyila*) 'acts as a reservoir of sensible impressions after the disappearance of the objects of sensation' and 'combines sensible impressions to form a complex sensible image'.[58] This faculty must also be developed to its perfection in prophets in order to receive revelation: 'The man [viz. the prophet] who has that sight [when his imaginative faculty reaches its utmost perfection] comes to enjoy overwhelming and wonderful pleasure, and he sees wonderful things which can in no way whatever be found in other existents.'[59] Al-Farabi argues that the rational as well as the imaginative faculties are highly developed in prophets. He emphasises that this is a special ability gifted by God to His prophets, enabling them to receive abstract knowledge from the Active Intellect, and to transform this knowledge into figurative images, by means of parables, examples or metaphors, that could be understood by most people.[60]

Like al-Farabi, Ibn Sina believes that there are three faculties that are essential to prophetic activity, namely, the rational power (*al-quwwa al-ʿaqliyya*), the imaginative power (*al-quwwa al-mutakhayyila*) and the effective power (*al-quwwa al-muaththira*).[61] These powers are not only limited to prophets, since all people possess them to some degree, but prophets require the utmost degree of all these powers to receive revelation from God. Ibn Sina and al-Farabi hold in common that prophetic revelation involves the reception of particular images through a process of emanation from the lowest of the celestial intellects aided by the Prophet's strong imaginative faculty. Unlike al-Farabi, however, Ibn Sina argues that the Prophet is also blessed with a strong capacity for intuition (*ḥads*), which is much stronger than that possessed by ordinary human beings.[62] The Prophet's strong intuition enables him to attain instantaneous knowledge from the Active Intellect. Ibn Sina asserts:

> [The prophet] will be receptive to the inspiration of the Active Intellect in all things, and the forms contained in the Active Intellect will be imprinted in him concerning all things, either all at once or nearly so. This imprinting will occur not by conforming to conversion but rather in an orderly manner that includes the middle terms . . . This is a kind of prophecy, or rather the highest of the prophetic faculties, and this faculty is most worthy of being called a 'holy faculty'. It ranks highest among the human faculties.[63]

Prophetic revelation does not necessarily occur at the end of the various stages of intellectual actualisation. As Deborah Black has noted, for Ibn Sina, the prophet's intuition 'does not come in episodic flashes; rather, he receives *all* intelligibles from the agent intellect in a single instant'; that is, the prophet does not lack 'comprehension of the intelligible truths that he receives . . . since they are already rationally ordered and logically arranged insofar as they include the middle terms of the syllogisms that demonstrate their truth'.[64]

Returning now to the initial question about how Islamic philosophical teachings, in particular those developed by al-Farabi and Ibn Sina (and occasionally al-Kindi), have influenced Rahman's theory, I focus in the following section on five aspects of the theories of revelation presented by these philosophers and Rahman himself: (1) the nature of revelation; (2) the Prophet's preparation for receiving revelation; (3) the involvement of the Prophet and the angelic figure in the process of revelation; (4) the potentiality of the Prophet in receiving revelation; and (5) the Prophet's power of transmitting God's Word to his audiences.

The nature of revelation

As discussed, al-Farabi and Ibn Sina share the idea that knowledge is the product of a process of emanation from the Active Intellect to mankind. Prophets are no exceptions to this rule. They receive knowledge through a process of emanation from the Active Intellect after the prophet's faculty of intellect has been prepared for its reception. Along similar lines, but in less detail, al-Kindi argues that the connection between God (the First Cause) and human beings is only established through the process of emanation. He asserts:

> As the First Cause, Most High, is connected with us through His emanation and as we are not connected with Him in any way except through His emanation, it is, therefore, possible for the receiver of His emanation to apprehend Him only to the extent of the powers bestowed on him.[65]

Like al-Farabi and Ibn Sina, Rahman uses the term 'emanation' in his writings when speaking about revelation. Revelation, in Rahman's theory, emanates from God. God does not simply send His message to the Prophet as traditionally understood; instead, revelation emanates or flows from the ultimate source of all beings upon the Prophet's soul: 'God's prophets or human messengers are recipients of some special or extraordinary power which emanates from the ultimate source of all being.'[66] For Rahman, 'the Revelation emanated from God', on the one hand, and was 'intimately connected with his deeper personality' on the other hand.[67]

Rahman's idea that revelation consists of non-physical and non-acoustic words is also rooted in the writings of al-Farabi and Ibn Sina. From the theory of revelation proposed by them, we can conclude that revelation consists of images, symbols and visions which do not necessarily include words in acoustic form, meaning that the prophet did not simply receive a verbal revelation. The prophetic revelation involves the reception of particular images and mental sounds from the celestial souls by the prophet's imaginative faculty. For al-Farabi, the prophet receives 'an overflow of intelligibilities into his imagination, where they become subject to symbolic imitation'. These intelligibilities consist of 'symbols and images'.[68] As Muhsin Mahdi notes, in Farabi's theory, 'revelation means the reception of the theoretical intelligibles or forms' because 'the mediating human power in the contact with the active intellect . . . is the acquired intellect, and this is apparently a theoretical intellect'.[69] Similar to al-Farabi, Ibn Sina argues that 'the concepts and intellectual ideas become images and symbols of deeper reality' as well as 'creative insights' for the prophet.[70] Although Rahman does not explain what he understands to be the nature of revelation in as much detail as al-Farabi and Ibn Sina, his idea that prophetic revelations include the reception of non-physical and non-acoustic words by the Prophet are found in the latter's writings.[71]

Prophet's preparation in receiving the revelation

Rahman's idea that the Prophet's mind should be in a receptive state and must improve its potential powers to become the recipient of revelation is rooted in al-Farabi's writings more than Ibn Sina's. As discussed, for Ibn Sina, prophets do not need necessarily to go through various stages of actualisation before receiving knowledge from the Active Intellect, while al-Farabi argues that a human mind should prepare its potential intellect for the emanation of the Active Intellect. Indeed, Ibn Sina recognises the possibility of achieving instantaneous knowledge without necessarily following procedures for gaining this knowledge, whereas for al-Farabi prophethood is granted to a person after he has gone through a long process of intellectual comprehension. Along al-Farabi's line of thought, Rahman, as already pointed out, argues that although revelation emanates from the divine source, it is conditioned by a human's intellectual preparation.[72] Indeed, what Rahman seems to have borrowed from al-Farabi is the idea that the contribution of the Prophet's mind and the preparation of his potential intellect are necessary preconditions for receiving divine revelation.

The involvement of the Prophet and the angel in the process of revelation

Both al-Farabi and Ibn Sina tended to explain the phenomenon of revelation within the discipline of philosophical psychology.[73] They share the idea that prophecy is an office that a prophet acquired through his faculty of intellect and his power of imagination. Accordingly, in addition to the prophet's involvement in the preparation of his potential intellect, his contribution to revelation also includes the involvement of his faculty of imagination and intellect within the process of revelation. Hence, another viewpoint that these philosophers and Rahman have in common has to do with the active participation or involvement of the prophet's human faculties and efforts in the process of gaining knowledge or prophetic revelations. Further, Rahman's view about the role of the angelic figure (in particular, the idea that the angel of revelation is the Spirit, not a physical being) is close to al-Farabi's and Ibn Sina's ideas. Al-Farabi attempted to explain the nature of the agent of revelation with a reference to the Active Intellect and Spirit, rather than by relying on the traditional Islamic view that recognises him as Gabriel. At the beginning of his *Political Regime*, al-Farabi explicitly states that the agent of revelation ought to be identified with the 'Trusted Spirit' or the 'Holy Spirit'.[74] For him, revelation is the product of emanation and the conjunction between the Active Intellect and the prophet's soul, and thus the angel is nothing but the Active Intellect itself.[75] This understanding of the process of revelation does not leave any room for assuming that the angel had a physical nature. More importantly, neither Rahman nor the above philosophers read the Qur'ānic verse Q 2:97 (stating that the Angel Gabriel brings down revelation to the Prophet's heart) literally, and each reads this verse in a way that identifies the angel of revelation as the Spirit.[76] Like al-Farabi, Ibn Sina identifies the Active Intellect with the Spirit and the angel of revelation. The angel of revelation, for Ibn Sina, is an 'emanating power': 'Revelation is the emanation and the angel is the received emanating power that descends on the prophets as if it were an emanating continuous with the universal intellect.'[77] Indeed, Ibn Sina considers the appearance of the angel and the hearing of his voice as an event that occurs in or through the imaginative faculty of the prophet, and thus regards it as a purely mental phenomenon.[78]

The potentiality of the Prophet in receiving the revelation

In Rahman's account, prophets are identified as possessing extraordinary power, gifted by God, which enables them to receive divine messages. Although the Prophet had to improve his potential powers to receive divine revelations, Rahman argues, he had a 'potential revelation in him'.[79] Along similar lines, al-Farabi and Ibn Sina consistently emphasise in their writings that the prophet had 'potential powers' that he had to develop before he could receive the revelation. According to al-Farabi, the prophet has been endowed with an 'extraordinary intellectual gift', and his intellect develops with the aid of divine power. Ibn Sina similarly asserts that the prophet has an extraordinary power of imagination and intellectual capacities, both of which are endowed by God.[80]

As discussed, Rahman likens the revelatory experiences of the Prophet to poetic or mystic inspiration insofar as their processes are concerned, but argues that the former is a unique phenomenon due to its divine origin. This idea is also rooted in the writings of al-Farabi, Ibn Sina and al-Kindi, but with a minor modification. From al-Farabi's and Ibn Sina's point of view, one can conclude that the prophetic experience can also be shared, though to a lesser degree, by other people, especially philosophers, in the sense that 'what the philosopher knows by reason, the prophet knows by revelation', as John Walbridge has argued.[81] A true prophet, for these philosophers, is a philosopher too. Indeed, the theories presented by the philosophers in question tend to describe revelation and philosophy as different ways of reaching the same truth – an idea which sharply contrasts with the traditional Islamic view of revelation. According to al-Farabi, the main difference between philosophers and prophets is that the philosophers reach the level in which they are prepared enough to receive revelation through reflection and meditation and with the aid of external sources, whereas prophets arrive at it through their extraordinary power of imagination and intellect gifted by God and without the need of a human instructor.[82] Ibn Sina also maintains that philosophers experience lesser degrees of intuitive ability than prophets, and thus are unable to receive the Active Intellect's emanation without the prior aid of a human teacher. Likewise, al-Kindi argues that philosophers must engage in long study, and may intend to answer the questions that are placed before them about 'true matters' with great effort and by delving into sciences such as logic and mathematics.[83] On the other hand, as al-Kindi suggests, 'God inspires him [the prophet] and enlightens his soul without resorting to the use of any first principles.'[84]

The similarity between Rahman's and the philosophers' views about the relationship between revelation and mysticism (or poetry) and between revelation and philosophy is that revelation and prophecy are considered a natural rather than a supernatural phenomenon. Just as Islamic philosophical tradition tends to liken revelation to philosophy, Rahman tends to liken it to poetry and mysticism. This implies that for the former the prophet is a kind of philosopher, and for the latter the prophet is a kind of mystic or poet. Indeed, in keeping with the philosophical teachings presented by al-Farabi, Ibn Sina and al-Kindi, Rahman tends to explain revelation in terms of psychology, with the least possible reliance on supernatural assumptions. Insofar as their psychological processes are concerned, there is no distinction between prophecy, poetry, mystical inspirations and philosophy for both Rahman and the philosophers. Prophecy is described in the theories of revelation presented by Rahman and the philosophers in question more in terms of a natural psychological phenomenon in which human intellection reaches its culmination, since it requires appropriate effort and preparation on the prophet's part. The difference between prophecy, on the one hand, and poetry, mysticism and philosophy on the other hand, is related mainly to their ultimate sources of origination, since the prophet's mind necessarily develops by the aid of the divine power. Further, in both accounts – that developed by Rahman and those developed by the philosophers – stress has been placed on the uniqueness of the Prophet's talents and capacities, all of which have come together in his personality.

The Prophet's power of transmitting words

As discussed, for Rahman, the Prophet has the power of transforming his revelatory experience into words that are familiar for his immediate audiences. This is an essential characteristic of all prophets because they have to 'get their message across'.[85] Rahman goes on to state that 'this power determines them upon a course of action that changes the lives of whole peoples'.[86] Accordingly, prophets shook people's 'consciousness from a state of traditional placidity and hypomoral tension into one of alertness'.[87] For Rahman, one of the main characteristics of the Prophet Muhammad was that he was able to change the 'idea-words' into 'sound-words' through which the life and the worldview of people of Hijaz radically changed.

Such ideas have their roots partly in al-Farabi's and Ibn Sina's writings. The discourse of the philosophers in question tends to involve the idea that prophets, unlike philosophers, are able to transfer the emanating knowledge received from the Active Intellect to other humans in clear, simple and succinct ways. In addition, a prophet must revolutionise his society with his dynamic personality and his effective power. Prophets were founders of political communities and did their best to get their message across. Ibn Sina asserts that the 'intellectual ideas become images and symbols of deeper personality and so gain strength to move people to act in a specified manner'.[88] For Farabi, 'the prophets' most important achievement is . . . their ability to cast theoretical knowledge in a figurative and metaphorical language that most people can understand', as Griffel argues.[89] Therefore, the philosophers in question believed that prophets should be able to formulate their religious consciousness or their revelatory experience into a definite pattern of life for people to follow. This is the way through which prophets revolutionised their societies. As a result, what Rahman and the philosophers in question have in common is that (1) the prophet has the power of transferring the knowledge he has received in the process of revelation in a succinct way, and that (2) the words the prophet expresses are so effective that they change the lives of people.

What I have argued in this section centres on one idea: Rahman's humanistic approach to revelation is indebted to the philosophical Islamic discourse on revelation. Like al-Farabi and Ibn Sina, Rahman believed that the Prophet was not a passive recipient of revelation, but had an active role in the process. It should be noted that the views of these philosophers about revelation have not, in general, been used by them to interpret the Qurʾān, because they were not Qurʾānic interpreters (*mufassir*). Their ideas concerning revelation, however, have a number of consequences about approaches to the Qurʾān, some of which the philosophers themselves might not have considered, and may even go beyond what they themselves intended. For example, the immediate consequence of al-Farabi's and Ibn Sina's theories of revelation is that the Qurʾān is to be understood as containing 'philosophical truths', and is replete with figurative language, metaphors, parables and even visual descriptions of past or future events. As Walbridge has noted, from such philosophical perspectives, the Qurʾān 'is essentially an imaginative rhetorical phenomenon . . . in which philosophical truths are cast in a form that will [even] be convincing to people without the ability to follow philosophical argument'.[90] Another consequence that results from the ideas of these philosophers about revelation is that any legal-oriented hermeneutic approach to the text put forward by theologians and religious jurists is subordinated to the rational philosophical-hermeneutical principles of philosophers. As such, 'the disciplines surrounding religious doctrine and law – *kalām* and *fiqh* – are subordinated to philosophy'.[91] While Rahman shares many of the philosophical ideas about revelation developed by the aforementioned philosophers, he does not necessarily share some of their implications and ramifications.

The connection between revelation and Qurʾānic hermeneutics

My analysis of Rahman's theory of revelation in the first section now becomes relevant to a broader formulation of what elements an interpreter must take into account when approaching the Qurʾānic text. The aim of this section is to examine the impact of Rahman's theory of revelation on his interpretive discourses. I first argue that Rahman historicises the Prophet's revelatory experiences in his writings. Then, I discuss two hermeneutical approaches that could be found in Rahman's writings, arguing that they are intimately connected to his ideas about revelation.

Historicisation of revelation and the Qur'ān

Rahman's theory is characterised by an attempt to transfer the concept of revelation from a metaphysical and ahistorical phenomenon to a historical one. Revelation is described as a semi-mutual process in Rahman's writings – that is, it is not viewed as a one-sided relation of transmission from God to Muhammad, but rather a two-sided relation between God and Muhammad, since the latter is seen as an organic part of the revelation. For Rahman, although revelation originates from God, the locus of revelation, namely the Prophet's heart, is where it is vouchsafed in historical time. The idea that revelation must be understood within historical time is further affirmed when Rahman gives a less supernatural view of the agent of revelation. The Spirit 'which develops in the Prophet's heart . . . comes into actual revelatory operation when needed'.[92] Indeed, Rahman suggests that the Prophet communicated revelation to his audience within an appropriate historical context. Other features of Rahman's account of revelation are to be approached as a set of principles whose goal is to historicise revelation. Rahman's account of the nature of revelation, his emphasis on the personality of the Prophet, and his idea that Muhammad's revelatory experiences required the preparation of his potential human intellect are several elements that support his historicised account of revelation. There is indeed an intimate connection between the Prophet's personality and his mission, his revelatory experiences and the text of the Qur'ān in Rahman's theory of revelation. He states:

> When one reviews the performance of Muhammad . . . and studies the Qur'ān closely as the document of his revelatory experiences, one cannot fail to perceive that an inner unity and an unmistakable sense of direction are displayed in the Prophet's activity and the Qur'ānic guidance. I am, of course, talking not of the actual effect this teaching had upon Muhammad's early or late followers . . . but of the nature and the quality of this teaching, viewed in its setting, with reference to its historical context on the one hand and the personality of the Prophet on the other.[93]

Rahman's theory sharply contrasts with the traditional view that the Qur'ān was inscribed in the Preserved Tablet (*lawḥ al-maḥfūz*) as something written before the creation of mankind. The Qur'ān did not exist before the time when the Prophet experienced the moral problems of his society. This is why the Qur'ān is to be considered a product or document of the Prophet's revelatory experiences. According to Rahman, the failure of the majority of Muslim scholars to examine the close relationship between the Prophet's role in revelation and the genesis of the Qur'ān resulted in a failure to see the Qur'ān as the Word of God and also the word of Muhammad.[94] This resulted in their failure to implement appropriate hermeneutical approaches when interpreting the Qur'ān. Within classical Islam, insisting on the externality of the Qur'ān in relation to the personality of the Prophet Muhammad, his experiences and feelings often resulted in the task of interpretation of the Qur'ān becoming a mere linguistic exercise, or the interpretation of the Qur'ān by the Qur'ān.

Rahman's first hermeneutic

Strongly related to this historicisation of the Qur᾽ān is the idea that the Qur᾽ān took shape within a historical setting and was directly relevant to its immediate context. The intimate relationship between Muhammad's mind and the process of revelation in Rahman's argument involves a complete affirmation of the interconnectedness of the Qur᾽ān and its historical context. By drawing a close connection between the Prophet's mind and revelation, Rahman's thesis provides a strong basis for establishing a link between the Qur᾽ān and its immediate context. It is in this sense that the Qur᾽ān is, for Rahman, 'God's response through Muhammad's mind (this latter factor has been radically underplayed by the Islamic orthodoxy) to a historic situation (a factor likewise drastically restricted by the Islamic orthodoxy in a real understanding of the Qur᾽ān)'.[95] This implies that the Qur᾽ān was shaped within a specific context in a certain period of time, and thus is inevitably bound to the world of the Prophet – namely the conditions of the seventh-century Hijazi society: 'the Qur᾽ān and the genesis of the Islamic community occurred in the light of history and against a social-historical background'.[96]

From this point, Rahman develops the view that in order to interpret the Qur᾽ān, one must be aware of the circumstances in which the text emerged. That is, the first key hermeneutic Rahman uses in his approach to the Qur᾽ān is that Qur᾽ānic verses must be interpreted within the broader context of their revelation, meaning that understanding the Qur᾽ān requires some knowledge of 'its proper context which is the struggle of the Prophet and the background of that struggle'.[97] Indeed, a proper interpretation of the Qur᾽ān should involve the recognition of the Prophet's *Sitz im Leben* – a term which stands for the alleged context in which a text has been created. Rahman goes so far as to state that recognition of the norms, values and practices of pre-Islamic Arabian society in which Islam came into being as a new religion should be taken into full consideration in any interpretation of the Qur᾽ān, since the political, economic and social problems encountered in Meccan and Medinan society provided the natural context for the messages contained in the text.[98]

Rahman approaches the discipline of 'the occasions of revelation' (*asbāb al-nuzūl*) in a way different from what is traditionally understood. He states that 'although most Qur᾽ānic commentators were aware of the importance of these situational contexts', this was 'either because of their historical significance or for their aid in understanding the point of certain injunctions', concluding that most Qur᾽ānic commentators never realised the 'full import' of the discipline of occasions of revelation.[99] Although Muslim scholars traditionally were engaged in discovering occasions of revelation, there were no major discussions on the significance of context in approaching the Qur᾽ān. Unlike Rahman, one of the main goals of most Muslim scholars in engaging with the *asbāb al-nuzūl* literature was to develop certain laws and injunctions. Rahman's emphasis on the notion of context is also related to his ideas about the discipline of *naskh* (abrogation). Abrogation, for Rahman, must be understood as supporting the notion of evolution of Qur᾽ānic themes in a given context. Given that revelation took place in a historical context, both *nāsikh* (abrogating) and *mansūkh* (abrogated) verses came into being as responses to the circumstances that the Prophet and the nascent Muslim community confronted. Rahman indeed rejects one of the most widely acknowledged interpretive methods, according to which the most recently revealed verses provide the final verdict on a particular issue and should be taken to be the ultimate Word of God. For him, interpreters of the Qur'ān must consider all passages of the text – be they abrogating verses or abrogated verses – and understand them against the background of their historical context.[100]

Rahman's second hermeneutic

Rahman's second hermeneutic is based on the idea that the Prophet's life experience and his deep moral-spiritual consciousness, which he developed from the earliest age, played a key role in his revelatory experiences. As discussed, according to Rahman, the appalling social and moral conditions that characterised seventh-century Meccan society, which included widespread socio-economic inequality, deeply affected the Prophet's own inner life.[101] Indeed, 'What issued from his experience in the cave [of Hira] was not merely the demolishing of a plurality of gods, but [also] a sustained and determined effort to achieve socioeconomic justice.'[102] Muhammad's concern for the social, economic and moral issues of his society continued after his prophetic mission began. His concern was so severe that 'when Muhammad's moral intuitive perception rose to its highest point and became identified with the moral law itself . . . the Word was given with the inspiration itself'.[103] That is, revelation was the culmination of an inner process through the Prophet's mind in response to the moral crisis of his society. Muhammad's prophetic career was inclined towards resolving this moral crisis and improving people in 'a concrete and communal sense, rather than [simply] toward the private and metaphysical'.[104]

The implication of this idea is that Muhammad's mission was geared towards 'social reform in terms of strengthening the socio-economically weak and depressed classes', including orphans, slaves and women.[105] To emphasise the significance of the Prophet's concern with socio-moral issues in the context of his prophetic mission, Rahman focuses on the theme of *zakāt* (almsgiving) in his writings. According to Rahman, by imposing the *zakāt* tax, Muhammad attempted to improve the status of the poor and the weak. *Zakāt* was one of the ways by which the Islamic 'socio-moral order' was established.[106] The importance of the theme of social justice in Muhammad's mission is also evident from the attitude of his opponents in Mecca. The Meccans were threatened by the message of Islam not only because of its insistence on monotheism, but also because of Muhammad's emphasis on social justice through condemnation of usury and the Prophet's call for *zakāt*. They were indeed threatened by Islam's message that wealth should be shared equally, and thus feared losing sources of their income.[107]

A key implication that follows from making such a connection between the revelation and the Prophet's personality, for Rahman, is that the Qur'ān is not only a divine response to the social conditions of Arabian society of the seventh century, but also a response to the moral issues encountered at the time. Thus, he writes, 'the Qur'ān is the divine response, through the Prophet's mind, to the moral-social situation of the Prophet's Arabia'.[108] In addition to monotheism, 'the basic *élan* of the Qur'ān is moral'.[109] In fact, an emphasis on the significance of the Prophet's moral concerns since an early age leads Rahman to conclude that the Qur'ān, at its core, is a text dealing with ethical values. In other words, there is an intimate relation between the Prophet's concern for establishing a moral order and the central message of the Qur'ān about ethical matters. The Qur'ān must be approached in a way that this 'unity [i.e. its emphasis on ethical matters] will emerge in its fullness'.[110] For Rahman, 'the Qur'ān is a unity and not a jumble of isolated or mutually contradictory ideas'.[111] Expanding this idea to the social arena, Rahman argues that the aim of the Qur'ān is to emphasise socio-economic justice and human egalitarianism.[112] Therefore, a key element of Rahman's interpretive method is that themes of ethics and justice give the Qur'ān a certain unity, meaning that ethics must be included as an essential focus in any interpretation. That is, the main pivot of the Qur'ānic verses is an ethical one, especially when it comes to the socio-legal passages of the text. It is in this sense that Rahman argued that there was a general failure of Islamic thought in the course of history in identifying the underlying unity of the Qur'ān, namely themes of ethics and justice.[113] This failure was mainly related to the approach of the majority of Muslim scholars who privileged the objectivity and verbal character of prophetic revelation and ignored the intimate relation between revelation and the inner reality of the Prophet's life.

Combination of the two hermeneutics: socio-legal passages of the Qur'ān

There are two implications that follow from Rahman's methodology. First, since the Prophet's mind was occupied with the moral crisis of his society, he became a moral reformer, and as such his mission was not primarily motivated or shaped by legislative issues. The Prophet, as Rahman himself points out, 'seldom resorted to general legislation as a means of furthering the Islamic cause'.[114] Accordingly, in the Qur'ān 'general legislation forms a very tiny part of Islamic teaching'.[115] Therefore, the Qur'ān should not be approached as a legal manuscript or document made up of specific rules and literal injunctions: 'The Qur'ān is primarily a book of religious and moral principles and exhortations, and is not a legal document.'[116] This shows that Rahman invoked the challenge to the classical Muslim jurists and those contemporary Muslim scholars who gave an importance to the Qur'ān's legal precepts: 'The Qur'ān is not a . . . legal document that Muslim lawyers have made it to be.'[117] That is, Rahman distanced himself from a legal-oriented hermeneutic – a method that aims to approach the Qur'ān from a legal perspective and to engage in law-finding exercises when interpreting the text. This is what Rahman partly shared with philosophers such as al-Farabi and Ibn Sina.

The second implication of Rahman's hermeneutics is that those verses of the Qur'ān dealing with legal matters must be approached and understood as fulfilling a moral purpose relevant to the time and circumstances in which they were revealed. The Qur'ān contains some legal enunciations, but they should be viewed against the backdrop of the social and historical context of their revelation. The applications of legal provisions of the Qur'ān have to be first examined within the broader context of the time of the Prophet, and then examined in light of the moral ideal that stands behind them. In other words, Qur'ānic legislations should be viewed in terms of their 'socio-historical background' and the 'moral objectives and principles' behind them.[118] What follows from this view is that the socio-legal passages of the Qur'ān should be approached in the light of the Qur'ān's overall movement towards greater social justice for human beings. Rahman indeed aimed to highlight in the Qur'ān a direction towards the progressive embodiment of the fundamental values of the text, such as justice and fairness. According to him, this 'moral ideal towards which the [early Islamic] society was expected to move'[119] was neglected by the majority of *fuqahā* and jurists in the course of Islamic history.

This combination of the hermeneutical approaches proposed by Rahman is particularly important in determining the relevance of the Qur'ān's teachings for Muslims today, and also raises questions about the issue of the mutability and immutability of certain socio-legal passages of the text. Rahman's methodology enables interpreters of the Qur'ān to contextualise its message as a response to the historical setting of seventh-century Arabian society. In the light of the socio-historical background of the Qur'ān, it would only be possible to deduce certain underlying ethical or moral principles as universal teachings, which must then be transposed to the conditions of the present-day Muslim world.[120] Indeed, for Rahman, one should distinguish between 'legal enactments' and 'moral injunctions'; for while the former are mutable or historical, the latter are immutable or normative.[121] This implies that the presumption that the message of Islam in relation to the social arena is somehow fixed and unchangeable is to be refuted because the legal provisions of the Qur'ān must be examined in light of the moral intentions or the *ratio legis* behind them: 'The implementation of the Qur'ān cannot be carried out literally in the context of today because this may result in thwarting the very purposes of the Qur'ān.'[122] Rahman therefore argues that one should not create a system of commandments and prohibitions based on the literal reading of Qur'ānic legal statements: 'To insist on a *literal* implementation of the rules of the Qur'ān, shutting one's eyes to the social change that had occurred and that is so palpably occurring before our eyes, is tantamount to . . . defeating its moral-social purposes and objectives.'[123] Strongly related to his methodology is the idea that the theological or metaphysical teachings of the Qur'ān belong to the realm of immutable or normative principles: 'For the theological or metaphysical statements of the Qur'ān, the specific revelational background is not necessary, as it is for its social-legal pronouncements.'[124]

As such, the immutable features of the Qur'ān that transcend the time and place of their revelation include its moral injunctions, the rationale or moral intentions that stand behind the socio-legal statements of the Qur'ān and the theological or metaphysical statements of the text (such as those related to the oneness of God and the theme of the afterlife). The mutable contents of the Qur'ān, on the other hand, denote principles that grew out of the specific socio-cultural milieu of their revelation, and thus should not be applied at all times and in all places. Rahman's distinction between normative and historical features of the Qur'ān, and in particular the distinction he draws between the socio-legal precepts of the Qur'ān and the ethical purposes that stand behind them, results from his views on revelation. This distinction opens the door to respond flexibly to the needs and circumstances of Muslims today. His methodology is indeed geared towards discovering how the intent of the Qur'ānic verses – especially those passages dealing with socio-legal issues – was laid down for the benefit of Muslims not only in the time of revelation, but also in the present. According to Rahman's thesis, it is only when the intention or the spirit behind Qur'ānic legal statements is taken into consideration that the revelation can maintain its relevance to a changing world. Moreover, in emphasising the mutability of the Qur'ānic legislations, Rahman's interpretive method stands in sharp contrast to the literalists' idea that the Qur'ān's legal stipulations should be applied at all times and in all places in the same way as they were applied to Muhammad's community or to the early Muslim communities.

Rahman's hermeneutics in practice

Before discussing how Rahman's hermeneutics are applied in practice, I compare his hermeneutics with Emilio Betti's (d. 1968) and Hans-Georg Gadamer's in order to situate Rahman's approach within a Western hermeneutic milieu. Some scholars of modern Islamic thought argue that Rahman has been influenced by Gadamer's hermeneutic approach,[125] while others believe that his interpretive method resonates more with Betti's 'Objectivity School' than with Gadamer's 'Subjectivity School'.[126] In Gadamer's hermeneutics, utmost emphasis is placed on the significant role of the interpreter's pre-knowledge in the process of understanding a given text. Leaning on the German philosopher Martin Heidegger's (d. 1976) analysis of *Dasein* (the human way to be), Gadamer argued that 'understanding is the original characteristic of the being of human life itself' and that 'the concept of understanding is no longer a methodological concept'.[127] For Gadamer, the readers of a given text are preconditioned by their socio-political and cultural milieus, which create a 'horizon' of understanding, and thus no interpretation is void of prejudice: 'The history of hermeneutics shows how the examination of the texts is determined by a very precise fore-understanding.'[128]

Unlike Gadamer, Betti places some distance between the subject and object of interpretation since a given text, for him, retains its intimate relation with its author's intentions. Betti's objectivist hermeneutic is based on the idea that one should seek to achieve the stable meaning of the text. Pursuing this line of thinking, Betti criticises Gadamer since the latter's approach 'inevitably leads to both subjectivism and relativism, with the consequence that hermeneutics is unable to adjudicate between correct and incorrect interpretations'.[129] Betti does not ignore the fact that any interpreter may understand the text from his/her own perspective, but he believes that every text has a determinate meaning attached to its author's intention that could be retrievable independently of the interpreter's subjectivity and historical context. For Betti:

> While recognizing that the interpreter will understand things in terms of his or her own experiences, every effort must be made to control one's 'prejudices' and to subordinate one's experiences to the meaningfulness that the interpreted object seeks to communicate.[130]

Returning to the initial question about how Rahman's interpretive method is related to Western hermeneutical milieu, I argue that his hermeneutics resonates more with Betti's objectivity school than with Gadamer's subjectivity school. Rahman's hermeneutics sharply contrasts with Gadamer's idea that interpreters are preconditioned by their prejudices during the process of understanding a text. For Rahman, Gadamer undermines the objectivity of the text by placing an utmost emphasis on the subjective conditions that play a role in the interpreter's approaches to it.[131] Rahman's interpretive method echoes aspects of Betti's hermeneutics in that an interpreter is able to capture the original intent of the author of the text. In line with the task of objectively discovering the original meaning of the Qur'ān, Rahman, as shown, highlights the significance of the ethical message of the text, as well as the context in which it emerged. This hermeneutic method, as discussed, is the result of Rahman's belief about how revelation came into being. By highlighting the role of context in shaping the revelation, Rahman, unlike Betti, believes that the original meaning of the text 'cannot be attributed simply to [its] author', and that the situation to which the Qur'ān was responding should also be taken into consideration.[132] That is, in the case of the Qur'ān, where God is considered the 'author', getting to the author's intentions is somehow problematic, and thus one is able to understand the original meaning behind the text from the context of the Qur'ān's emergence and the text's ethical message.

As such, in regard to Rahman's hermeneutics, little attention has been given to thinking about the role of the subjectivity of an interpreter in the act of interpretation. In fact, Rahman does not supply further amplification of his hermeneutic approach on a level that takes the roles of prejudices and pre-understandings of the interpreter into account. As such, his approach is unable to comprehend how the meaning of the text can also be produced based on the interests, expectations and the cultural episteme of the interpreter. In addition, his hermeneutic is not concerned with how classical Muslim scholars' interpretive discourses are, by and large, embedded in a pre-modern *Weltanschauung*, and shaped by the confines of the epistemological framework of their societies. Rahman's project is not oriented around the history of the reception of the text, and thus ignores the fact that the socio-political context of the pre-modern period did not leave much room for commentators to appreciate the kinds of understanding that their counterparts in the modern era seem to attach to certain Qur'ānic themes.[133] I demonstrate this in the following section.

Rahman's approach to Qur'ānic legislations in practice

To recap Rahman's hermeneutics, interpreters must determine the ultimate reasons (or what he refers to as the *ratio legis*) for which a Qur'ānic injunction relating to the social arena came into being. This *ratio legis* is 'a general principle which is presented as the essence of the law . . . it is the moral value that the law seeks to embody and realize'.[134] For Rahman, the Qur'ān should be treated 'as a whole' and 'as a set of coherent [ethical] principles or values where the total teaching will converge'.[135] Strongly related to this approach is the idea that the ethical-moral foundations of Qur'ānic laws must be discovered, meaning that 'actual effective orientation and ethical engineering'[136] are of particular importance for approaching Qur'ānic legislative injunctions. Therefore, Qur'ānic legislation on a given subject must satisfy both the Qur'ān's unitary teaching and the ultimate purpose (or the *ratio legis*) that stands behind it.

To show how Rahman applies his hermeneutics in practice (especially in defence of the mutability of most Qur'ānic *aḥkām*), I give a brief overview of his views on issues such as slavery, *riba* (usury) and cutting a thief's hand. In terms of the prohibition of usury, Rahman links the Qur'ānic condemnation of *riba* to its moral-ethical aspects and the historical context of the seventh-century Arabian society. The Qur'ān denounces *riba* in the context of the economic injustice of Meccan society, where the unethical commercial practices were prevalent and exploitation of the poor and needy through interest on debt was widespread. That is, the spirit behind the prohibition of *riba* was to prevent injustice.[137] By highlighting the importance of the ethical purpose that sits behind the prohibition of *riba*, Rahman downplays the importance of its legal aspects. This mirrors his idea that the Qur'ān is not a legal document. Rahman further states that the Qur'ānic condemnation of *riba* does not mean that the Qur'ān prohibited bank interest in today's context. Indeed, the idea that all forms of interest must be banned stands in sharp contradiction to the spirit behind the condemnation of *riba* in its original place. Since moderate rates are one of the fundamental principles of today's economy, and since Muslims must participate in the global economy, prohibition of interest is not only 'foolish', but is also 'un-Islamic'.[138]

Another example deals with the institution of slavery. According to Rahman, the Qur'ān permitted the pre-Islamic institution of slavery, but imposed a reformed set of regulations for slaves in a way that could eventually lead to a society in which slavery does not exist. The Qur'ān could not eliminate slavery in a short period of time, since it was 'ingrained in the structure of society' and its overnight disposal would have created problems.[139] Accordingly, the institution of slavery should not be seen as an eternal injunction, but rather must be viewed as the progressive embodiment of an ethical-moral injunction which ultimately results in its eventual disappearance in light of evolving social conditions. This again mirrors Rahman's hermeneutic approach, which says that the interpreter should seek to understand the 'direction' towards which a particular Qur'ānic commandment was leading – in this case, improving the conditions of slaves.

Another example of how the Qur'ān legalises an existing practice is that of the amputation penalty for theft. For Rahman, cutting off a hand of a thief in the context of a nomadic society is quite reasonable because 'the right of possession is strongly associated with an accentuated sense of personal honor', and thus theft was not primarily considered an 'economic crime, but as a crime against values of personal honor and its inviolable sanctity'. In urbanised societies in which there are visible shifts in values, this law is not applicable.[140] In another example, on the question of murder, although the Qur'ān confirms the pre-Islamic Arab forms of settlement either by blood money or retaliation (*qiṣāṣ*), Rahman refers to verse 5:32 in the Qur'ān ('if any saves one person, it is as though he has saved all humanity'), concluding that since murder is a crime against society rather than a private crime, *qiṣāṣ* is not applicable and must be replaced by new legislation in specific contexts.[141] Leaning on the significance of ethical-moral foundations of Qur'ānic legislations, the Qur'ān itself states that it is best to forgive.[142]

The Qur'ān on women's issues and rights

The significance of advancing women's rights in the modern period lies not only in the fact that this half of the population must be given equal rights to men; it is also rooted in the idea that the development of civil society and democratic institutions is impossible without promoting gender equality. Scholars have often recognised the close relation between the democratisation process and promoting gender equality. Referring to the context of modern Iranian society, Jahanshahrad states that 'there is a direct relationship between gender equality and democratization . . . women's demands for equal rights can theoretically be recognized as part of the general demands of Iranians for democracy'.[143] In a similar vein, a number of Egyptian writers during the Arab Spring called for revolutionists' immediate action towards supporting women's rights, thus defying gender inequality, since they believed that Egyptian women were able to play a central role in developing civil society through bringing about substantial changes in the social and political spheres.[144] In what follows, I show how the contextualist approach proposed by Rahman provides a solid theoretical framework for advancing women's rights and gender equality.

On the issue of polygamy, Rahman rejects the idea of the majority of Muslim jurists who consider 'the polygamy permission clause as having legal force'.[145] Emphasising the social circumstances in which the Qur'ānic injunction of polygamy was revealed, Rahman states that 'neither monogamy nor polygamy can be regarded as the unique and divinely ordained order for every society in every season and that either institution may apply according to social conditions prevailing'.[146] According to him, during pre-Islamic times, polygamy was accepted as a social norm among Arabs because of a disproportionate decrease in the number of men compared to women due to tribal wars.[147] Rahman's reading of the Qur᾿ānic passage 4:3 leads him to argue that polygamy with up to four wives within the historical context of its revelation is a legitimate form of matrimony, meaning that the ideal form of relationship between men and women within the Qur᾿ānic worldview is that of a monogamous matrimony. In other words, the Qur᾿ān's ultimate aim is not to maintain the institution of polygamy, but rather to eliminate it. Rahman applies his hermeneutical approaches to the Qur᾿ānic injunction of polygamy. Distinguishing between the legislations of the Qur᾿ān and the moral rationale behind them, he concludes, 'the sanctions put on polygamy were in the nature of a moral ideal towards which the society was expected to move, since it was not possible to remove polygamy legally at one stroke'.[148] Therefore, what must be taken into consideration concerning the Qur᾿ānic injunction of polygamy is the intention and guiding direction towards which Qur᾿ānic revelation was moving, which is to say that the Qur᾿ān permitted polygamy only as 'a legal solution of the situation', but regarded monogamy as 'the moral law for long-term achievement'.[149] It follows that 'the overall logical consequence of [Qur᾿ānic] pronouncements is a banning of polygamy under normal circumstances'.[150] In addition, in approaching the Qur᾿ānic verses concerning polygamy, what should be considered is the social objectives or moral principles – namely justice – implied in that legislation. Rahman states:

> The Qur᾿ān is talking of polygamy in the context of treating orphaned girls who had come of age but to whom their guardians were unwilling to give back their properties. Instead, they would like to marry their wards, so that they could continue to use their properties . . . [Polygamy] is certainly in keeping with the purposes of the Qur᾿ān concerning social justice in general and with regard to women's justice in particular.[151]

According to Rahman, the Qur᾿ānic verses that seem to emphasise men's authority or superiority over women (Q 4:34; Q 2:228) must be reinterpreted when their appropriate social context is taken into account. The superiority that the Qur᾿ān speaks about in these verses is that of a 'functional' and 'not inherent superiority'.[152] This is due to the fact that during the time when the Qur᾿ān was revealed, men were the 'primary socially operative factors' and were responsible for 'defraying household expenditure'.[153] In this sense, the notion of superiority or authority mentioned in the Qur᾿ān is not inherent in the nature of sexes, but rather based on certain qualities that men acquired within specific socio-economic contexts of Arabian society at the time of revelation: 'If a woman becomes economically sufficient . . . and contributes to the household expenditure, the male's superiority would to that extent be reduced.'[154] Rahman's conclusion is that since today's context has changed, its associated religious precepts concerning the superiority of men over women must change accordingly.

The Qur'ānic verse stating that a credit transaction should be written down either in the presence of two male witnesses, or one male and two female witnesses (Q 2:282), is also to be approached in its appropriate historical context. Rahman criticises the traditional law that the testimony of a woman is considered half of that of a man on the ground that 'women in those days were normally not used to dealing with credit' due to the social framework in which they lived.[155] He asks: 'how can one deduce from this a general law to the effect that under all circumstances and for all purposes, a woman's evidence is inferior to a man's?'[156] Given that today's context is different from that of the revelation era, this legislation is not applicable in the present context. In a similar vein, the Qur'ānic statement about women's inheritance is closely related to the economic roles assigned to men and women in tribal society. Inheritance reflects 'the function of their actual role in traditional society'.[157] Rahman reasons: 'With social change, however, changes in shares must follow, since in a detribalized society social functions undergo radical changes.'[158] This shows that Rahman is unconvinced of the logic of the 'dowry argument' presented by some contemporary Muslim scholars such as Muhammad Iqbal.

As such, much of the gender inequality found in the Qur'ān is rooted in the cultural norms and standards of the early Islamic society, but 'when the situation so changes that the law fails to reflect the *ratio*, the law must change'.[159] According to Rahman, the history of Muslim legal pronouncements concerning women's rights shows that jurists often ignored the fact that 'each legal or quasi-legal pronouncement is accompanied by a *ratio legis* explaining why a law is being enunciated'.[160] Instead of considering the fact that Islam lifted women's status and removed certain abuses to which women were subjected in pre-Islamic times,[161] jurists have often 'freezed' Islamic regulations about women's issues due to their literal understanding of the text. Indeed, what jurists often ignored is the 'direction' in which the early Islamic community during the Prophet's time was moving.

As shown, Rahman manages to apply his hermeneutical approaches to the realm of women's issues and rights. However, we recall that in Rahman's hermeneutic there is not much emphasis on the particular context of the interpreter or the interpreter's *pretext* – conditioned by factors such as class, gender, religious orientation and ethnicity – in the practice of exegesis. Expanding this to women's issues, there is no discussion in Rahman's writings about why the views of most Muslim scholars of pre-modern times concerning women's rights lack the kinds of understanding of some commentators in the modern era. In fact, Rahman's hermeneutic does not appreciate how the interpretation of certain Qur'ānic verses about women in early Islamic history and in the modern period are closely related to the specific context or condition of their time. Hence, while Rahman's hermeneutic manages to reinterpret some Qur'ānic injunctions concerning women's issues in light of the modern context (due to his humanistic approach to revelation), it does not identify well enough the epistemic limits of pre-modern Qur'ānic commentators in interpreting such injunctions.

The application of Rahman's hermeneutics in the political arena

This section focuses on the implications of Rahman's hermeneutic in regard to the political arena, specifically when it is related to notions of democracy and *shūrā* (consultation). It is first of all important to provide a brief overview of the institution of *shūrā*. The practice of consultation by which a tribal chief (the sheikh) received advice from the most prominent members of his tribe was known to the Arabs during pre-Islamic times. The pre-Islamic institution of *shūrā* continued to be practised in the period in which the Prophet lived and the Qur'ān was revealed. The Qur'ān itself refers to *shūrā* in three verses: 'Consult with them about matters' (Q 3:159); '[For those] whose affairs are determined by mutual consultation' (Q 42:38); and 'If they desire to wean the child by mutual consent and consultation, there is no blame upon them' (Q 2:233). While the first two verses have a broader socio-political context, the last verse deals mainly with a more personal matter, namely the need for the parents' consultation in regard to the care of their children.

Most Muslim scholars in the contemporary era can be loosely grouped into one of three main categories when they discuss the relation between democracy and *shūrā*. The first group, often identified as 'liberal' Muslims, believes that democracy is inherently compatible with the fundamental teachings of Islam since the Qur'ān supports the concept of *shūrā* (consultation). From their viewpoint, democracy is equivalent to *shūrā*, and thus it has its roots in the Qur'ān itself.[162] The second group, often recognised as fundamentalists, rejects the idea that the Qur'ānic teachings and democracy are harmonious or compatible, and thus maintains the corresponding argument that there is no need for Muslim societies to adopt a Western democratic method of governance.[163] Finally, certain Muslim scholars believe that democracy is an extra-religious matter, and thus argue that it is not derivable from the Qur'ān – an argument which inevitably leads them to conclude that democracy and *shūrā* are not necessarily equivalent – though they strongly support the idea that Muslims should incorporate modern democratic norms into their methods of governance in today's context.[164]

Rahman's idea about democracy is consistent with the first category of scholars grouped above. Rahman criticises the Islamist scholar ʿAbul Aʿla Mawdudi (d. 1979), who rejects democracy and equates it with *shirk*, arguing that democracy and a representative form of government are necessary for Muslims in today's context.[165] Although Rahman states that the 'concept of *shūrā-ijmāʿ* is not quite compatible with a multi-party system as it is practiced in modern democracies',[166] the weight of his argument manifested in his works tends towards equating democracy with *shūrā*, since he considers 'the principle of democracy as embodied as the Qur'ānic *shūrā*'.[167] Rahman himself states that his argument is in line with the 'modernist' scholars who 'have contended that the only valid Muslim rule is through shūrā, which in the world of today means a representative form of government'.[168] For Rahman, 'the democracy of Islam was expected to be based upon the mutual discussion (*shūrā baynahum*) of the members of a community who had proper awareness of Islamic purposes'.[169] Rahman equates *shūrā* with democracy and thus maintains the corresponding argument that 'all human rights, universally recognized, are automatically vouchsafed and guaranteed by a Government based on *shūrā*'.[170] This implies that he considers the concept of *shūrā* as a sufficient basis for establishing a democratic structure in today's context.

From Rahman's argument, we can conclude that he considers democracy an appropriate mode of governance, but his main reason for the necessity of the implementation of democratic norms in today's context derives mainly from the Qur'ānic injunction that Muslims should conduct their affairs through the principle of *shūrā*.[171] Rahman's method does not leave much room for acknowledging the importance of an extra-Qur'ānic grounding of democracy and does not take as much account of the significance of democracy beyond its religious justifications. Sam Shirazi identifies the importance of grounding democracy and human rights on extra-religious principles: 'Muslims should be able to determine the proper role of human rights [and by its extension, democracy] in their societies without having to rely solely on Islamic revelation.'[172] He suggests that the notions of democracy and human rights 'should not be [only] valued because Islam mandates so, but just because they rationally make sense and because all human beings are entitled to them'.[173] Rahman, however, attempts to find theological justifications for supporting democratic norms. Although he believes that the Qur'ān is primarily a book of moral principles and is not a legal document,[174] since it does not provide its readers with 'many general principles',[175] he does not exclude the possibility of deriving modern democratic norms for governing today's society from the Qur'ānic injunctions of *shūrā*. As such, Rahman implicitly suggests that traditional Islamic teachings could be sufficient to formulate the laws for governing societies in today's context.[176]

My criticism of Rahman's political ideas is not only that he sees the notion of *shūrā* as a sufficient basis for establishing a democratic structure; I also believe that Rahman's argument for equating democracy with *shūrā* weakens his proposal that the Qur'ān is a response through the Prophet's mind to the socio-ethical problems of seventh-century Arabia, and that the Qur'ānic themes dealing with socio-political matters should be approached within the constraints of the context of the Qur'ān's revelation and its 'epistemic schemes'.[177] In other words, equating *shūrā* with democracy goes against Rahman's thesis, which argues that Muhammad's mind is historically situated. Since the revelation occurred within a specific historical context and within the limits of the Prophet's worldview and that of his contemporaries – well before the development of modern notions of democracy – it is unconvincing to simply equate the latter with a concept prevalent in seventh-century Arabia, namely the institution of *shūrā*. While it is possible to offer some scriptural support for democratic ethics, the broader socio-historical context of Arabian society and the worldview of the immediate addressees of the Qur'ān did not allow for the rise of democratic norms in the modern sense of the word. Equating democracy with *shūrā*, therefore, would essentially divorce revelation from the prevailing epistemic framework within and through which it emerged, and thus result in a way of viewing revelation as an event that stands outside the historical or the contextual framework of its emergence.

In sum, Rahman's commitment to democracy is not based on an extra-religious justification. Although Rahman recognises democracy as an appropriate form of governance, he does not apply his hermeneutic approach in the context of advancing such political arguments. The fact that the institution of *shūrā* is pointed out in the Qur'ān does not necessarily mean that the Qur'ān supports or rejects democracy, since the modern notions of democracy and human rights were inconceivable during the Prophet's time. Therefore, while Rahman's hermeneutic allows for flexibility in terms of a practical application of religious injunctions concerning women's issues and rights, his hermeneutic leans towards traditionalism, and so arguably stands in tension with his contextualist approach when applied to the political sphere.

Conclusion

This chapter has argued that Rahman's understanding of the revelation and of the Qur'ān's nature, which are humanistic, and based on the theories of revelation presented by medieval Muslim philosophers (especially al-Farabi and Ibn Sina), has led him to develop two hermeneutical approaches to the Qur'ān. Rahman's first hermeneutic is based on the idea that the socio-political and cultural elements of Arabian society during the revelation era should play a key role in the process of interpretation of the Qur'ān. Rahman's second hermeneutic indicates that the Qur'ānic message was intimately bound up in Muhammad's personality and his concern for the creation of a moral order, meaning that the basic message of the Qur'ān is ethico-moral. This shows how Rahman's hermeneutics are related to the issue of the mutability and immutability of Qur'ānic rulings. Qur'ānic legislations can only be properly understood in light of their historical context, their *ratio legis* and by considering the ethical goals towards which the message of the Qur'ān is directed.

This chapter has also argued that Rahman's hermeneutic functions appropriately in practice when applied to the discourse of women's rights, and has the capability of promoting gender equality in the realms of testimony, inheritance and marriage. While I do not agree with those scholars who argue that Rahman 'has never really put his exegetical approach into practice',[178] I argue that his hermeneutic has not been well applied in his arguments concerning the political arena, especially when it is related to equating democracy with *shūrā*. Indeed, while Rahman understands revelation and the Qur'ān in a humanistic way – which places him in sharp contrast to other 'liberal' or 'modernist' Muslim scholars – his understanding of the term *shūrā* does not differ very much from that of the latter. Therefore, although Rahman's contributions are valuable in reformulating traditional theories of revelation and in identifying the human aspects of the Qur'ān, his hermeneutic, when applied in practice, is not wholly different or separable from the position of mainstream modernist Muslim scholars.

Notes

1. I borrowed the term 'ordinary sense' from Völker in her 'Two Accounts of Qur'anic Revelation', p. 273.
2. Rahman, *Major Themes*, p. 99.
3. Ibid.; among the verses mentioned, the most related verse is Q 12:108, which states: 'Say: This is my path – I call people to God on the basis of a clear perception.'
4. Saeed, *Reading the Qur'an in the Twenty-First Century*, p. 54.
5. Rahman, 'Muhammad and the Qur'an', p. 10.
6. Rahman, *Islam*, p. 33.
7. Ibid.
8. Rahman, *Major Themes*, p. 100.
9. Rahman, *Islam*, p. 33.
10. Rahman, 'Muhammad and the Qur'an', p. 11.
11. Ibid.
12. Rahman, *Major Themes*, p. 91.
13. Ibid.
14. Völker, 'Two Accounts of Qur'anic Revelation', p. 275.
15. Rahman, *Major Themes*, p. 85.
16. Ibid.
17. Ibid.
18. Ibid., p. 98.
19. Rahman, *Major Themes*, p. 97; another Qur'ānic verse that supports such an idea, according to Rahman, is Q 2:92.
20. Rahman, 'Muhammad and the Qur'an', p. 10.
21. Ibid., p.10. See also Saeed, *Reading the Qur'an in the Twenty-First Century*, p. 54.
22. Rahman, 'Muhammad and the Qur'an', p. 10.
23. Rahman, *Major Themes*, p. 97.
24. Ibid., p. 99.
25. Ibid.
26. Rahman, 'Muhammad and the Qur'an', pp. 10–11.
27. Rahman, *Major Themes*, p. 95.
28. Rahman, *Islam*, pp. 31–2.
29. Rahman, 'Translating the Qur'an', p. 24.
30. Rahman, *Major Themes*, p. 99.
31. Rahman, 'Divine Revelation and the Prophet', p. 111.
32. Rahman, *Major Themes*, p. 101.
33. Rahman, 'Divine Revelation and the Prophet', p. 114.
34. Ibid.
35. Rahman, *Major Themes*, p. 80.
36. Ibid., p. 98.
37. Ibid., p. 97.
38. Rahman, 'Muhammad and the Qur'an', p. 10. As Denny noted, this is one of the main characteristics of a genuine religious experience: 'a man who has a genuinely religious experience is automatically transformed by that experience' (Denny, 'Fazlur Rahman', p. 93).
39. Rahman, *Islam*, p. 31.
40. Fazlur Rahman, 'Some Islamic Issues in the Ayyub Khan Era', p. 299.
41. Rahman, *Major Themes*, p. 80.
42. Rahman, *Islam*, p. 33.
43. This is also noticed by Völker, 'The Qur'an and Reform', p. 54.
44. For details, see Martin, Woodward and Atmaja, *Defenders of Reason in Islam*, p. 77. See also Saeed, 'Fazlur Rahman', p. 42.
45. Martin, *Defenders of Reason in Islam*, p. 203.
46. For details of Rahman's view on *naskh*, see Sonn, 'Fazlur Rahman and Islamic Feminism', pp. 128–9; Völker, 'The Qur'an and Reform', p. 135.

47. A number of scholars have acknowledged that Rahman has been influenced by some medieval Muslim philosophers in regard to his theory of revelation. Jahanbakhsh holds that Rahman's theory of revelation is 'more or less of the same nature that characterized medieval philosophical' debates over the nature of *kalam-e Bari* (Jahanbakhsh, 'Introduction', p. xxix). Völker has attempted to find some aspects of Rahman's theory of revelation in Ibn Sina's understanding of *imagination* or *intellectualisation* (Völker, 'The Qur'an and Reform', p. 57).
48. His thesis is published under the title *Avicenna's Psychology*.
49. Berry, *Islam and Modernity*, p. 43.
50. Rahman, *Prophecy in Islam*.
51. Rahman, 'My Belief-in-Action', pp. 154–5.
52. For details of Rahman's interest in philosophy, see Kersten, *Cosmopolitans and Heretics*, p. 71.
53. Griffel, 'Muslim Philosophers' Rationalist Explanation', p. 162.
54. For a general overview of Islamic form of Neoplatonism, see Leaman, *A Brief Introduction to Islamic Philosophy*, pp. 3–5; Miyan Sharif, *A History of Muslim Philosophy*, p. 458.
55. For detail of this idea, see al-Farabi, *On the Perfect State*, pp. 165–6.
56. al-Farabi, *On the Perfect State*, p. 244; for a detailed discussion, see Mahdi, *al-Farabi*, pp. 153–6.
57. al-Farabi, *On the Perfect State*, pp. 244–5; al-Farabi, *al-Siyāsa al-Madaniyya*, pp. 79–80. For details, see Griffel, 'Muslim philosophers' rationalist explanation', p. 166. As noted by Mahdi, the Acquired Intellect is not 'identical with the divine mind. It is rather the upper limit of human intellection . . . Farabi never admits that the two [Acquired Intellect and divine mind] can be united. This would of course set him apart from such contemporary mystical figures as al-Hallaj'. Mahdi, *al-Farabi*, p. 154.
58. Ibid., p. 134.
59. al-Farabi, *On the Perfect State*, p. 225.
60. al-Farabi, *al-Siyāsa al-Madaniyya*, p. 80; see also Griffel, 'Muslim Philosophers' Rationalist Explanation', pp. 166–8.
61. Ibn Sina, *al-Mabda' va al-Ma'ād* [The Origin and The Return], pp. 112–16; For details, see Okumus, 'The Influence of Ibn Sina', p. 400. For al-Farabi's ideas on human faculties, see al-Farabi, *Fuṣūl al-Madanī* [Aphorisms of the Statesman], pp. 29–31.
62. Ibn Sina consistently refers to the intuitive power of the Prophet, as well as his rational and imaginative power, in his works. Even in his *Treatise on Psychology*, he refers to such powers possessed by the Prophet. See Ibn Sina, *Treatise on Psychology*, pp. 28–30; Griffel, 'Muslim Philosophers' Rationalist Explanation', pp. 171–2. There are also other differences between al-Farabi's and Ibn Sina's theories of revelation. Ibn Sina, unlike al-Farabi, addresses the question of the miracles performed by prophets.
63. Ibn Sina, 'On the Soul', p. 32; see also Ibn Sina, *al-Mabda' va al-Ma'ād*, p. 116.
64. Black, 'Psychology', p. 320. See also Fakhri, *A History of Islamic Philosophy*, p. 164.
65. Cited in Atiyeh, *Al-Kindi*, p. 220.
66. Rahman, *Major Themes*, p. 98.
67. Ibid., p. 100. In comparing the ideas of Fazlur Rahman with those of philosophers, I use 'prophet' or 'prophets' when referring to the philosophers' ideas as they often speak about prophet in general terms.
68. Black, 'Psychology', p. 313.
69. Mahdi, *al-Farabi*, p. 156.
70. Qadir, *Philosophy and Science*, p. 84.
71. Throughout his *Prophecy in Islam*, Rahman refers numerous times to the idea of Muslim philosophers that the Prophet did not receive verbal revelation (Ibid., pp. 38, 72, 74).
72. See section 'The connection between Prophet's personality and revelation'.
73. I deliberately used the term 'philosophical psychology' since medieval philosophical writings were concerned mainly about the study of the soul and not only mental faculties, as is the focus of the modern discipline of psychology. The term is also used by John Walbridge, *God and Logic*, p. 72.
74. See Mahdi, *al-Farabi*, pp. 155–6.
75. Rahman himself explains al-Farabi's idea in his *Prophecy in Islam*, p. 34. For a primary source, see al-Farabi, *al-Siyāsa al-Madaniyya* [The Political Regime], p. 181.
76. For the philosophers' reading of Q 2:97, see Griffel, 'Muslim Philosophers' Rationalist Explanation', p. 167.
77. Avicenna, 'On the Proof of Prophecies', p. 115. See also Rahman and de Boer, ''Akl'.
78. This is what was attested by Rahman himself in *Prophecy in Islam*, p. 38.
79. Rahman, *Major Themes*, p. 101.

80. Qadir, *Philosophy and Science*, pp. 82–4.
81. Walbridge, *God and Logic*, p. 70.
82. For some discussions about this, see Ibid.; Qadir, *Philosophy and Science*, p. 83; Brown, *A New Introduction to Islam*, p. 151.
83. Adamson, 'al-Kindi and the Reception of Greek Philosophy', p. 46.
84. Atiyeh, *Al-Kindi*, p. 99.
85. Rahman, *Major Themes*, p. 80.
86. Ibid., p. 98.
87. Ibid., p. 80.
88. Qadir, *Philosophy and Science*, p. 84.
89. Griffel, 'Muslim philosophers' rationalist explanation of Muhammad's Prophecy', p. 168. Likewise, al-Kindi asserts that prophets have the power of presenting their message to ordinary humans in a way that is briefer and clearer than that of philosophers. Atiyeh, *al-Kindi: The Philosopher of the Arabs*, p. 28.
90. Walbridge, *God and Logic*, p. 80. See also Griffel, 'Muslim Philosophers' Rationalist Explanation', p. 167.
91. Walbridge, *God and Logic*, p. 72.
92. Rahman, *Major Themes*, p. 97.
93. Fazlur Rahman, *Islam and Modernity*, p. 13.
94. Rahman, *Islam*, p. 31.
95. Rahman, *Islam and Modernity*, p. 8.
96. Ibid., p. 5.
97. Rahman, 'Interpreting the Qur'an', p. 46.
98. Ibid., p. 45.
99. Rahman, *Islam and Modernity*, p. 17.
100. For Rahman's ideas about *naskh*, see Sonn, 'Fazlur Rahman and Islamic Feminism', pp. 128–9.
101. Rahman, *Major Themes*, p. 85; Rahman, *Islam*, p. 11.
102. Rahman, *Islam and Modernity*, p. 15.
103. Rahman, *Islam*, p. 33.
104. Rahman, *Islam and Modernity*, p. 2.
105. Rahman, 'Islam and Political Action', p. 153.
106. Rahman, *Islam*, p. 37; Rahman adds that *zakāt* is so important that even prayer is seldom mentioned in the Qur'ān without being associated with *zakāt* (Ibid.).
107. Rahman, *Islam*, p. 15; Rahman, 'Islam's Origin and Ideals', p. 12.
108. Rahman, *Islam and Modernity*, p. 5.
109. Rahman, *Islam*, p. 33.
110. Rahman, *Major Themes*, p. 15.
111. Rahman, 'Law and Ethics in Islam', p. 13.
112. Rahman, *Islam and Modernity*, p. 19; Rahman, *Major Themes*, p. 37.
113. Rahman, *Islam and Modernity*, p. 3.
114. Rahman, 'Concepts Sunnah, Ijtihad and Ijma in the Early Period', pp. 10–11.
115. Ibid., pp. 10–11.
116. Rahman, *Islam*, p. 37.
117. Rahman, 'Law and Ethics in Islam', p. 8.
118. Fazlur Rahman, 'Islam: Challenges and Opportunities', p. 326.
119. Rahman, *Major themes of the Qur'ān*, p. 48.
120. This is Rahman's 'double movement theory'. The 'double movement' theory involves moving from the present situation to the time of the revelation of the Qur'ān and then moving back to the contemporary circumstances. Indeed, this theory has its roots in Rahman's understanding of revelation. See Rahman, *Islam and Modernity*, p. 20; Fazlur Rahman, 'Islam: Legacy and Contemporary Challenge', p. 415.
121. Rahman, *Major Themes*, p. 47; Rahman, *Islam and Modernity*, p. 141.
122. Fazlur Rahman, 'The Impact of Modernity on Islam', p. 127.
123. Rahman, *Islam and Modernity*, p. 19.
124. Ibid., p. 154.

125. See for example, Waugh, 'The Legacies of Fazlur Rahman', pp. 31–2; Sonn, 'Fazlur Rahman and Islamic Feminism', p. 126.
126. For example, see Moosa, 'Introduction', p. 19; Rahman, 'The Qur'ān in Egypt', p. 251.
127. Gadamer, *Truth and Method*, p. 250.
128. Ibid., p. 296.
129. Ormiston and Schrift, *The Hermeneutic Tradition*, p. 19.
130. Ibid.
131. Rahman, *Islam and Modernity*, p. 9.
132. Ibid., p. 8.
133. In this sense, I disagree with Sonn that 'Fazlur Rahman offered a comprehensive and systematic methodology for understanding revelation' (Sonn, 'Fazlur Rahman's Islamic Methodology', p. 213).
134. Rahman, 'Law and Ethics in Islam', p. 9.
135. Rahman, *Islam and Modernity*, p. 20.
136. Ibid., p. 7.
137. Rahman, 'Riba and Interest', p. 3.
138. Rahman, 'Islam: Challenges and Opportunities', p. 326. For a comprehensive discussion of Rahman's ideas on *riba*, see Sonn, 'Fazlur Rahman and Islamic Feminism', p. 124.
139. Rahman, *Islam*, p. 38.
140. Rahman, 'Islamic Modernism', p. 330.
141. Rahman, *Islam and Modernity*, p. 144.
142. Ibid.
143. Jahanshahrad, 'A Genuine Civil Society', p. 244.
144. For an examination of this issue, see Natour, 'The Role of Women in the Egyptian Revolution', pp. 80–1.
145. Rahman, 'The Status of Women in Islam', p. 301.
146. Rahman, *Islam*, p. 29.
147. Rahman, 'The Status of Women in Islam', p. 300.
148. Rahman, *Major Themes*, p. 48.
149. Rahman, *Islam*, p. 29.
150. Ibid., p. 38.
151. Rahman, 'The Status of Women in Islam', pp. 299–301.
152. Rahman, *Major Themes*, p. 49.
153. Rahman, 'The Status of Women in Islam', p. 294.
154. Rahman, *Major Themes*, p. 49.
155. Ibid., pp. 48–9.
156. Rahman, 'The Status of Women in Islam', p. 292.
157. Ibid., p. 297.
158. Ibid.
159. Rahman, *Major Themes*, p. 48.
160. Ibid.
161. Rahman, *Islam*, p. 38.
162. For instance, Jamal al-Dan Afghani maintains that the democratic-parliamentary system is similar to a modern version of *shūrā*. In a similar vein, Rashid Rida argues that *shūrā* contains the main element of Western-style democracy. See Soage, 'Shūra and Democracy: Two Sides of the Same Coin?', pp. 96–7.
163. Prominent among these thinkers has been the Pakistani scholar, Abul Ala Maududi. He states that 'the world has not been able to produce more just and equitable laws than those given 1400 years ago . . . it is saddening to realize that Muslims nonetheless often look for guidance to the West' (Mayer, *Islam and Human Rights*, p. 61).
164. As I demonstrate in the next chapters, Abdolkarim Soroush, Muhammad Mujtahed Shabestari and Nasr Hamid Abu Zayd fall in this group.
165. Rahman, 'The Islamic Concept of State', p. 264.
166. Ibid., p. 262.
167. Rahman, 'Islam and Political Action', p. 157.
168. Rahman, 'Law and Ethics in Islam', p. 11.

169. Rahman, 'Non-Muslim Minorities', p. 19.
170. Rahman, 'The Islamic Concept of State', p. 265.
171. Rahman, 'Law and Ethics in Islam', p. 6.
172. Shirazi, 'Pineapples in Paradise', p. 25.
173. Cited in Shirazi, 'Pineapples in Paradise', p. 32.
174. Rahman, *Islam*, p. 37.
175. Rahman, *Islam and Modernity*, p. 20.
176. Völker has also drawn the same conclusion from Rahman's writings. According to her, what can be deduced from Rahman's understanding of the Qur'ānic term *shūrā* is that it is 'a sufficient basis for a democratic structure' (Völker, 'Qur'an and Reform', p. 179).
177. The term 'epistemic scheme' is used by Dahlen in *Islamic Law, Epistemology and Modernity*, pp. 64–84.
178. Amirpur, 'The Expansion of Prophetic Experience', p. 436.

4

Abdolkarim Soroush: The Prophet's Revelatory Experiences

This chapter examines Abdolkarim Soroush's theory of revelation and its influence on his approach to Qur'ānic exegesis. It first explores Soroush's theory of revelation in order to examine how he understands the role of the Prophet in the process of revelation, and secondly, the way in which he emphasises human aspects of the Qur'ān. It then examines the extent to which his account of revelation is rooted in either pre-modern Muslim philosophical teachings or in modern Western scholarship. The remainder of this chapter addresses Soroush's approaches to Qur'ānic exegesis and its applications to certain Qur'ānic passages or themes. In order to show how Soroush's theory of revelation and his hermeneutics function in practice, I focus on three themes that appear in his work, namely religious pluralism, discourses of women's rights and the relation between state and religion.

Soroush's theory of revelation

This section focuses on Soroush's understanding of the nature of revelation, and the way he links the Qur'ānic revelation to the circumstances that Muhammad confronted during his prophetic mission. In particular, it examines how Soroush emphasises the human dimension of revelation by arguing that there are two levels of historicisation of the concept of revelation in his theory.

Soroush on the nature of revelation

Soroush's fundamental assumption in his theory of revelation is the idea that revelation is, in its very nature, the same as the 'religious experience' of prophets.[1] This idea is valid for all the prophets of God since 'prophethood was [essentially] a kind of [human] experience':[2] 'Religious experience is exactly that which, in the case of the prophets, is known as reception of revelation.'[3] In other words, revelation, as a fundamental aspect of religion, is essentially linked to a form of human experience. Soroush states that all prophets have undergone inward religious experiences through which they became prepared 'for performing their awesome task in the world'.[4] One source Soroush draws on to make this argument is Abu Hamid al-Ghazali's *Deliverance from Error*, a well-known spiritual autobiography written in the eleventh century of the Common Era.[5] Having relied on this source, Soroush argues that religious experience is the most important and defining aspect of a prophetic mission; that is, he makes the case that prophets must be recognised from their religious experiences, and not – as most thinkers of classical Islam hold – merely on the basis of their ability to perform miracles.[6] As Frank Griffel argues, Ghazali had clearly distanced himself from the classical Ashʿari view that prophecy could only be verified through miracles.[7] For Soroush, the prophecy of Muhammad, like that of other prophets, is essentially a matter of individual human experience. What distinguishes Ghazali from Soroush, however, is that the former's discussion of religious experience was not oriented around developing specific methods to approaching the Qur'ān, but rather remained confined to a defence of prophecy as such. As will be discussed, Soroush's perspective, unlike Ghazali's, on the theme of experience became a basis for developing various hermeneutical approaches to interpreting the Qur'ān.

For Soroush, the Prophet did not simply hear the Word of God during the process of revelation, but had an inner experience of the divine through which the Qur'ān came into being. The Prophet's 'experience' of the divine did not simply consist of hearing physical and acoustic words, as traditionally understood, but rather included 'reveries, insights and illuminations'.[8] Soroush distances himself from the traditional account of revelation, which 'has almost univocally described the phenomenon [of revelation] as auditory' (as Madigan noted[9]), but rather focuses on visual aspects of revelation in his theory. In fact, Soroush's emphasis on experiential features of revelation leads him to argue that the Prophet was semi-conscious in the process of revelation, and was able to see autonomous forms, visions and images through his strong imaginative faculty. The idea that Muhammad experienced revelation in the sense that *waḥy* contained visual aspects – in the form of visions and images – is more strongly emphasised in Soroush's most recent works. For example, when referring to the Qur'ānic verse, 'And to God prostrates whoever is within the heavens and the earth' (Q 13:15), Soroush states that 'Muhammad was not told that everything glorifies God, but he himself experienced everything as glorifying God', and makes the case that 'one fascinating revelatory experience of the Prophet was that he saw everything in the earth and the heaven and their shadows prostrating to God day and night'.[10] Soroush writes:

> Muhammad is a narrator [*rāvī*]. That is, he is not [simply] addressed by voices that he hears in his inner ear, which ask him to transfer their message to humanity. Muhammad conveys his experiences as an observer of the visions he himself has seen [in the process of revelation].[11]

In order to explain the nature of revelation in detail, Soroush, like Rahman, likens the revelatory experiences of prophets to those of poets and mystics:

'To understand the unfamiliar phenomenon of revelation we can use the more familiar phenomenon of the creation of poetry and artistic creativity in general.'[12] From Soroush's writings one can conclude that there are three similarities between prophecy and poetry. First, like poets who feel that they receive inspiration from a source external to them, prophets, too, receive inspiration or revelation from an external source. Second, poetry and divine revelation are both related to the possession of a kind of talent. Soroush argues that poets and prophets possess extraordinary talents, including those of articulation and imagination.[13] Third, like a prophet, a poet 'can open new horizons for people; he can make them view the world in a different way'.[14] Despite these similarities, Soroush distinguishes prophecy from poetry (or mysticism). He acknowledges that religious experience in itself does not make one a prophet. Even the mere sight of an angel does not instil one with a prophetic mission. For example, the Qur'ān speaks about the story of Mary's encounter with the angel, and about how the sight of the angel frightened her, but Mary did not become a prophet.[15] Therefore, religious experience is a necessary condition for a person to become a prophet, but is not a sufficient one. Further, there is an element of mission which distinguishes the prophetic experience from the experience of mystics and poets: 'The difference between prophets and other people who undergo similar experiences is that they do not remain confined within this personal experience.'[16] Another difference between the revelatory experiences of prophets and similar types of experiences is that the former are of a divine essence, while the latter do not have roots in a divine source. Therefore, in an approach not dissimilar to that of Fazlur Rahman, Soroush argues that mystics, poets and prophets experience similar incidents only insofar as the psychological processes of revelation are concerned, and their revelatory experiences are different in terms of their ultimate sources. Soroush concludes that the revelatory experience of the prophet excels that of poets and mystics: 'Revelation is higher poetry.'[17]

The first level of historicisation of revelation: the Prophet's role in revelation

Strongly related to Soroush's notion of religious experience is the idea that the Prophet was not a mere passive receiver of revelation, but rather played an active role in his revelatory experiences: 'In the process of revelation, the Prophet is an active agent, not a passive means.'[18] Soroush rejects the traditional account of revelation according to which the Prophet is reduced to a channel for the transmission of God's Word. In what follows, I argue that there are three themes in Soroush's theory which are associated with the Prophet's role in revelation: (1) the Prophet's heart and mind are two faculties that were actively involved in the revelation process; (2) the Prophet's personality played a central role in revelation; and (3) the Angel Gabriel was part of Muhammad, or appeared in his imaginative faculty, and thus was not an external being vis-à-vis the Prophet.

The role of the Prophet's heart and mind in revelation

Like Rahman, Soroush makes a case that the process of revelation was internal. One of the main problems with the traditional account of revelation, according to Soroush, is that it reduces to zero the involvement of Muhammad's heart and mind in revelation. Soroush places an emphasis on the role of the Prophet's heart in the process of revelation and believes that the Qur'ān descended onto the Prophet's heart, not onto his tongue (Q 26:193–4).[19] In addition, as will be explained later, following some Muslim philosophers, Soroush states that the Prophet's power of intellect and imagination also played an important role in the process of revelation.[20] That is, it was impossible for the Prophet to receive revelation without the involvement of his intellectual and imaginative faculties. Revelation, for Soroush, 'was the effervescence within Muhammad's mind and the tumult within his heart'.[21]

The role of the Prophet's personality

As stated, Soroush maintains that it was the inner experience of founders of religious traditions that shaped those religions. Strongly related to Soroush's theme of 'experience' is the idea that the Prophet's personality played a far greater role in the formation of the Qur'ān than the traditional accounts of revelation acknowledge. Much like Rahman, who saw Muhammad's personality as much more than an instrument in the event of revelation, Soroush places the Prophet's personality at the very centre of revelation and shows a similar appreciation of it: 'The Prophet's personality is the core; it is everything that God has granted to the Muslim community. Religion is woven through and through with this personality.'[22] The Prophet's moods, ranging from his joy to his sadness, played a pivotal role in the revelations he received. In one of his interviews, Soroush says that Muhammad's personal history, 'his father, his mother, his childhood and even his moods', played a significant role in shaping the text.[23] The Prophet was sometimes jubilant and highly eloquent while at other times he was bored: 'All those things have left their imprint on the text of the Qur'ān. That is the purely human side of revelation.'[24] Although Soroush argues that Muhammad's personality and feelings played a central role in the process of revelation, he consistently makes the case that the Prophet's personality was exceptional, since it was 'divinely sanctioned', and thus Muhammad had the potential to receive revelation.[25] Such an approach is reminiscent of Rahman's idea that the Prophet Muhammad had 'the potential Revelation in him'.[26]

The role of the angelic figure in revelation

In regard to the role of the angelic figure in revelation, Soroush distances himself from the ideas proposed by traditional Muslim scholars, as he rejects the total otherness and the externality of the angelic figure vis-à-vis the Prophet. Soroush makes the case that the angelic figure was internal to the Prophet, having only appeared in Muhammad's faculty of intellect.[27] In keeping with Rahman's theory of revelation, Soroush considers the angel of revelation to be a part of the Prophet, and not a physical and external being vis-à-vis the Prophet.[28] When the traditional account speaks of the winged angels, Soroush interprets this as meaning that 'angels are not corporeal beings that can have wings . . . it is . . . in the Prophet's imagination [that] angels appeared to have wings', and thus concludes that 'the angel's arrival, the delivery of revelation and the like are events that occur within the Prophet's being'.[29] In line with his approach, which involves considering the phenomenon of revelation within the framework of the Prophet's personality, Soroush states that 'Gabriel is lost in Muhammad's grandeur'[30] and that 'it was not he [Muhammad] who was under Gabriel's sway, but Gabriel who was under his sway'.[31]

The Prophet's role in releasing God's Words

Soroush argues that revelation was a 'formless phenomenon' whose content was not understandable to others.[32] This is due to the fact that revelation was a form of 'experience' that did not merely consist of verbal words. As such, the Prophet had to 'explain' or 'interpret' his revelatory experiences in a human language that would be understandable to his audiences. In other words, God gave a non-verbal inspiration to His Prophet and it was left upon him to 'translate' it for others:

> The Prophet is also the creator of the revelation in another way. What he receives from God is the content of the revelation. This content, however, cannot be offered to the people as such, because it is beyond their understanding and even beyond words. It is formless and the activity of the person of the Prophet is to form the formless, so as to make it accessible . . . the Prophet transmits the inspiration in the language he knows, the styles he masters and the images and knowledge he possesses.[33]

Soroush likens again revelation to mystical inspirations in order to highlight the significance of the Prophet's role in articulating his revelatory experiences. After receiving or experiencing a mystical inspiration, the mystic must interpret it for others, meaning that he should clothe his experience in human words. For Soroush, 'putting the experiences into words and describing them, using concepts, is itself an interpretation [of a mystical experience]'.[34] In a similar vein, prophets must express their revelatory experiences in the language that they and their audiences understand. Indeed, one of the special skills that all prophets, including Muhammad, possessed was to give a 'form' or 'face' to 'formless' or 'faceless' truths.[35] That is, Soroush distinguishes the nature of revelation from the words of the Qur᾽ān by arguing that the formless meaning is from God and the form belongs to Muhammad, or that 'the breath is from God and the reed-pipe is from Muhammad; the water is from God and the jug is from Muhammad'.[36] The Qur᾽ān is indeed Muhammad's words and expression of his revelatory experiences. As Soroush puts it, 'God wrote Muhammad and Muhammad wrote the Qur᾽ān'.[37]

The second level of historicisation of revelation: revelation from experience to a historical event

As shown so far, Soroush attempts to historicise the notion of revelation – an approach which emphasises that revelation was the product of Muhammad's human experiences and is intimately related to his personality. Soroush takes one step further than Rahman in historicising the notion of revelation. His conception of revelation as an individual experience of the Prophet Muhammad is another point of departure for his argument about both the historical and this-worldly dimensions of revelation and its gradual expansion.

If revelation is a form of experience, then that experience, like any form of experience, is subject to expansion, evolution and enrichment. When humans experience something, there is always a possibility that the experience may grow and deepen in quality. Like other forms of human experiences, prophetic experiences do not mature all of a sudden, but grow gradually: 'A poet becomes more of a poet by writing poetry. A speaker becomes more of a speaker by delivering speeches. This can be said of any experience . . . as the experience endures, so, too, will it gain in excellence.'[38] In this respect, 'just as anyone who gains any experience can become more skilled and more experienced, a prophet, too, can gradually become more of a prophet'.[39] According to Soroush, the Qur᾽ān confirms that the Prophet Moses was at first frightened when the cane was transformed into a serpent, but he gradually became accustomed to his revelatory experiences and miracles.[40] Similarly, Muhammad became gradually acquainted with his prophetic mission and his role as God's prophet. He became more confident, resilient and steadier in the performance of his duties: '[T]he blessing of revelation rained down upon him constantly, giving him ever greater strength and flourishing. Hence the Prophet grew steadily more learned, more certain, more resolute, more experienced; in a word, more of a prophet.'[41] Soroush's conceptualisation of the term 'experience' becomes clearer here as he attaches it to the Prophet's personality. For him, as the Prophet's experiences grew and expanded, so too did his personality, and vice versa.[42] This emphasis on the evolutionary nature of Muhammad's prophecy confirms the human side of revelation, and the importance of Muhammad's human character in shaping it.

Soroush uses a number of sources to support his idea about the gradual expansion of prophetic experience. For him, Q 20:114, which states, 'O my Lord, increase me in knowledge', confirms the gradual development of prophetic experience.[43] He also relies on the writings of two celebrated medieval Muslim scholars, al-Tabari and Ibn Khaldun. Soroush cites Ibn Khaldun as saying, 'the Prophet's endurance for revelation gradually grew. Initially, when the verses of the Qur᾽ān were being revealed to him, his endurance would rapidly expire.'[44] To cite a short passage from Ibn Khaldun's *Introduction to History*, 'revelation causes pain, since it means that an essence leaves its own essence and exchanges its own stage for the ultimate stage . . . gradual habituation to the process of revelation brings some relief'.[45] Soroush takes Ibn Khaldun's idea as an adequate reason for supporting the fact that the Meccan chapters and verses of the Qur'ān are short, whereas the Medinan ones are longer. Drawing on Ibn Khaldun, Soroush sees revelation as a psychological phenomenon with an experiential nature.[46] However, unlike Soroush, Ibn Khaldun does not, in general, challenge the traditional understanding of revelation because he believes there is a huge gap between the human sphere and the divine realm, considering the Prophet's mind passive during the revelation process. In fact, although Ibn Khaldun initially attempts to approach the Qur'ān by questioning how revelation took place in Muhammad's psyche, he does not establish a systematic link between the Prophet's revelatory experience and its immediate context – a theme that is recurrent in Soroush's writings. Soroush also cites al-Tabari, stating that, after the revelation of the initial verses of *sūrah al-ʿalaq*, which is traditionally considered the first chapter of the Qur'ān revealed to Muhammad, the Prophet was frightened and could not grasp what had been revealed to him, but gradually became accustomed to his revelatory experiences.[47] Soroush concludes from Ibn Khaldun's and Tabari's accounts that the Prophet's ability to bear his revelatory experiences increased gradually. These accounts show that the Prophet's inward religious experience was subject to expansion, and did not emerge instantly.

For Soroush, the revelatory experiences of the Prophet did not take shape in a vacuum. Like any other experiences, such as mystical ones, Muhammad's revelatory experiences did not develop on their own, but in a particular context. Soroush rejects the British philosopher Walter T. Stace's (d. 1967) idea that mystical experiences are unmediated and ineffable by asserting that there is no pure or context-free experience.[48] Soroush's idea echoes aspects of the American philosopher Steven Katz's contextualist approach to mystical experiences. To quote Katz, 'There are no pure (i.e. unmediated) experiences. Neither mystical experience nor more ordinary forms of experience give any indication, or any grounds for believing, that they are unmediated.'[49] For Katz, a proper evaluation of mystical experiences includes 'acknowledging that the experience itself as well as the form in which it is reported is shaped by concepts which the mystic brings to, and which shape, his experience'.[50] In other words, according to Katz, mystical experience, like any other religious experience, is shaped by the subject's cognitive conditions as well as his cultural environment, religious training and historical circumstances. In a similar vein, Soroush asserts that the nature of mystical experiences is shaped in a socially constructed context.[51] From this premise, he explains why there exist various mystical experiences, rejecting Stace's view that 'all mystical experiences are the same and doctrine is later interpreted into the experience'.[52] Soroush believes that 'the Prophet did not adapt abstract experiences to reality';[53] instead, the actual existing world of the Prophet's time played a crucial role in shaping, and in the development of, his revelatory experiences. Muhammad encountered various circumstances during his prophetic mission. As these circumstances altered, Muhammad's experiences and his personality evolved.

Soroush makes the case here that the Prophet's external experiences affected his inward revelatory experiences: 'The Prophet's interaction with the outer world undoubtedly allowed his mission and prophetic experience to expand and flourish.'[54] Indeed, as the Prophet's external situation, namely his societal life and conditions, changed, his internal experiences, namely his intellectual and spiritual capabilities, evolved and expanded. This shows that Soroush sees prophecy as a natural phenomenon with its roots in history.

By developing this discussion, Soroush gives the Qur'ān a historical nature and sees it as having come into being within specific socio-historical circumstances. In order to discuss further how Muhammad's outward experiences affected his internal religious experiences, and to conclude that prophecy should not be seen as a phenomenon outside but rather within history, Soroush likens the Prophet to a lecturer. The relationship between a lecturer and his students is similar to that of the Prophet and his audiences. This relation in both cases is that of an 'interaction or dialogue'.[55] The relation between a teacher and his students is not a 'unilateral process of inculcation. It is not as if the teacher only speaks and the students only listen.'[56] The lecturer encounters unexpected questions that must be answered, and thus he does not exactly know what will occur in the classroom. Indeed, the students are not passive in the classroom because they are able to divert the teacher from his intended subject. A clever teacher also encourages his students to 'take their turn center stage, so that they may all advance together'.[57] According to Soroush, the Prophet of Islam was in a similar position among his audiences, i.e. the residents of Mecca and Medina. Muhammad's audiences, and the circumstances he constantly encountered during his prophetic mission, had an impact on his revelatory experiences. This notion of the 'dialogical nature of prophetic experience' is intimately close to the evolutionary feature of prophethood. Soroush writes:

> Someone would go to the Prophet and ask him a question. Someone would insult the Prophet's wife. Someone would set alight the flames of war. Someone would accuse the Prophet of being insane. Someone would spread rumors about the Prophet marrying Zayd's wife. Someone would overlook their duties during the sacred months . . . All of this would find an echo in the Qur'ān and the Prophet's words.[58]

The Qur'ān, which is the product of the Prophet's revelatory experiences, has a dialogical nature since many verses of the text came into being as responses to the questions posed to the Prophet by his community.[59] This idea echoes aspects of Ebrahim Moosa's approach to revelation and the Qur'ān. Moosa states that 'the Qur'ān as revelation requires an audience of listeners and speakers. In other words, a community is integral to it being a revelation . . . This audience is not a passive audience, but an interactive audience that engages with a performative revelation.'[60] In order to show the intimate relation between revelation and its audience, Soroush says:

> If they had not accused Aisha of having an adulterous relationship, would we have the verses at the beginning of the al-Nour Sura (Chapter 24)? If the war of the confederate tribes had never occurred, would we have the al-Ahzab Sura (Chapter 33)? If there had been no Abūlahab or if he and his wife had not displayed enmity towards the Prophet, would we have the al-Masad Sura (Chapter 111)? These were all contingent events in history whose occurrence or non-occurrence would have been much the same. But, having occurred, we now find traces of them in the Qur'ān.[61]

An important corollary of this discussion is that day-to-day events played a central role in shaping Muhammad's internal religious experiences, and accordingly in the formation of the Qur'ān. By making a connection between the revelation on the one hand, and the biography and life of the Prophet on the other hand, Soroush intends to bring to light the historicity of the Qur'ān and the contingencies of its verses. The Qur'ān emerged as a result of the Prophet's interactions with his society and people, meaning that it was shaped in response to specific historical events occurring within his society. This conclusion is very close to Rahman's, although Soroush takes a different route to prove it.

From what has been discussed so far, we can conclude that Soroush's theory of revelation is even more 'humanistic' and 'historicized' compared to Rahman's. Soroush, unlike Rahman, focuses on the idea that revelation in its essential nature can be linked to a type of human experience. Further, for Soroush, in addition to the role of the Prophet's personality and feelings in shaping the content of revelation, the Prophet played a key role in articulating his revelatory experiences. While in Rahman's theory the extent to which the Prophet played a role in articulating the revelation in Arabic words remains somehow unclear, in Soroush's theory, the Prophet had an absolute role in wording his revelatory experiences in the Arabic language to his community. The Qur'ān, for Soroush, is not only the product of the Prophet's extraordinary personality, but is also the result of the Prophet's utterance of his revelatory experiences in human language (Arabic). Therefore, for both Rahman and Soroush, the Qur'ān has both divine and human aspects; however, Soroush emphasises the human dimension of the Qur'ān to an even higher degree than Rahman.

Soroush's theory of continuity of revelation

The last theme in Soroush's theory is the doctrine of continuity of revelation, which plays an important role in Soroush's hermeneutic. One of the central elements in Soroush's account of revelation is the idea that the Prophet's religious experience is capable of being expanded and evolved not only over his lifetime, but also in the course of history by other Muslims.[62] The doctrine of the continuity of revelation is developed in Soroush's paper entitled 'The Last Prophet', which was published in two parts. Soroush here argues that the notion of the finality of prophethood means that no other founder of a religion will appear to propagate a new faith. The finality of prophethood refers to the idea that the responsibility of a prophetic mission will never be placed on anyone's shoulders again, and thus there would be no prophetic mission after the Prophet's death.[63] Having placed an emphasis on the importance of the Prophet's personality, Soroush asserts:

> Muhammad, as the Seal of the prophets, had a particular personal characteristic that rendered him worthy of being the last: it was that he had scaled all the necessary and possible stations of vision and revelation, such that there was nothing left to be unveiled.[64]

However, since prophetic experiences are expandable to other human beings (especially mystics and poets, as shown), people of following generations are able to experience revelation, though to a lesser degree. Soroush again bases his argument here on al-Ghazali's idea that regular Muslims might 'possess a token of' the prophetic state in their dreams.[65] However, al-Ghazali's discussion of dreams, unlike Soroush's argument, was not oriented around the notion of an individual's relation to the divine, but rather confined to a defence of prophecy, as already pointed out. In contrast to al-Ghazali, however, Soroush argues that the doctrine of the finality of prophethood does not imply that 'personal prophetic experiences will cease to occur'.[66] An important corollary of this idea is that the path to the Prophet's religious experience is open to all of his followers. Indeed, Soroush emphasises Muhammad's human subjectivity in the process of revelation in order to argue that the door to prophetic experience is equally open to individual Muslims.

In the theory of the expansion of prophetic experience, as discussed, Soroush argues that the message of the revelation changed on a par with the development of the Prophet's personality and with the change in circumstances and events that the Prophet and his community encountered. Therefore, people played a role in the gradual genesis and formation of Islam. Just as Muslims in the time of the Prophet played a role in shaping Muhammad's revelatory experiences, and thus formation of the Qur'ān, Muslims during the post-prophetic period should also play a key role in expanding and enriching the religion.[67] In the same way that Muhammad's experience was shaped in line with his socio-historical context, today's Muslims should develop the prophetic experience in light of contemporary knowledge. In today's context, religious experience 'must interact and engage with the actions of the actors of this age'.[68] This is how Soroush establishes a link between the Prophet's time and the history of the following generations, up to the present-day context. In his book entitled *Loftier than Ideology*, Soroush asserts that 'revelation continuously descends upon us, in the same way that it hailed Arabs [during the time of the Prophet], as if the Prophet were chosen today'.[69] For him, 'we are in the same position that the companions of the Prophet were placed'.[70] It follows that 'in the absence of the Prophet, the inward and outward prophetic experiences must expand and grow, thereby enriching and strengthening religion'.[71] A religion that emerged through interactions and conflicts of its time will continue to exist and develop through new interactions and conflicts, thereby adding to the wealth of previous experiences. Soroush concludes that 'the era of prophetic mission is over, but the opportunity remains for the expansion of the prophetic experience, both spiritually as well as socially'.[72] Muslims should develop and enrich the prophetic experience by engaging with the realities of their time, as the Prophet himself expanded his religious experiences within his historical setting and in the light of his contemporary realities.

The sources of Soroush's ideas about revelation

Soroush's account, like Rahman's theory, challenges the established traditional understanding of revelation. His theory reflects the Muʿtazili's position in regard to revelation only insofar as it emphasises the *createdness* of the Qur'ān and its historicity, since there is no main emphasis on the experiential features of revelation and the Prophet's articulation of his revelatory experiences in the Muʿtazili's accounts of revelation.[73] Soroush (as he himself acknowledges) 'takes one step further and says . . . that the Qur'ān is God's creation means that the Qur'ān is the Prophet's creation'.[74] I pose in this section the question about how various aspects of Soroush's theory correspond to pre-modern and modern Muslim and non-Muslim scholars' views on revelation. I specifically compare Soroush's theory of revelation with the ideas proposed by certain Muslim philosophers and certain orientalists of the twentieth century, and also Shah Wali Allah's account of revelation. The theme of 'experience' (which is central in Soroush's theory) and its corresponding theories within Islamic and Western religious scholarship will be examined in the next chapter when I discuss Mujtahed Shabestari's account of revelation.

The influence of Islamic philosophical tradition

Soroush's view on the role of the Prophet's heart and mind in the process of revelation is close to that of Rahman. Further, like Rahman, Soroush argues that revelation was deeply internal, and that the angel of revelation was a mere faculty or power developed inside the Prophet. Thus, one can make a case that Soroush, like Rahman, has been heavily influenced by some Muslim philosophers' accounts of revelation. Soroush himself defends his theory of revelation as being consistent with those proposed by some medieval and early-modern Muslim philosophers. His idea that the Prophet himself played a significant role in shaping the content of revelation is grounded on some Islamic philosophical teachings, as he himself acknowledges that 'Islamic philosophers, ranging from al-Farabi to Ibn Sina, from Nasir al-din Tusi to Sadr al-din Shirazi, have considered it impossible to grasp revelation without the involvement of his faculty of imagination'.[75] That is, reminiscent of the philosophical concepts of rational agency (*al-quwwa al-ʿaqliyya*) and the power of imagination (*al-quwwa al-mutakhayyila*), Soroush's theory places the greatest emphasis on the active role of the Prophet's mind in the process of revelation.

As discussed in the previous chapter, according to the theories of revelation proposed by medieval philosophers (in particular al-Farabi, Ibn Sina and al-Kindi), the Prophet did not receive a verbal revelation, but rather received images, symbols and visions which were then transformed into verbal modes, thanks to the Prophet's strong imaginative faculty. Rahman's idea that the content of revelation consisted of 'idea-words', as argued in the previous chapter, implicitly suggests that what the Prophet received during the process of revelation included forms and images, and thus his account partially agrees with medieval philosophers' theories of revelation. Compared with Rahman, Soroush's idea that prophetic revelation included 'reveries, insights and illuminations' is even more in line with the views of medieval Muslim philosophers. However, the notion of likening revelation to poetry (or mysticism) in Soroush's writings is by and large similar to Rahman's view, and both seem to have strongly relied on the philosophical distinction between prophecy and philosophy. Soroush's idea that prophetic experience is expandable, though to a lesser degree, after the Prophet's death also reflects the significance of a key Islamic philosophical-mystical theme that 'while prophecy has ceased, Muhammad being the seal of the prophets, messages of divine origin can still be communicated through dreams, albeit on a smaller scale than prophecy'.[76]

Soroush's views about the nature of the angel of revelation and his emphasis on the inner psychological processes of revelation have their foundations in some philosophical Islamic teachings. In addition to the ideas of some medieval Muslim philosophers, especially those of al-Farabi and Ibn Sina, Soroush seems to have relied on the views of Sadr al-Din Shirazi (more commonly known as Mulla Sadra (d. 1571/1640), the well-known Shiʿi philosopher of the seventeenth century of the Common Era) when developing his ideas about the angel of revelation. When challenged by Ayatollah Jaʿfar Sobhani, his most ardent critic in Iran, Soroush borrowed from Mulla Sadra to support his theory of revelation. He cited Sadra as saying:

> Do not ever imagine that the Prophet heard the word of God from Gabriel in the same way that you hear the word of the Prophet. And do not ever imagine that the Prophet imitated Gabriel in the same way that Islamic nation imitates the Prophet.[77]

Further analysis of Sadra's writings shows other similarities between Soroush's and Sadra's accounts of revelation. Like Soroush, Sadra rejects the idea of the physicality of the angel of revelation and his wholly-otherness or externality vis-à-vis the Prophet. For Sadra, through his extraordinary power of imagination, the Prophet makes contact with the Active Intellect, from whom he receives the divine knowledge. This knowledge then descends from the Prophet's intellect to his other faculties and enables him to 'see' and 'hear' the angel.[78] However, seeing and hearing the angel do not take place, in Sadra's account, through the Prophet's physical senses such as his eyes and ears.[79] Sadra's refutation of the existence of the angel in a material form is attested here:

> In the vision of the angel and in the hearing of inspiration – a vision and a hearing that are pure and evident – the effusion comes down from the world of the Imperative to the soul, which thus acquires the vision of something from the Malakut in an immaterial fashion.[80]

This suggests that revelation was an internal process in which the Prophet was able to see the angel of revelation and to hear his voice, but only within his faculty of imagination. More importantly, Soroush's idea that the Prophet's will is not subordinate to that of the Angel Gabriel is also rooted in Sadra's account of revelation. Sadra states that the Prophet does not simply follow the angel's words; he knows the mind of the angel due to his active contact with the intellective level of the angel.[81] Sadra also grounds his argument on the idea that the Prophet has a 'reasoned' knowledge, not just an 'imitative' knowledge. Considering the Prophet as a mere follower of the Angel Gabriel is inconsistent with the idea that the Prophet possesses such reasoned knowledge and reduces the intellectual faculty of the Prophet to an imitative level. Sadra states that one should not think that 'the Prophet is a blind follower of Gabriel . . . Blind following can never constitute knowledge at all.'[82]

The influence of Shah Wali Allah

Among the topics in which Rahman and Soroush have been clearly influenced by Shah Wali Allah (d. 1762),[83] we may point to the role of the Prophet's personality, feelings, heart and mind in the event of revelation. Both Soroush and Rahman found Shah Wali Allah's account of revelation interesting, and both have referred to it in some of their writings. Rahman published an essay in August 1968 in which he defended his idea of revelation as an extension of the ideas of a number of Muslim reformers such as Shah Wali Allah.[84] For his part, Soroush speaks about Shah Wali Allah's ideas concerning 'the causes of the revelation of religious laws' to support his theory of revelation.[85] Central to Shah Wali Allah's theory is the idea that the Prophet's personality and feelings played a role in the divine revelations he received: 'The Prophet's own intent, his eager and earnest quest for something, his supplications, craving and pleading for it is also a strong cause for the revelation of the Divine decree in that respect.'[86] This corresponds to Rahman's and Soroush's emphasis upon the role of the Prophet's personality in revelation.

One can also observe Shah Wali Allah's influence on Soroush and Rahman in regard to the role of the Prophet's heart in receiving the revelation. As discussed, to refute the traditional theories of revelation, both Rahman and Soroush argued that the Qurʾān descended onto the Prophet's heart (referring to Q 26:193–4). Shah Wali Allah uses the same Qurʾānic verse to argue that 'the divine blessings descended upon the heart of the Apostle'.[87] For him, 'revelation means the breathing into the heart through a dream or by creating the necessary knowledge in it at the time when man concentrates upon the Unseen'[88] – an idea which implies that the heart is the locus of revelation.

In regard to the relation between humans and God, Shah Wali Allah asserts that 'when man progresses and gains nearness to God, he may be endowed with a higher conception of God's Attributes'.[89] In this respect, one's religious perceptions grow 'more and more extensive according to his proximity to the Reality',[90] meaning that in the course of one's progress in the approach to God, a natural foundation for the formation of higher conceptions is developed. Shah Wali Allah argues that prophets are no exception to this general rule. In one of his books, Shah Wali Allah states that there was a constant progress in the Prophet's spiritual and moral ascension. That is, the religious dispensation granted by God to the Prophet was subject to evolution and growth, as a result of which the Prophet's personality grew and developed.[91] Muhammad's revelatory experiences were not unvarying during his prophetic mission, but were rather subject to expansion and development in accordance with his external experiences. This shows the influence of Shah Wali Allah on Soroush's theory of expansion of prophetic experience. I will demonstrate this influence in greater detail later in this chapter.

Possible influences of orientalism

At this point, it is useful to compare Soroush's theory of revelation with the theories of revelation developed by some orientalists of the twentieth century. Although there is no direct evidence showing that Soroush has been influenced by such accounts, the similarities between Soroush's and orientalists' theories of revelation may give us some indications that he has been inspired by them. To begin with, Soroush's idea that Muhammad's religious experience had a historical basis and was subject to evolution and expansion reflects Tor Andrae's argument that Muhammad's relation to his revelatory experiences became more 'stylized' and 'objectivized' in the course of his prophetic mission.[92] In a similar vein, in an approach not dissimilar to that of Soroush, Maxime Rodinson discussed Muhammad's revelation within the broader context of mystical experience, drawing comparisons between the Prophet's experience and that of other mystics.[93]

Soroush's theory is closest to Montgomery Watt's idea of revelation. Watt considers the revelation that Muhammad received during his prophetic mission as a 'human experience',[94] but distinguishes it from other forms of human experience by asserting that 'it is God who takes the initiative in revelation [and thus] . . . the form of words in the consciousness of the prophet contains truth from God'.[95] Like Soroush, Watt places an emphasis on the Prophet's personality in shaping his revelatory experiences. He holds that the Prophet required a special form of personality to 'fit him to be a recipient of revelation'. Muhammad's temperament, according to Watt, affected 'the imaginal form of the revelation', and thus there was a close relation between the Prophet's personality and the content of his revelatory experiences.[96] Further, like Soroush, Watt believed that the Prophet had a central role in wording his revelatory experiences: 'The general content of the utterance was perhaps "revealed" from without, but it was left to Muhammad to find the precise words in which to speak.'[97]

Watt's account comes very close to Soroush's when he holds that the revelatory experience of the Prophet is subject to expansion and development. For Watt, as new circumstances arose and his experience developed, the Prophet's understanding of revelation became deeper, and thus his revelatory experience grew.[98] Like Soroush, Watt is of the view that revelation was influenced by 'the intellectual and cultural outlook of the community to which it is addressed, and in which the prophet shares'.[99] This idea is similar to Soroush's view that 'people were never mere observers, even in the loftiest aspect of religiosity, such as revelation itself'.[100] Like Soroush, Watt had argued that Muhammad's understanding of his mission became steadier as his community grew, concluding that revelation was subject to change and expansion over time: 'As this community grew and met opposition, it required further guidance; and this came in the fresh revelations received by Muhammad from time to time.'[101] These revelations were 'certainly the adaptation of the revealed message to the life of a growing community'.[102]

Both Soroush and Watt hold that the character of revelation is at once divine and human because, although the ultimate source of revelation was God, it evolved and developed through the Prophet's experiences, and within the broader cultural and intellectual horizons of his community and audiences.

Soroush's hermeneutics

It has been shown so far that by incorporating various ideas proposed by a number of classical and early-modern Muslims and orientalists, Soroush developed a theory in which revelation is historicised in two steps. First, he developed the notion that revelation is not a supernatural but rather a historical phenomenon, in the sense that the Prophet played an active role in shaping its content. In this context, Soroush tends to distance himself from describing the event of revelation in a way that relies heavily on metaphysical assumptions, instead considering the appearance of the angel of revelation as an internal phenomenon, or one that took place in the Prophet's psyche. Second, by considering revelation as an experience, Soroush established an intimate link between the experimental and evolutionary nature of revelation, meaning that the Qur'ān has a historical nature that came into being through a gradual process and under specific socio-historical circumstances. For Soroush, 'the Qur'ān was revealed and realized gradually; in other words, it had a historical genesis.'[103] This theory does not negate the meta-historical aspects of the revelation since, for Soroush, it is natural that when revelation enters the domain of history, it is suited to the natural law and becomes particular and culturally-historically specific: 'Everything that enters nature, including religion and revelation, bends to its ways. Everything that enters human society becomes social and human.'[104]

The purpose in bringing attention to such an understanding of revelation in Soroush's writings is to highlight areas where it is applied for the purpose of developing new interpretive methods when approaching the text of the Qur'ān. As I discuss in this section, Soroush's theory of revelation has important consequences, especially in regard to opening up a more flexible space for the Qur'ān's interpretation.

Soroush's first hermeneutic

In his article 'The Prophet's Mission and Identity Crisis', Soroush's account of revelation is used to develop an approach to interpreting the Qur'ān. In the first part of the article, the historicity of the religious experience of the Prophet is stressed again:

> When we look at the uprising of the dear prophet of Islam, we cannot overlook the historical background to his uprising. The prophet appeared in a certain place, among a special people and in a special cultural environment, consequently, some of his teachings were related to the factors that existed in the environment. The prophet had to announce his mission in a language that could be understood and comprehended by those around him. The people that he was addressing had a special intellectual outlook, culture, attitudes and customs. The prophet could not have begun from 'nowhere'. He could not have shot his arrow into darkness. He could not have talked to abstract and imaginary audiences.[105]

According to this view, the socio-cultural circumstances of Arabian society at the time of the emergence of Islam affected Muhammad's religious experience and the formation of the Qur'ān. The Prophet was obliged to use the language of his people as a means of communication with them. The Qur'ān was worded by the Prophet and in doing so he had to deal with the historical limitations of the language, meaning that he could only use terms and concepts that would be familiar and understandable to his audiences. In addition, in order to address the people he was encountering, he had to conform to the cultural codes of his society. Therefore, in addition to the day-to-day events that he constantly encountered throughout his prophetic mission, his mission was also highly affected by the specific linguistic and cultural norms that were dominant in his society prior to the rise of Islam. 'One of the difficulties of the mission of all prophets', Soroush points out, is that 'they must declare a supra-historical message within a historical context . . . Today, if we wish to understand the meaning and the content of the prophet's message, we must put ourselves in that cultural context.'[106] The verses of the Qur'ān are in keeping with the Arab environment of the time, and thus any responsible hermeneutics has to first take into account the history, culture and context of Arabian society.

Soroush's theory of essentials and accidentals

Soroush's theory of the 'essentials and accidentals' of religion is rooted in this approach. According to this theory, since many aspects of the Qur'ānic revelations took shape within a specific historical and cultural environment, they must be referred to as accidental, contingent and mutable. The accidental (*arazī*) aspects of Islam include 'something that could have been other than it is and appeared in some other form', while the essential (*zātī*) aspect of religion is 'that which is not accidental; anything without which religion would cease to be religion and the alteration of which would be a negation of religion itself'.[107] Accordingly, essential matters of religion cannot be deducted from its contingent elements.[108] The essential aspects of religion include the statements that are related to the foundations of belief, such as the unity of God, the prophecy of Muhammad and the belief in life after death, and thus they are valid for all times and places.[109] The essentials also include the ethical scope of religious experience.[110] By contrast, the accidentals functioned only within the specific 'cultural, social and historical environment of the delivery of the main message',[111] and thus they are not valid for all times and places. According to Soroush, to be a Muslim 'demands belief and commitment to the essentials [of religion], [not to its accidentals]'.[112] There are five main domains in Soroush's writings that belong to the realm of accidentals, as discussed below.

(1) Soroush considers the Arabic language of the Qur'ān as an accidental aspect of religion. He says, 'it would have been enough for the Prophet of Islam to have been born an Iranian, an Indian or a Roman for his language to become Persian, Sanskrit or Latin'.[113] This idea differs from the beliefs of many pre-modern Muslim scholars who regarded the Arabic language of the Qur'ān as an essential feature of the Qur'ānic text. Ibn Qutayba (d. 276/889), for instance, states that no other human language is comparable with Arabic, since it is the language in which God had decided to send down his last message to human beings.[114] The emphasis on the absolute linguistic purity of the Qur'ānic text led some pre-modern Muslim scholars to argue against the validity of any translation. For example, the medieval Andalusian jurist and theologian Ibn Hazm (d. 456/1064) says, 'Non-Arabic isn't Arabic; so [the Qur'ān's] translation is not the Qur'ān.'[115] Soroush, however, believes that the Qur'ān was worded by the Prophet, and thus that the language of the text is not God-given.

(2) The Arab culture in which Islam emerged is another accidental aspect of religion: 'Had the beloved and great Prophet of Islam received his mission in a different environment, the book of revelation', Soroush points out, would have 'taken on an altogether different hue.'[116] In other words, if the Prophet had lived in another society, his religious experience, and consequently its product – that is, the Qur'ān – would have been different, while the essence of his message would have remained the same. This is due to the fact that revelation in its metaphysical sense is formless, but when it enters the domain of human beings it must take a form; culture provides the religion with a particular form.

(3) Soroush states that all the concepts, notions and theories that are used in the Qur'ān and were part of the Arab worldview at the time of the Prophet belong to the realm of accidentals.[117] In this context, in his *Prophet's Mission and Identity Crisis* Soroush says that certain terms such as 'the path, the road, guidance, being lost, desert, provisions, straight path and many other similar terms' that are constantly used in the Qur'ān deal with a life based on caravans.[118]

(4) Another accidental aspect of religion consists of the historical events and stories (such as wars, protests, enmities, hypocrisies and objections) recorded in the Qur'ān and hadith literature. The questions posed to the Prophet by believers and their opponents and the answers given to these questions also belong to the realm of accidentals.[119] The entry of these accidentals into the Qur'ān shows its 'dynamic, interlocutory nature'[120] because they demonstrate how the Qur'ān came into being alongside the Prophet's actual experiences and the issues or problems that the Prophet and the nascent Muslim community encountered.

(5) The entry of some scientific terms related to (for example) medicine and astronomy into the Qur'ān and other Islamic sources is another accidental aspect of religion: 'There are many *hadiths* . . . concerning treatment of diseases, but nobody really considers them essential to Islam because that is not what makes people needy of prophets.'[121] In a similar vein, '[t]he Ptolemaic theory of the seven heavens is neither essential to Islam, nor the only way of depicting God's beneficence and power'.[122] In facing the realities confronting believers in the modern period, these accidental dimensions of religion could be replaced by modern theories since they are not normative and absolute. Soroush goes on to state that believers should not expect to learn natural sciences such as physics, astronomy and cosmology from religious sources, since they are not among the essential features of religion: 'religion was neither intended for teaching us science nor do we have such an expectation of it'.[123] This idea also has its roots in Soroush's use of the term 'religious experience'. By focusing on the experiential character of religiosity, Soroush finds an independent realm for religion, securing it from a variety of worldly affairs such as scientific knowledge, and thus recognises science and religion as autonomous bodies of knowledge. As discussed, prophecy, for Soroush, is a matter of individual experience, and 'what the prophets introduced to us contained the products of their discoveries and experiences'.[124] It is in this sense that Soroush states, 'Religion is not identical with science, nor is it a progenitor, an arbiter, or a guide for it.'[125] Therefore, believers should neither approach scientific knowledge through religious scriptures, nor consider religious texts as a source of scientific knowledge.

The immediate implication of the aforementioned discussions is that if the Prophet had lived in another society, the majority of the Qur'ānic rulings (which later became the basis of the growth of the *shari'a* laws), such as the precepts of blood money, ritual cleanness, men's and women's clothing, as well as the rights of men, women, slaves and non-slaves, would have taken on different forms, while the essential message of Islam would still have remained the same.[126] The Prophet was even obliged to maintain many aspects of pre-Islamic rules. Such ideas echo Shah Wali Allah's approach to Qur'ānic rulings. Shah Wali Allah holds that the form and the substance of the Qur'ānic rulings have vital links with the culture and customs of pre-Islamic Arabia and thus regards many socio-legal precepts of Islam as an accidental element of Islam. Shah Wali Allah is of the view that the Prophet did not generally introduce new laws and institutions, but rather accepted the majority of the existing regulations of the society, only introducing minor modifications to them. Indeed, instead of negating the entire customary law of Arabian society, the Prophet applied certain modifications which made those customs compatible with the essential tenets of his religion.[127] In a similar vein, Soroush, by contextualising the message of revelation, concludes that 'most of the precepts of *fiqh* and even its basic tenets are accidentals'.[128]

The fundamental aspect of what I identify as Soroush's first hermeneutic is that it is crucial to distinguish the essentials of the Qur᾿ān from its accidental aspects: 'The task of the modern-day religious scholars and students of Islam is to . . . identify a whole range of accidentals that penetrated to the very core of the essence of Islam and imposed their own nature and physiognomy on it.'[129] In this respect, the interpreter must be engaged in 'culturally translating' these accidentals in facing the realities of the modern world because the messages of prophets are 'both local and time-bound, as well as being universal and eternal'.[130] Strongly related to Soroush's first hermeneutic is the notion of mutability and immutability: while the accidental aspects of religion are historically and culturally specific and thus are not absolute and universal, the essentials are universally applicable and do not change under different circumstances. Soroush's thesis argues for a rethinking of the traditional concept of revelation by accepting a humanistic view of the Qur᾿ān on the grounds that an interpreter today is able to propose a responsible hermeneutics when he/she determines which aspects of the revelation are relevant to Muslim life in the present day.

Soroush's second hermeneutic

Soroush also bases his hermeneutics on the temporal contingencies of religious knowledge. He argues in his theory of the expansion and contraction of religious knowledge (*Qabz va Basṭ-e Te᾿orīk-e Sharī῾at*) that one must distinguish between the content of revelation on the one hand, and the human interpretation of it on the other. For Soroush, revelation is divine and perfect since it is initiated by God, whereas any human understanding of revelation is contingent and fallible. Indeed, central to Soroush's theory is the notion of the difference between the essence of religion and our understanding of religion (religious knowledge or *fahm-e dīnī*):[131] 'Religion is in no need of reconstruction and completeness. Religious knowledge and insight that is human and incomplete, however, is in constant need of reconstruction.'[132] Soroush further asserts that 'it is up to God to reveal a religion, but up to us to understand and realize it. It is at this point that religious knowledge is born, entirely human and subject to all the dictates of human knowledge.'[133] The influence of John Hick's (d. 2012) use of a Kantian distinction between the noumena and the phenomenon in his discussion of the ultimate Real is evident here. In his *An Interpretation of Religion*, Hick had arrived at the conclusion that one must distinguish between ultimate reality in itself and ultimate reality as interpreted in human experience.[134] Soroush, in a similar vein, asserts, 'Whatever the reality may be [in itself], we are faced with complications and difficulties in terms of its verification [for us].'[135] If we replace the concept of religion with that of reality, then Soroush's idea becomes clearer. In the same way that we should distinguish between reality and our interpretation of reality, we should distinguish between a given text such as the Qur'ān and our interpretation of it.

Before I explain what I identify as Soroush's second hermeneutic in greater detail, I emphasise that Soroush himself does not establish a link between his theory of the expansion of prophetic experience, developed in the late 1980s, and that of the expansion and contraction of religious knowledge, developed in the 1990s and early 2000s. However, the former inevitably entails the latter, though the latter does not necessarily lead to the former. The reason why there is no systematic relation between these two theories in Soroush's writings is that he was initially interested in epistemology and the relation between religious knowledge and other modes of human knowledge, whereas he later became increasingly concerned with developing new theories about revelation and the formation of the Qur'ān. While he first developed a theory based on the contingencies of religious knowledge, he later developed the theory of the expansion of prophetic experience that is based on the contingencies of the accidental aspects of religion and the human elements of revelation. I believe that the epistemological contingencies of religious knowledge can be understood within the context of the historical and cultural contingencies of revelation and divine scripture. In fact, Soroush's theory of the expansion and contraction of religious knowledge is an organic extension of his first hermeneutic and the theory of the continuity of revelation. If there was an interactive relation between revelation, the Prophet's subjective faculties and the context of the Qur'ān's emergence, and if revelation continuously descends upon us 'as if the Prophet were chosen today', then interpretation of the Qur'ān in today's context should differ from the Qur'ān's exegesis in previous eras, since it must inevitably take into consideration the socio-historical context of the present society. Not only is the discourse of religious experience but also that of religious knowledge and today's interpretive corpus dependent on their societal and historical contexts. This is due to the fact that by entering into the human domain, revelation became 'interpretive'. In Soroush's theory, the Qur'ān has a subjective-interpretive nature in the sense that it is already an interpretation of the Prophet, and is not the direct Word of God. Consequently, it is natural that an interpreter approaches the Qur'ān from his/her subjective position, which includes his/her presuppositions.

Soroush's theory of expansion and contraction of religious knowledge also coheres with his identification of religion as a human experience. Soroush states that 'a person who has religious experience is like a sculptor who is never satisfied with the figure he sculpts. He is constantly chipping away at it, remoulding it and shaping it into a new form.'[136] Soroush refers here to the ever-changing nature of religious experience, arguing that religious experience is always an incomplete project. Just as religious experience results in a feeling of incompletion and dissatisfaction, and thus is always open to renewal and change, religious knowledge is imperfect and incomplete, and thus must be open to criticism and revision. In other words, there is contraction and expansion in our experience and understanding of the sacred, meaning that every generation would inevitably experience and understand Islam's revelations anew. For Soroush, both religious experience and religious knowledge take shape within the broader context of their emergence, and thus are subject to change, progress and historical mutation.[137]

Returning now to the theory of expansion and contraction of religious knowledge, religious knowledge, Soroush points out, is a mundane form of knowledge and depends on many variables (including when and where interpretation takes place) and thus is contingent to other human knowledge and sciences. Soroush indeed puts forward the concept of the dependency (*tābe'īyyat*) of religious knowledge to other forms of human knowledge, arguing that religious knowledge theoretically contracts and expands by being in dialogue with other modes of knowledge.[138] Knowledge, according to Soroush, is always in a state of transformation and each area of knowledge inevitably influences other modes of knowledge: 'Different modes of knowledge including human sciences, natural science, philosophy and religious discipline are all related and interconnected.'[139] Religious knowledge is historically changeable, and how it changes is dependent on the evolution of our scientific understanding of the physical world: 'Human understanding of religion, like his understanding of nature, is subject to a flow and change.'[140] This implies that 'all non-religious modes of knowledge have an inevitable influence on religious knowledge, and change in our epistemic knowledge in one arena will lead to change in our understanding and knowledge in another realm'.[141] The corollary of this approach is that in religious knowledge, as in any other field of human knowledge, no particular conception is sacred and beyond questioning and criticism: 'This is', Soroush points out, 'equally true in *fiqh* and exegesis as it is in chemistry, for example.'[142]

Compared to Rahman, Soroush acknowledges the human epistemic limits associated with interpreting the Qur'ān in each generation. While Rahman believes that we are able to attribute to the text a certain objectivity which remains somehow unaffected by the interpreter, Soroush acknowledges our inability to discover an objective meaning within the Qur'ānic text. While Rahman ignores, by and large, the role of interpreters' biases in the act of interpretation, Soroush believes that the discipline of interpretation operates at a human epistemological level, and thus is by default subject to the interpreters' prior knowledge. The difference between the two scholars' hermeneutic approaches can be attributed to their different understandings of revelation. While in Soroush's theory of revelation the Prophet's subjectivity has been given a significant role in shaping the text, and thus the text is identified as having a subjective-interpretive nature, in Rahman's theory the Prophet's subjectivity is not considered to have played such a significant role that the Qur'ān comes to be viewed as the Prophet's own words.

Therefore, Soroush's hermeneutic is not only limited to considering the socio-historical context of revelation (such as the values, norms and context of the era of revelation) but is also oriented around the context in which the Qur'ān is being interpreted (such as the values, norms and context of the specific times and places in which the text is being read), as well as the interpreters' prior knowledge, pre-understandings and prejudices. According to Soroush, even the questions that are posed to a text including the Qur'ān are the products of our prior knowledge, and our responses, too, are understandable in the light of our existing knowledge.[143] Soroush pays serious attention to the contextual nature of interpretation, concluding that the interpretation of the text is temporal and provisional, and inevitably influenced by other branches of knowledge. Soroush's second hermeneutic is oriented around what Safdar Ahmed identifies as 'a subject-centered notion of truth' – an idea which claims that 'truth' is 'not something that travels in a straight line from the text to the interpreting subject'.[144] Soroush even suggests that the Qur'ān is *hungry for* rather than *impregnated with* meaning and thus concludes that meaning is given to the text rather than extracted from it.[145] Therefore, Soroush's second hermeneutic coheres more with Gadamer's methodological approach (in contrast to Betti's hermeneutics), which claims that any interpretation of a given text depends on the interpreter's subjectivity.

The implications of Soroush's hermeneutics

In this section, I show how Soroush's account of revelation and hermeneutics function in practice, especially in relation to a number of themes such as religious pluralism, women's rights and political matters. The immediate implication of Soroush's theory of revelation – in an approach not dissimilar to that presented by Rahman – has to do with the contingency of Qur'ānic legal statements and rulings. This contingency is based on the idea that Qur'ānic rulings are shaped within the cultural and intellectual context in which they emerged, and thus they do not fall under the category of essentials, but rather belong to the realm of accidentals, as described above. Like Rahman, Soroush distances himself from a legal-oriented hermeneutics and provides a new insight that challenges the literalist understanding of the Qur'ān. As Sadri notes, the lesson that one could draw from Soroush's writings is to 'seek the spirit of the religion rather than its literal content'.[146] This implies that Muslims should not get tied up in legalistic details derived from the Qur'ān, because the Qur'ānic verses dealing with socio-legal issues are to a large extent the direct result of the accidents of the prophet's life.[147]

Soroush's emphasis on the theme of experience also leads him to criticise the heavy reliance of Muslim jurists on legal statements of religion for establishing laws. For him, placing an emphasis on the objectivity of legal precepts of the Qur'ān, and a focus on the essential role that these provisions may play in shaping social structures, undermines the very heart of religion. Indeed, by focusing on the experiential features of religion, Soroush views religion in minimalist terms, especially in relation to legal matters and jurisprudence. In Soroush's words, 'a maximalist religion undermines religion itself'.[148] To him, even 'the guidance offered by religion is minimalist guidance . . . and not maximalist'.[149] He argues that following the Prophet should not involve simply doing what he enjoined or abstaining from actions as he proscribed, but rather reproducing the Prophet's spiritual experiences. This position poses a fundamental challenge to the widely accepted jurisprudential discourse that legalistic provisions constitute the most significant part of religion. For Soroush, these provisions were not essential to religion, even during the period of revelation, let alone in the context of the modern world. Soroush here comes even closer to Rahman's idea that the Qurʾān is not a legal document. As Ahmed notes, unlike legal-oriented readings of Islam, Soroush's emphasis on religious experience promotes 'openness and change', especially in relation to matters concerning jurisprudence, and thus fosters 'a spirit of engagement'.[150] This provides a strong basis for the ever-changing reality of faith, opening the way to the idea that religion has the capability of being reinterpreted and of adapting itself to the conditions and needs of every era.

Religious pluralism

Soroush's theory of revelation – in particular his emphasis on the theme of experience – has a significant consequence that appears in his writings. This section argues that Soroush's philosophy of religious pluralism[151] has its foundation in his conception of faith and revelation as forms of religious experience. Before exploring this issue, I indicate that, following a number of scholars such as Eck, Sachedina, Said and Funk, I use the term 'religious pluralism' in the sense of an active effort between followers of different religions to arrive at mutual 'understanding', rather than simply referring to a form of 'tolerance' towards others' religion.[152] 'Religious pluralism calls for active engagement with the religious other not merely to tolerate, but to understand. Toleration does not require active engagement with the other. It makes no inroads on mutual ignorance.'[153] The issue of religious pluralism is of crucial importance, as Sachedina asserts, in the present context 'in which religious differences . . . have been manipulated to burn bridges between communities'.[154] That is, the significance of religious pluralism lies in the fact that it 'is a fundamental recourse that can be tapped by humankind to establish peace and justice in any contemporary society'.[155] Indeed, the emphasis upon religious pluralism results in the entrance into dialogue with one another, creating a paradigm for developing a democratic social order.

As discussed earlier, the starting point of Soroush's investigation into the nature of religion is the idea that revelation is tantamount to the Prophet's experience of divinity. Soroush considers 'religiousness and religiosity and their continued endurance to hinge on religious experience',[156] and regards the Prophet as the recipient of such experiences. It is in this context that Soroush prioritises experiential religiosity (*tajribat-andīsh*) over other forms of religiosity such as expedient or pragmatic religiosity (*maṣlaḥat-andīsh*) and gnostic or learned religiosity (*maʿrifat-andīsh*). While expedient religiosity is based on heredity, emulation and obedience,[157] learned religiosity is identified by 'a lack of dogma or by a sense of rational wonder'.[158]

Experiential religiosity, or what the Prophet experienced within the process of revelation, and which ultimately resulted in the creation of the Qur'ān, is placed in the highest order of religiosity.[159] That is, the most desired form of religiosity is the form created by the Prophet himself, since it is 'passionate, revelatory . . . individualistic, deterministic, quintessential, reconciliatory, ecstatic, intimate, visual and saintly'.[160]

For Soroush, since religion is, by its nature, formed on the basis of an inner experience of the divine, it is inherently plural. Soroush does not consider religious faith as merely a category of knowledge; rather, he defines it as 'the exclusive experience and private property of the individual', and thus 'while there might be collective rituals, there are no collective faiths'.[161] Religious faith gives 'one's heart to someone along with trust and reliance to that one and to know that one as good and to love that one'.[162] This type of faith is to be considered part of an interior and individualistic form of religiosity, and is distanced from faith as traditionally understood since it can increase or decrease as love can also increase or decrease. Considering religion as a kind of experience leads Soroush to avoid inserting 'certainty' as an element of faith, thereby opening the way for religious pluralism.[163] In fact, his downplaying of the notions of 'religious truth' or 'absolute truth' is a fundamental theme in Soroush's theory, since faith and religiosity are intimately related to our experience of the divine, and shaped within a specific cultural paradigm. This coheres very well with the idea that even the Prophet Muhammad experienced divinity with his subjective faculties and within the specific socio-cultural paradigms of his era. As Ghamari-Tabrizi asserts, central to Soroush's understanding of faith and religiosity is the idea that 'faith, achieved through religious experience, is always fluid and conditioned by one's life circumstances; it is therefore practically conducive to pluralism.'[164] In sum, for Soroush, religiosity based on experience inescapably gives rise to pluralism.

Soroush goes on to state that the existence of various religious traditions is consistent with, and not contrary to, the Divine Will. The plurality of religions should be regarded as the manifestation and embodiment of different responses to the Divine, experienced in humans' various historical and cultural contexts.[165] Since the outward socio-historical conditions of prophets played a substantial role in shaping their religious experiences, various religions inevitably generated different contingencies and localities. This is why the languages, juridical pronouncements and teachings of everyday life found in various Sacred Scriptures are inevitably different from one another. Like Islam, other religions are comprised of essential (*zāti*) and accidental (*arazi*) aspects. Accordingly, while the essential dimensions of religions include similar principles, they differ in their contingent aspects. The main conclusion that the pluralist should draw from this premise is the need to promote the common principles found at the core of various religious traditions and to move beyond the differences that accidental aspects of religions have brought about. In an interview with Sasan Tavassoli, Soroush asserts that 'the essence of religion is for man to put down his own self and arrogance, and bow in worship to God. I love worship and I love to see that in church or mosque.'[166]

As a result, the plurality of religious traditions does not only mean that there are various ways to approach God, as the classical Sufis asserted, but that this plurality should also be seen as a reflection of different historical as well as cultural circumstances within which various religions emerged and evolved. Soroush's approach serves to fulfil the ultimate goal of religious pluralism, which, as discussed, encourages believers to arrive at mutual understanding rather than simply tolerating one another. The pluralist should take into consideration the different historical environments in which religions came into being. With such an understanding, no one considers his/her beliefs as the chosen ones, and those of others as falsehoods, leading one to consider the Truth as a shared asset. In other words, since Soroush's method involves viewing the particularities and localities of religious traditions as tied to the contingent context in which they appeared, it provides great impetus to the denial of any form of inherent superiority of one religion over another. Soroush emphasises that this idea by no means implies that rituals and beliefs of religions must be left aside in order to promote pluralism: 'This is not to say that the followers of all sects and religions should needlessly abandon their own practices, rituals and beliefs, and turn into a uniform mass.'[167] Therefore, while followers of various religious traditions are not expected to abandon their worshipping practices and rituals, they are expected to understand the diversity of religious rites and practices from historical perspectives and in the light of the contingent conditions of their emergence.

One may ask at this stage how Soroush, as a defender of religious pluralism, treats the Qur'ānic charges against Christians (such as that which includes Mary in the Godhead according to Q 5:119–20). This is an example where Soroush's ideas about a dialogical nature of the Qur'ān and the intimate relation between the text and its environment are applied. Soroush argues that the Qur'ānic charges against Christians were directed to the Christian communities present in Arabia at the time of the Prophet.[168] He points out that these Qur'ānic materials are historically conditioned and are considered accidental aspects of revelation. Accordingly, they are not applicable for all times and should not be viewed as directed against all Christians. These Qur'ānic materials only reflect the socio-historical circumstances that the Prophet encountered during his prophetic mission. It is in this context that any commentator on the Qur'ān should question whether a contextually appropriate Qur'ānic observation for the seventh century should be applied as a rule in the twenty-first century. Although Soroush does not deal in great detail with the issue of the Qur'ān's ostensibly hostile response to Christians and Jews, his approach can be used to read such verses as Q 9:5 as well as those which seem to have limited the salvific promise to Islam as the only true religion (such as Q 3:19; 3:85; 5:3) within their own historical context. Even the wars that raged between Muslims and non-Muslims during the Medinan phase of Muhammad's prophetic mission and the Qur'ānic verses that are related to them should be attributed to the inevitably hostile environment in which the new religion arose. Soroush's thesis, if appropriately put in practice, aptly considers religious pluralism as a modern phenomenon, and recognises that the Qur'ān's use of polemical language against the Jews and

Christians in some of its Medinan verses is related not only to the polemical environment within which Muhammad continued his prophetic mission; but this polemic should also be attributed to Muhammad's and the Qur'ān's concern for distinguishing the identity of the community of believers from other religious communities concurrent in Arabia.[169]

Religious pluralism, for Soroush, is also based on the plurality of the interpretation of religious scriptures. If encounters with the transcendent can take place in a variety of ways, and if everyone is able to conceptualise the divine with his/her own subjective faculties, then various understandings and interpretations of religious texts will inevitably arise. Soroush's emphasis on our human epistemic limits in reading religious texts (indicated in his second hermeneutic) results in a diversity of interpretations, implying that the interpretation of religious scriptures 'is subject to expansion and contraction according to the assumptions preceding them and/or the questions enquiring them'.[170] This idea allows for multiple interpretations of a given religious text, thereby justifying religious pluralism within a particular religion. The broader context in which a sacred text such as the Qur'ān is being interpreted plays a key role in the act of interpretation, and thus, as the time and context change, it is absolutely natural that countless interpretive texts that differ from each other come into existence.[171] This theme has also been emphasised by Muhammad Mujtahed Shabestari, whose ideas will be examined in the next chapter.

Although in establishing the principle of religious pluralism, Soroush drew on the tradition of medieval Islamic mysticism – especially Jalal ad-Din Muhammad Balkhi, known commonly as Rumi (d. 672/1273) – he also borrowed heavily from the well-known Christian scholar of Religious Studies John Hick.[172] As Ghamari-Tabrizi and Dahlen also observe,[173] Soroush's philosophy of religious pluralism is close to Hick's. Both Soroush's and Hick's point of departure in their philosophy of religious pluralism is the notion of 'experience', and both make a close connection between religious experiences of prophets and the emergence of associated religions.[174] Like Soroush, Hick asserts that 'the great world traditions constitute different conceptions and perceptions of, and responses to, the Real from within the different cultural ways of being human'.[175] For Hick, the nature of ultimate Reality is beyond our human concepts, and thus whatever we perceive of it is inescapably 'humanly thought and experienced'.[176] That is, the concept of religious truth is contextual and relational because no individual has direct access to the Real. Both Soroush and Hick believe that the contingent elements of religious traditions are inevitable responses to the entrance of the Divinity into the domains of human culture and subjectivity, experienced by our limited human mind. Soroush and Hick indeed distanced themselves from traditionalist circles by claiming that the human mind, due to its limitations, is unable to determine the superiority of one religious tradition or a particular belief over other religious traditions or beliefs. The implication of such an idea is that different religions must be seen as 'related kin' instead of 'rival strangers', working 'toward the same goal of human transformation in mutually complementary ways'.[177] This approach coheres very well with what Raimon

Panikkar identifies as 'true pluralism', a notion that challenges 'absolutism not by an (equally absolute) anti-absolutism, but by relativizing all absolutisms by means of searching for their contextuality',[178] which can be considered as a strong basis for pluralism in today's world.

Discourses of women's rights

Although Soroush has not dealt with the issue of women's rights in a substantial way, he has explored some aspects of this topic. This section argues that Soroush's hermeneutics are used in his discussion about the rights of women.

Soroush distances himself from the apologetic approaches adopted by many contemporary Muslim scholars about women's rights in Islam. He accepts the idea that some Qur'ānic passages as well as some prophetic traditions give men more rights than they give to women: 'It cannot be denied that there are many legal inequalities in Islam . . . including the inequality between the rights of men and women.'[179] Having analysed Imam Ali's letter to his son, Soroush concludes that the Imam's words are uncongenial to women.[180] Such problems, according to Soroush, 'cannot be resolved by providing new justifications to defend an outmoded worldview, hoping women will be lured back into accepting them'.[181] Not only do some Qur'ānic verses give men more authority than women, but also the majority of pre-modern Qur'ānic commentators interpreted the Qur'ānic verses dealing with women's issues in a highly patriarchal way. In line with his idea that understandings of religious texts are contextual and take shape in dialogue with other modes of knowledge, Soroush argues that the inequality between men and women accepted by pre-modern Qur'ānic commentators was in line with the macro context of the pre-modern period. Soroush writes, 'if Muslim scholars defined women's status in a way we find unacceptable today, it is not because they wanted to humiliate women or undermine their status, but because that is how they understood and interpreted the religious texts' based on their prior knowledge, which was compatible with the context in which they lived.[182] This mirrors his epistemological theory that 'the norms and values of every era should be placed within their context [of appearance] and we should not judge people of past generations by today's values and standards'.[183] In the pre-modern period, Soroush states, women accepted such patriarchal norms 'not because they were stupid or oppressed but because they had no problems with such understanding and interpretation'.[184] But 'today women don't accept or believe in such a position'.[185]

In such approaches to unpacking the legal rights of women, both of Soroush's hermeneutical approaches are applied. Soroush argues that the Qur'ānic verses dealing with women's rights are only reflections of the socio-historical circumstances of the Arabian society at the time of revelation. For instance, since the Qur'ān came into existence in line with the patriarchal norms of the Arab society of the seventh century, many of the blessings promised in paradise – such as black-eyed perpetual virgins – appeal only to men.[186] In an interview on the subject of women's rights entitled 'Contraction and Expansion of Women's Rights', Soroush says 'we should not devise rights and duties [for women] that their historical, biological and psychological existence has declared impossible, undesirable or inappropriate'.[187] This is to say, the concept of women's rights, as we understand it today, could not have taken shape in the context of Arabian society in the seventh century. Therefore, the inequality that existed between men and women in the text does not belong to the essentials of Islam, but is part of its accidentals since it came into being as a result of the seventh-century socio-cultural norms of Arabian society.[188] In addition, by applying his theory of expansion and contraction of religious knowledge, Soroush concludes that pre-modern Muslim interpretations of some Qur'ānic passages were formed within the patriarchal context of pre-modern societies and thus are in great need of new interpretations in the modern period. He states:

> In the past, this and many other issues were so much in line with popular culture that there was no need for thinking. In our time such [issues] have been dealt such devastating blows that no one finds it expedient to tackle them or to confront such a formidable torrent.[189]

This is compatible with Soroush's idea that every interpretation of the text carries within itself the interpreter's epistemic understanding of the world and his/her preconceptions and prior knowledge. As such, since the context of societies today is different from that of the pre-modern era, there is a need for reinterpreting those Qur'ānic verses that were used in the pre-modern period to justify the inequality of women.

Unlike Rahman, Soroush does not examine in great detail issues relating to women's inheritance, testimony and polygamy. The main similarity between Soroush's and Rahman's approaches is that the Qur'ānic verses that give fewer rights to women than those given to men must be approached within their specific social context, and not within today's context. That is, if the Qur'ān had been revealed in the twentieth or twenty-first centuries, it would have approached this issue in a different way. Unlike Rahman, Soroush explains the main reason for the dominant patriarchal interpretation of the Qur'ān among pre-modern commentators. Drawing on his second hermeneutic, Soroush maintains that the pre-modern interpretations of Qur'ānic verses dealing with women's status were only reflective of the socio-political circumstances in which interpreters lived. Last but not least, Soroush's second hermeneutic manages to explain why discourses of equality between men and women among feminist exegetes such as Amina Wadud and Asma Barlas emerged during the contemporary era, but did not appear during pre-modern times among Muslim scholars.

Islamic democratic order

As demonstrated, Soroush's second hermeneutic makes substantial advances towards more pluralistic interpretations of the religion, and this has some significant political consequences. Soroush's project protects the natural plurality of human understanding and interpretation of religion and considers the notion of religious absolutism hermeneutically naïve. He welcomes a variety of interpretations and sees any obstacle to this development as a hindrance to the growth of Islamic thought in this era because everyone approaches the holy scriptures with his/her own presuppositions. Perhaps the most significant consequence of Soroush's view on the contingent nature of religious knowledge is his argument against the 'official interpretation of religion' (*qerāʾat-e rasmī az dīn*) by the state and by the clergy in Iran. If interpretations of religious scriptures vary according to an individual's episteme, then there can be no single fixed interpretation presented by the state. According to Soroush, a religion turns into an ideology whenever one single interpretation of religion is declared to be the official one and adopted by a specific class as the true interpretation. Any claim to the *truth of Islam* transforms religion into an ideology: 'Pluralist society is a non-ideological society; it has no official interpreters or commentators.'[190] For Soroush, the official interpretation of religion gives rise to shutting 'the gates of thought'.[191] This type of interpretation is linked to the inflexible ideological understanding of the faith. Soroush writes:

> In an ideologized society, the official interpretation of ideology reigns, but in a religious society, there are several interpretations, not one single official interpretation of religion. In an ideologized society, ideology is left to the ideologues, whereas in a religious society, the relevance of religion (*amr-e dīn*) is much too great to be left to the official interpreters only. In a religious society, there is no person, no legal opinion that is above dispute, and no single knowledge of religion is thought to be the best and the final say.[192]

The doctrine of the relativity of interpretations results in the idea that nobody has the right to claim the primacy of one interpretation over another. The monopoly of those groups who view their own understanding of religion as the only true interpretation of Islam is fundamentally unacceptable because the *fuqahā*, too, are influenced by specific interests, preconceptions and pre-understandings when approaching the interpretation of the Qurʾān: 'No *faqīh* can approach religious texts with an empty mind (*zehn-e khālī*).'[193] Soroush's ideas concerning the construction of religious knowledge are of particular importance for discussions about the way religion is politicised in Iran and within the broader Muslim world. Recognising the multiplicity of meanings and the negation of any claim to a privileged access to the Word of God lays the foundation for a viable democratic Islamic politics. From one side, by submitting religious knowledge to the same reasoning which governs other areas of intellectual activity, Soroush makes the case that religion should participate in the civic sphere and thus should not be relegated solely to the private domain.[194] By applying his second hermeneutic, Soroush rejects secularism in its strict sense because, for him, it leads to the total elimination of religion from areas of society. From the other side, since the knowledge of religion is entirely human, no political party is authorised to speak or legislate on behalf of the Divine Will. 'Because the content of religion is human and non-divine . . . it cannot accommodate the sense of finality that accompanies the theology of Islamism.'[195] Indeed, any political body which claims to speak on behalf of the Divine Will would inevitably distort it. Soroush states that speaking on behalf of God transfers religion to a mere ideological device for organising a particular social order, meaning that he warns against any efforts that aim at politicisation of religion.[196] As a result, Soroush advocates a form of secularism in which religious values are protected within the social context, and thus religious discourses are not purged from the public sphere, but religion is freed from the ideological grip of the state and clerical elite – a notion distinct from the French *laïcite*, or more generally from the European experience of an absolute separation between church and state.

One main feature of Soroush's political theory which places him in sharp contrast to Rahman is that modern democratic norms such as human rights and democracy are extra-religious, meaning that they are not necessarily derivable from the Qur'ānic concept of *shūrā*.[197] We recall that Rahman equates democracy with *shūrā*, suggesting that modern democratic norms can be derived from primary sources of Islam, especially the Qur'ān. By contrast, Soroush argues that religion can only bolster individuals' moral sensitivities and that democracy cannot flourish without commitment to moral precepts. However, this does not mean that methods of governance in today's context as well as other modern political norms can be derived from the Qur'ān. Soroush states that the discourse of human rights 'is an extra-religious area of discourse . . . [and] lies outside of the domain of religion'.[198] Soroush avoids a projection of the present norms onto the past and makes a sharp distinction between *shūrā* and democracy. For him, it is important to move beyond the period in which some scholars have sought to extract democratic norms from the Qur'ān.[199] In Soroush's political thought, as Ghobadzadeh notes, 'governance is perceived in completely non-religious terms, which leaves subjects to determine their political system based on civic reasoning'.[200]

According to Soroush, modern democratic norms are the end products of modernity and the collective critical reasoning of humanity during the modern period, and thus could not have emerged in pre-modern societies due to the epistemological limitations of that era. The basic assumption behind this idea is that there is an ontological difference between pre-modern and modern societies. According to Soroush, humans in the modern world are rights-bearers whereas in the pre-modern era they were duty-bound subjects. By using the word *haqq* (literally meaning Right), Soroush states that 'one of the most decisive paradigmatic changes of the modern world is that most of its concepts and institutions are right-based, reflecting the shift in human self-perception from duty-bearing to right-bearing'.[201] Soroush's position here is consistent with his hermeneutic approach, which acknowledges that certain epistemic limits that existed during the pre-modern era played a significant role in shaping the text. That is, the Qur'ān came into being within a particular historical context and was shaped by the contingencies of the Prophet's situation and the language that he used to articulate the text; and more importantly, it was affected by the limitations of the epistemological framework and worldview of Muhammad's audiences and society. As such, the concept of *shūrā* in the Qur'ānic worldview does not carry the same implications that are associated with our contemporary notion of democracy, since they belong to two different epistemological paradigms. Therefore, in his discussion about an ideal form of governance, Soroush does not refer to Islamic principles such as *shūrā*, considering governance a non-religious matter. His political idea, unlike Rahman's, acknowledges the necessity of extra-Qur'ānic grounding of democracy for governing a Muslim-majority society. Soroush's view represents a flexible approach to political governance insofar as it suggests that the governing frameworks of each period of history are to be derived from the ethical and intellectual norms of that era, and do not necessarily have to be developed by referring to religious sources.

Conclusion

This chapter has argued that Soroush's humanistic approach to revelation is used in his writings to interpret the Qur'ān in a way consistent with modern norms and standards. Soroush historicises the concept of revelation in two steps. He first revalorises revelation from being a mere metaphysical concept to a historical notion by highlighting the role of the Prophet in it and by emphasising its dialogical nature. Second, by considering revelation tantamount to the religious experience of the Prophet which is subject to change and expansion, Soroush establishes a link between revelation and the socio-historical context of the seventh-century Arabian society. This guides him to argue that an interpreter of the Qur'ān should distinguish between the essentials and accidentals of the text. He also argues that the discipline of Qur'ānic interpretation is not immune to change since knowledge of religion evolves along with other branches or modes of human knowledge. In this way, Soroush argues in favour of a flexible interpretation of the Qur'ān that is compatible with modern norms.

Soroush's hermeneutical approaches have led him to argue in favour of the contingent nature of the Qur'ān's socio-legal passages – an approach that distances him from a legal-oriented hermeneutic. I argued that Soroush's hermeneutical approaches function in three realms: the discourse of women's rights, religious pluralism and the influence of religion on methods of governance. In terms of the discourse of religious pluralism, Soroush's hermeneutics lead to both inter-religious and intra-religious pluralisms. As for the discourse of women's rights, although Soroush applied his epistemological theory to address why traditional interpretations of those Qur'ānic verses that seem to have given more rights to men than women should undergo substantial changes, he has not yet applied extensively his hermeneutics to issues such as women's inheritance and testimony. Compared to Rahman, Soroush's humanistic approach to revelation and his hermeneutics allow for more flexibility in developing a viable political theory within an Islamic context by challenging the approach which incorporates a maximal role for government in terms of religious values, and by highlighting the importance of extra-religious areas of discourse in approaching some modern political concepts such as democracy and human rights.

Notes

1. Soroush, *The Expansion of Prophetic Experience*, p. 4.
2. Ibid., p. 9.
3. Ibid., p. 199.
4. Ibid., p. 5. See also Soroush, *Ṣirāṭ-hāye Mostaqīm* [*The Straight Paths*], p. 9.
5. al-Ghazali, *Deliverance from Error*.
6. Ibid., pp. 6–7.
7. Griffel, 'Al-Ghazali's Concept of Prophecy', pp. 101–44.
8. Ibid., p. 19; Abdolkarim Soroush, 'Ta'abīr-e Ma'ād dar Ru'yā-hāye Rasūlāneh' [Interpretation of Resurrection in the theory of Prophetic Visions].
9. Madigan, *The Qur'ān's Self-Image*, p. 141.
10. Abdolkarim Soroush, 'Muhammad: Rāvī-e Ru'yā-hāye Rasūlāneh' [Muhammad: the Narrator of Prophetic Dreams].
11. Ibid.
12. Soroush, *The Expansion of Prophetic Experience*, p. 292.
13. Abdolkarim Soroush, 'The Word of Muhammad'. See also Soroush, *The Expansion of Prophetic Experience*, p. 328.
14. Soroush, 'The Word of Muhammad'.
15. Soroush, *The Expansion of Prophetic Experience*, p. 5.
16. Ibid.
17. Soroush, 'The Word of Muhammad'.
18. Soroush, *The Expansion of Prophetic Experience*, p. 295.
19. Ibid., p. 294.
20. Ibid., p. 296.
21. Ibid., p. 328.
22. Ibid., p. 16.
23. Soroush, 'The Word of Muhammad'.
24. Ibid.
25. Soroush, *The Expansion of Prophetic Experience*, p. 16.
26. See previous chapter.
27. Soroush, *The Expansion of Prophetic Experience*, p. 331.
28. Ibid., p. 293.
29. Ibid., pp. 331–2.
30. Ibid., p. 293.
31. Ibid., p. 12.
32. Ibid., p. 19.
33. Soroush, 'The Word of Muhammad'.
34. Soroush, *The Expansion of Prophetic Experience*, p. 125.
35. Ibid., p. 332.
36. Ibid., p. 295.
37. Ibid., p. 329.
38. Ibid., p. 11.
39. Ibid., p. 9.
40. Ibid., p. 11.
41. Ibid., p. 10.
42. Ibid., p. 14.

43. Ibid., p. 9.
44. Ibid., p. 10.
45. Ibn Khaldun, *The Muqaddimah*, p. 78.
46. For details on Ibn Khaldun's idea on revelation, see Ibid., pp. 70–8.
47. Soroush, *The Expansion of Prophetic Experience*, pp. 10–11.
48. Soroush, *Ṣirāṭ-hāye Mostaqīm*, pp. 11, 166–7.
49. Katz, 'Language, Epistemology and Mysticism', p. 26.
50. Ibid.
51. Soroush, *Ṣirāṭ-hāye Mostaqīm*, p. 167.
52. For details, see Ashk Dahlen, 'Sirat al-mustaqim – One or Many?', pp. 428, 444.
53. Soroush, *The Expansion of Prophetic Experience*, p. 22.
54. Ibid., p. 13.
55. Ibid., p. 14.
56. Ibid., p. 15.
57. Ibid., p. 15.
58. Ibid., pp. 16–17.
59. Ibid., p. 17.
60. Moosa, 'The Debts and Burdens of Critical Islam', p. 124.
61. Soroush, *The Expansion of Prophetic Experience*, p. 17.
62. For a discussion about this, see Soltani, 'Dīnshenāsī-e Abdolkarim Soroush' [Abdulkarim Soroush's Approach to Religious Studies], pp. 51–2.
63. Soroush, *The Expansion of Prophetic Experience*, p. 27.
64. Ibid., p. 34.
65. For evaluation of this idea, see Ormsby, 'Poor Man's Prophecy: al-Ghazali on Dreams', p. 145.
66. Soroush, *The Expansion of Prophetic Experience*, p. 27.
67. Ibid., p. 21.
68. Ibid., p. 23.
69. Soroush, *Farbeh-tar az Ideolojy* [Loftier than Ideology], p. 78.
70. Ibid., p. 77.
71. Soroush, *The Expansion of Prophetic Experience*, p. 19.
72. Ibid., p. 22.
73. Soroush himself has advocated the Muʿtazili position on the temporal nature of revelation: Soroush, *The Expansion of Prophetic Experience*, pp. 274–5.
74. Soroush, 'I am a Neo-Muʿtazilite'.
75. Soroush, *The Expansion of Prophetic Experience*, p. 331. See also Ibid., p. 296.
76. Sviri, 'Dreaming Analysed and Recorded', p. 252. al-Kindi is one of the first philosophers to have emphasised this theme. He argues, 'while asleep, the psyche is liberated from the senses and the sensible, and has direct access to the "form-creating faculty"'. (See Edgar, *The Dream in Islam*, p. 8).
77. Soroush, *The Expansion of Prophetic Experience*, pp. 330–1.
78. Mulla Sadra, *al mabdaʾ va al-maʿād* [the Origin and the Return], p. 605.
79. Mulla Sadra, *al-Asfār* [the Journeys], Vol. 3, p. 99.
80. Sadr al-Din Shirazi, *Tafsīr al-Qurʾān al-Karīm* [the Interpretation of the Qurʾān], p. 299, cited in Jambet, *The Act of Being*, p. 337.
81. Fazlur Rahman has written a book about Sadra in which this viewpoint is highlighted: Rahman, *The Philosophy of Mulla Ṣadra*, p. 187.
82. Mulla Sadra, *al-Asfār*, Vol. 3, p. 99.
83. Shah Wali Allah was a member of the Naqshbandi order and was one of the most influential Muslim scholars in the Indian subcontinent during the eighteenth century.
84. Even prior to the publication of this paper, Rahman had seen in Shah Wali Allah a thinker who had adopted the idea that religious ideas have to 'adjust themselves to and re-express themselves in terms of the genius of a particular age and of a particular people'. Rahman, 'The Thinker of Crisis', p. 45.
85. Soroush, *The Expansion of Prophetic Experience*, pp. 82–9.
86. Cited in al-Ghazali, *The Socio-Political Thought of Shah Wali Allah*, p. 205.
87. See Shah Wali Allah, *Sufism and the Islamic Tradition*, pp. 95–6.

88. Ibid., p. 59.
89. Cited in Halepota, *Philosophy of Shah Waiullah*, p. 229.
90. Ibid.
91. Shah Wali Allah, *al-Khayr al-Kathir* [the Great Benefit], pp. 98–103. For examination of this viewpoint in detail, see al-Ghazali, *The Socio-Political Thought of Shah Wali Allah*, p. 25.
92. Andrea, *Muhammad*, p. 66.
93. Rodinson, *Muhammad*, pp. 74–81.
94. Watt, *Islamic Revelation*, pp. 15, 108.
95. Watt, *Islam and Christianity Today*, p. 59.
96. Ibid., p. 66.
97. Watt and Bell, *Introduction to the Qur'an*, p. 22.
98. Watt, *Islam and Christianity Today*, pp. 68–9; Watt, *Islamic Revelation in the Modern World*, p. 46.
99. Watt, *Islam and Christianity Today*, p. 66.
100. Soroush, *The Expansion of Prophetic Experience*, p. 19.
101. Watt, *Islamic Revelation*, p.2 0.
102. Ibid.
103. Soroush, *The Expansion of Prophetic Experience*, p. 16.
104. Soroush, *Reason, Freedom and Democracy in Islam*, p. 61.
105. Soroush, 'The Prophet's Mission and Identity Crisis', pp. 2–3, cited in Aliabadi, 'Abdolkarim Soroush and the Discourse of Islamic Revivalism', p. 50.
106. Ibid.
107. Soroush, *The Expansion of Prophetic Experience*, p. 67.
108. Ibid., p. 91.
109. This does not appear in the English translation of Soroush's 'Essentials and Accidentals in Religion', which is a part of his *The Expansion of Prophetic Experience*, but is found in the original Persian text. See Soroush, *Basṭ-e Tajrobeh Nabavī*, p. 80. See also Soroush, 'The Changeable and Unchangeable', p. 10.
110. Soroush, *The Expansion of Prophetic Experience*, p. 104.
111. Soroush, 'The Evolution and Devolution of Religious Knowledge', p. 250.
112. Soroush, The Expansion of Prophetic Experience, p. 63.
113. Soroush, *The Expansion of Prophetic Experience*, p. 70. See also Soroush, *Farbeh-tar az Ideolojy*, p. 59.
114. Ibn Qutayba, *Ta'wīl Mushkil al- Qur'ān* [*Elucidation of Difficult Passages of the Qur'ān*], pp. 20–1.
115. Cited in Cook, *The Koran*, p. 94.
116. Soroush, *The Expansion of Prophetic Experience*, p. 71.
117. Ibid., pp. 72–3.
118. Soroush, 'The Prophet's Mission and Identity Crisis', p. 6.
119. Soroush, *The Expansion of Prophetic Experience*, pp. 80–1.
120. Ibid., p. 81.
121. Soroush, 'The Evolution and Devolution of Religious Knowledge', p. 250.
122. Soroush, *The Expansion of Prophetic Experience*, p. 78.
123. Ibid.
124. Soroush, *Nesbat-e 'ilm va Dīn* [The Relation between Science and Religion], p. 121.
125. Soroush, *Reason, Freedom and Democracy in Islam*, p. 60.
126. Soroush, *The Expansion of Prophetic Experience*, p. 89.
127. For further investigation of Shah Wali Allah's Concept of the Shari'a, see Miraj, 'Shah Wali Allah's Concept of the Shari'a', pp. 347–8.
128. Soroush, *The Expansion of Prophetic Experience*, p. 89.
129. Ibid., p. 77.
130. Soroush, 'The Prophet's Mission and Identity Crisis', p. 3.
131. Soroush, *Qabz va Basṭ-e Te'orīk-e Sharī'at*, pp. 106–7.
132. Soroush, *Reason, Freedom and Democracy in Islam*, p. 31.
133. Ibid.
134. Hick, *An Interpretation of Religion*, pp. 233–51. Kant points out that since the properties of something as experienced 'depend upon the mode of intuition of the subject, this object as appearance is to be distinguished from itself as object in itself' (see Dahlen, *Islamic Law, Epistemology and Modernity*,

p. 299). The *noumena*, for Kant, is an event that cannot be known by the use of the senses, while *phenomenon* refers to anything that appears to the senses. Translating this to the realm of religion, the reference becomes human experience and understanding of divine scriptures rather than an absolute law of God.

135. Soroush, *The Expansion of Prophetic Experience*, p. 157.
136. Ibid., p. 234.
137. There is, however, another feature in Soroush's theory of *Expansion and Contraction of Religious Knowledge* which is not necessarily developed from his theory of *Expansion of Prophetic Experience*. Soroush holds that knowledge in general is public and the 'creation of new knowledge is always in reference to the overall body of public human knowledge' (cited in Vakili, 'Abdolkarim Soroush and Critical Discourse in Iran', p. 154). See also Soroush, *Qabz va Basṭ-e Te'orīk-e Sharī'at*, p. 229. Thus, Soroush considers religious knowledge, like other branches of human knowledge, as a collective endeavour: 'religious knowledge is not a personal knowledge of a single individual but a branch of human knowledge that has a collective and dynamic identity' (Soroush, *Reason, Freedom and Democracy in Islam*, p. 34). This suggests that religious knowledge has a collective nature while religious experience is highly individualistic. Soroush in general believes in the concept of the accumulation of knowledge over time. This notion of collectivity echoes Quine-Duhem's proposal that all forms of knowledge are inevitably collective (Ibid., p. 16).
138. Soroush, *Qabz va Basṭ-e Te'orīk-e Sharī'at*, p. 165.
139. Ibid., p. 187.
140. Ibid., p. 167.
141. Ibid.
142. Soroush, *The Expansion of Prophetic Experience*, p. 123.
143. Soroush, *Qabz va Basṭ-e Te'orīk-e Sharī'at*, p. 265.
144. Ahmed, 'Progressive Islam and Qur'anic Hermeneutics', p. 84.
145. Soroush, *Qabz va Basṭ-e Te'orīk-e Sharī'at*, p. 271.
146. Sadri, 'The Iran Situation'.
147. Ibid.
148. Soroush, *The Expansion of Prophetic Experience*, p. 115.
149. Ibid., p. 112.
150. Ahmed, 'Progressive Islam and Qur'anic Hermeneutics', p. 89.
151. The concept of pluralism was first coined by Enlightenment philosophers Christian Wolff and Emmanuel Kant (Riis, 'Modes of Religious Pluralism under Conditions of Globalization', p. 21). Subsequent theories about pluralism emerged during the nineteenth and twentieth centuries, having resulted in countless explicit and implicit definitions. Edward Craig defines pluralism as 'a broad term, applicable to any doctrine which maintains that there are ultimately many things or many kinds of thing' (Craig, 'Pluralism', p. 463). This broad definition sets the stage for more specific forms of pluralism in three realms: cognitive, moral and religious pluralism.
152. Eck, *A New Religious America*, pp. 70–1; Said and Funk, 'Dynamism of Cultural Diversity', pp. 21–2.
153. Sachedina, *The Islamic Roots of Democratic Pluralism*, p. 35.
154. Ibid. For a report on an urgent need for religious pluralism, see Hussain, 'Muslims, Pluralism, and Interfaith Dialogue', pp. 264–7.
155. Sachedina, *The Islamic Roots of Democratic Pluralism*, p. 11.
156. Soroush, *The Expansion of Prophetic Experience*, p. 203.
157. Ibid., p. 183.
158. Ibid., p. 186.
159. Ibid., p. 190.
160. Soroush, *The Expansion of Prophetic Experience*, p. 190.
161. Dahlen, *Deciphering the Meaning of Revealed Law*, p. 218.
162. Soroush Dabbagh, *Ayīn dar Ayīneh* [Religion in the Mirror], p. 124.
163. Tavassoli, *Christian Encounters With Iran*, p. 145.
164. Ghamari-Tabrizi, *Islam & Dissent in Post-revolutionary Iran*, p. 232. As I argue in the next chapter, Muhammad Mujtahed Shabestari raised similar viewpoints throughout his writings.
165. Soroush, *Farbeh tar az Ideolojy*, p. 194.

166. Tavassoli, *Christian Encounters with Iran*, p. 144.
167. Soroush, *The Expansion of Prophetic Experience*, p. 142. This is again due to the fact that worshipping provisions of religion such as 'the form and appearance of rites of worship and other rites' are considered as contingent and accidental (Ibid., p. 88).
168. Tavassoli, *Christian Encounters with Iran*, p. 139.
169. For an evaluation of Qur'ānic polemics and their relation to its context, see Sirry, *Scriptural Polemics*, pp. 33–45.
170. Soroush, 'The Evolution and Devolution of Religious Knowledge', p. 245.
171. Soroush, *The Expansion of Prophetic Experience,* p. 137.
172. For Soroush's referring to Hick, see Soroush, *Ṣirāṭ-hāye Mostaqīm*, pp. 19–24; Soroush, *The Expansion of Prophetic Experience,* pp. 131–4.
173. Ghamari-Tabrizi, *Islam & Dissent in Post-revolutionary Iran*, p. 225; Dahlen, 'Sirat al-mustaqim – One or Many', pp. 429–33.
174. In the next chapter, I discuss in great detail Hick's ideas on 'religious experience'.
175. Hick, *An Interpretation of Religion*, p. 376.
176. Hick, 'Christianity Among the Religions of the World', p. 21.
177. Ghamari-Tabrizi, *Islam & Dissent in Post-revolutionary Iran*, p. 225.
178. Panikkar, 'The Crosscultural Dialogue', p. 253.
179. Soroush, 'The Prophet's Mission and Identity Crisis', p. 4.
180. Mir-Hosseini, *Islam and Gender*, p. 223.
181. Ibid., p. 230.
182. Ibid.
183. Soroush, *Qabz va Basṭ-e Te'orīk-e Sharī'at*, p. 260.
184. Mir-Hosseini, *Islam and Gender*, p. 230.
185. Ibid., p. 223.
186. Ibid., pp. 228–9.
187. Soroush, 'Contraction and Expansion of Women's Rights'.
188. Soroush, 'The Prophet's Mission and Identity Crisis', p. 4.
189. Mir-Hosseini, *Islam and Gender*, p. 226.
190. Soroush, *The Expansion of Prophetic Experience,* p. 152.
191. Soroush, *Farbeh-tar az Ideolojy*, pp. 135–41.
192. Soroush, 'Ḥokūmat-e demokrātīk-e dīnī', p. 20 Cited in Amirpur, 'The Expansion of Prophetic Experience', p. 422.
193. Soroush, *Qabz va Basṭ-e Te'orīk-e Sharī'at*, p. 487.
194. Ahmad, *Reform and Modernity in Islam*, p. 214.
195. Ibid., p. 213.
196. While Soroush does not prevent the clergy and religious scholars from participating in political affairs of their society, he believes that the state must place them on an equal footing to all citizens in any competition for political leadership (see Ghobadzadeh, *Religious Secularity*, p. 206).
197. Extra-religious is a form of knowledge based in the natural and social sciences as well as the humanities.
198. Soroush, *Reason, Freedom and Democracy*, p. 128.
199. Ghobadzadeh, *Religious Secularity*, p. 62.
200. Ibid., p. 66.
201. Cited in Aliabadi, 'Abdolkarim Soroush and the Discourse of Islamic Revivalism', p. 68.

5

Muhammad Mujtahed Shabestari: How the Prophet Saw the World

This chapter examines the extent to which Muhammad Mujtahed Shabestari highlights discourses of contextualisation in his writings as a result of his reconsideration of various features of traditional theories of revelation. It first explores how Shabestari understands revelation, examining the extent to which his account is rooted in either pre-modern Islamic or modern Western theological discourses. It then explores how Shabestari has developed his hermeneutics of Qur'ānic exegesis on the basis of his understanding of revelation and the nature of the Qur'ān. Then I pose a question about how Shabestari uses his hermeneutical theories in his interpretation of certain texts or themes of the Qur'ān. I also ask the extent to which his contribution to religious reformist discourse in Iran is grounded in his hermeneutics. To address these questions, I focus on three main themes that appear in Shabestari's writings: the issue of the mutability/immutability of Qur'ānic socio-legal precepts, the concept of religious pluralism, and the relation between state and religion.

The need for reconsideration of the traditional account of revelation

The point of departure for Shabestari in his reform project concerns the need for re-examination of various aspects of traditional accounts of revelation. The importance of re-examining theological issues, including those related to the nature of revelation, stems from the fact that Iran is a religious society. According to Shabestari, religious belief plays a major role in, and represents the main point of departure for, the conduct of affairs in the domains of culture and political governance in Muslim societies, including in Iran. Therefore, Shabestari believes that any reform project in Iran, and by extension Muslim-majority countries, must begin with a substantial revision of religious discourses.[1] According to Shabestari, the Islamic movements which have operated over the past 150 years failed to offer a comprehensive reform project because they 'were political movements more than anything else and not movements for the revival of Islamic faith'.[2] Shabestari's project is oriented around the idea that reform or reconstruction in religious thought and within the realm of theology should precede socio-political change in a religious society. This situates Shabestari within the same framework as the other scholars surveyed in this book.

It is within this context that the traditional understandings of revelation come under severe attack in his writings. Shabestari clearly distances himself from the classical Islamic position concerning the person of the Prophet being a passive channel of communication between the divine realm and the human one.[3] He also distances himself from the classical line of thought that prophecy could only be verified through miracles.[4] Given that the traditional understanding of revelation does not lead to a 'theologically sound account of the relation between God and the Prophet' from Shabestari's perspective, he concludes 'we have no options left but to have a different perspective towards our understanding of God's Word'.[5]

Shabestari's theory of revelation

Shabestari's theory is based on the idea that revelation was transmitted from God to His Prophet through 'signs' and 'perceptions' (*eshāreh*).[6] For Shabestari, Muhammad received a *Blick*, a German term meaning an 'attitude' or an 'outlook' on existence, during the event of revelation. The main function of revelation was to give the Prophet a particular worldview, namely a monotheistic worldview, which in turn enabled him to understand the world and mankind in a certain way. As the Iranian scholar Katajun Amirpur notes, *waḥy* is described in Shabestari's theory as 'an aptitude given the Prophet by God. It is this aptitude that enables Muhammad to carry out God's work, that is, to summon to faith.'[7] In this sense, Qur'ānic verses were not originally revealed to the Prophet in the (verbal) form that they are now; they were only 'signs' and 'informative' of the way Muhammad reacted to revelation: 'Revelation is God's sign to the Prophet.'[8]

Shabestari goes on to say that noticing these 'signs' provided an experiential content for the Prophet: 'Witnessing a divine sign is certainly an experience for the person involved. Even the Prophet himself experienced God's call and signs sent to him.'[9] For Shabestari, 'in early Islam we encounter a person [Muhammad] who speaks of an experience'.[10] As Jahanbakhsh notes, central to Shabestari's account is the idea that *Blick* formed the content of revelation, and that the prophethood is nothing but an 'experience of the *Blick*'.[11] According to Shabestari, when the Qur'ān states in Q 24:35, for example, that 'God is the light of the heavens and the earth', this suggests that 'the Prophet has experienced the essence of God in the form of light'.[12] Much like Soroush, Shabestari frequently uses the term 'experience' when referring to revelation, arguing that faith in its very essence has an experiential nature: 'Faith does have a knowledge-based dimension, an element of sovereign subjectivity in it. However, this knowledge must stem from a core experience.'[13] Accordingly, to follow the Prophet is to catch the *Blick* of revelation, as the Prophet did. That is, believers should try to conceptualise and follow Muhammad's spiritual and internal experience.

God's Word, its 'Wholly Otherness' characteristic and the nature of language

Shabestari does not regard the Prophet as a mere passive transmitter of God's message. For him, even the Prophet 'never claimed [himself] that the meaning and wording of [Qurʾānic] verses come directly from God and he only narrates them to his audiences'.[14] The Prophet was not similar to 'a Qurʾānic reciter who does not play any role in the creation of the words and meanings of the Qurʾān and only recites the verses, or . . . an audio channel that only transmits voices to its addressees'.[15] Paralleling Soroush's theory of revelation, Shabestari argues that the Qurʾān grew out of the Prophet Muhammad's personal experience of revelation. That is, the Qurʾān has to be understood as the product of Muhammad's religious experience, rather than a word-for-word revelation from God.[16] While Shabestari has not given specific consideration to the role of the Prophet's personality in shaping the content of revelation, his understanding of the nature of revelation and the Qurʾān is basically humanistic due to its emphasis on the Prophet's human subjectivity in its relation to the divinity. The *Blick* theory suggests that God's message was not delivered to the Prophet verbally, and that any encounter between God and His Prophet could only take place through experience and perception. For Shabestari, it is not possible to conceive of God's speech in the same way that we understand humans' speech.[17] He goes on to state that there is no Word of God in the true sense of the term because it implies anthropomorphism. Speech is, in its very nature, the product of humans, and is specifically connected to the times and places in which humans live. In his work, Shabestari retells the German philosopher Albert Keller's (d. 2010) definition of language:

> Language consists of a system of expressions and signs (*ezharāt*) that has been founded and then evolved by human beings. Mankind has formed this system to express himself, to make himself understandable to others, and to understand others. Language is a system through which human beings systematize their knowledge and inform others about it, and to conceptualize or deal with reality.

Shabestari criticises those scholars who believe that the words and statements of the Qurʾān are the exact speech of God.[18] Leaning also on the Austrian philosopher Ludwig Wittgenstein's (d. 1951) central idea that linguistic expressions are intimately connected to human praxis and bound up with human life and attitudes, Shabestari concludes that human language can only exist in the human world and within a specific social context, meaning that language – be it the language of a sacred scripture or that of other mundane texts – is essentially a socially constructed phenomenon.[19] This stands in sharp contrast with the ideas of those scholars who regard the Arabic language of the Qurʾān as sacred.[20] For Shabestari, in addition to the speaker from whom the language originated and the listener or the addressee to whom the language is directed, language requires a social context.[21]

If God's Word is not like literal human speech, what characteristics does it have? Leaning on Karl Barth, Shabestari states that the Word of God is 'wholly other' (*be kolī dīgar*).[22] God's Word must open a 'horizon' (*ofoq*) for its listeners; even 'with the sign of God to the Prophet the horizon of the Prophet was opened up. His ordinary horizon changed to a revelatory and prophetic horizon.'[23] In addition, leaning on the medieval mystic Ibn ʿArabi (d. 638/1240), Shabestari states that 'in order to realize the revelatory nature of a statement, one should consider the effects it brings about on its addressees which other statements do not bring about'.[24] Therefore, certain statements could have a revelatory nature for one person but not for another person, since they do not have the same effect on all people: 'A word is revealed only when it becomes wholly other', and thus 'there is no such thing as "revelation in itself for all people and all times"'.[25] What is of particular importance here is Shabestari's emphasis on the subjective nature of revelation. His idea about the 'wholly otherness' of revelation is consistent with his emphasis on the experiential character of revelation. That is, due to its experiential nature, God's messages, unlike worldly affairs, must be 'horizon-opening' (*ofoq-goshā*) and 'wholly other'.

The Prophet's role in wording his revelatory experiences

For Shabestari, prophethood is a way or a channel through which the content of revelation is delivered to humanity.[26] The Prophet's role was to guide people to the metaphysical truth he experienced in his *Blick* and to inform them about it. The Prophet had to 'translate' or 'interpret' his revelatory experiences into human language since this is the only way by which revelation becomes understandable for the Prophet's audiences. This is one of the most crucial aspects of Shabestari's theory: the Qurʾān is the articulation of the *Blick* in human language by the Prophet, meaning that it is the Prophet's human speech (*kalām-e insanī-e payāmbar*).[27] Like every other human being who articulates his/her own experience, the Prophet had to deal with the historical limitations of language, and thus used a language that he and his contemporaries were familiar with.[28] The Qurʾān should indeed be seen as an attempt to inform its readers or lead them to grasp the content of revelation, or what the Prophet saw through his *Blick*. It follows that the Qurʾān is an 'interpretive' text in its very nature.

In sum, for Shabestari, the content of revelation must be distinguished from the Arabic words of the Qurʾān; for while the former is of divine origin and is initiated by God, and most importantly, wordless, the latter consists of the Prophet's own words. Thus, Shabestari argues that the Qurʾān is the product of *waḥy* and 'not *waḥy* itself'.[29] Although the Prophet used his own words for transferring God's message to humanity, these words were in conformity with the signs descended from 'above', implying that the Qurʾān has a dual nature (divine and human). Therefore, while the Qurʾān is not a text authored by the Prophet himself, it is not word-for-word God's speech either. In order to emphasise the divine nature of revelation, Shabestari also argues that Muhammad was divinely empowered in a way that enabled him to articulate his prophetic experience in human words, and concludes that although the words of the Qurʾān are the Prophet's, the power of transmitting his revelatory experiences into words has been endowed to Muhammad as a 'special gift' by God.[30] *Waḥy* must be understood as an ability given to its recipient to speak the word (*tavānāsāzi be sokhan goftan*).[31]

Shabestari emphasises that the Qur'ānic expressions *inzāl waḥy* and *inzāl al-kitāb* (the descent of revelation/Book) do not necessarily show that the Prophet played no role in creation of the text. To confirm this theory, Shabestari refers to the Qur'ānic verse 25:48 stating that 'we send down (*anzalnā*) from the sky pure water'. The fact that God sends down rain from the sky, according to Shabestari, does not necessarily show that the Qur'ān ignores the natural causes of raining. In a similar vein, the verses referring to *inzāl waḥy* and *inzāl al-kitāb* do not necessarily indicate that human and social elements had no role in shaping the text.[32] For Shabestari, the fact that verses of the Qur'ān are originated from God does not mean that they should not be attributed to the natural cause of the verses, which is the Prophet himself and the context in which he launched his prophetic mission.

Human aspects of the Qur'ān

Compared to Soroush's theory, Shabestari's *Blick* theory is less historicised because it does not give ample consideration to the role of the Prophet's personality in shaping his revelatory experience.[33] In addition, in this theory, 'there is no . . . explanation of Muhammad's capabilities and readiness as a human recipient of this experience', as Jahanbakhsh has noted.[34] Indeed, unlike Rahman and Soroush, Shabestari is not interested in putting forward a philosophical argument about how the Prophet's human state of mind had to be suitably prepared for receiving revelation. However, Shabestari's approach to the Qur'ān, as discussed, is basically humanistic and historical, and coheres very well with what I already identified as a 'reform theology'. Shabestari himself states that 'some consider revelation an unusual and metaphysical phenomenon which is connected to metaphysics. Personally, I do not agree with this definition of revelation.'[35]

This humanistic approach stems from Shabestari's view of the process of the formation of the text from at least three aspects. First, for Shabestari, God did not give His Prophet a verbal revelation, and thus He is not the word-for-word author of the Qur'ān. Second, the Qur'ān is the product of the Prophet's human speech, or his 'interpretation' of the event of revelation. The Qur'ān is a 'monotheistic reading of the world [conducted by the Prophet] in light of *waḥy*'.[36] Therefore, the objectivity of the Qur'ān as highlighted in traditional theories is transferred in Shabestari's theory to the subjective response and interpretation of the Prophet. Finally, the human aspect of the Qur'ān, according to Shabestari, is related to the dialogical nature of the text or its inseparability from the society in which it came into being. The conversations and discussions between the Prophet and his listeners/audiences are all reflected in the Qur'ān.[37] 'The Qur'ān', according to Shabestari, 'expresses the prophetic interpretation of the social life of the people of Hijaz, and the religious precepts [of the text] are the products of this interpretation'.[38] Shabestari concludes that 'the Qur'ān is a historical text (*matn-e tārīkhī*), not a metaphysical text (*matn-e māvarā' al-tabiyee*)'.[39] In short, much like Soroush, Shabestari views revelation as having both divine and human characteristics at the same time:

'Religion is a two-dimensional phenomenon. One aspect of it is rooted in the other-worldly realm and another in the realm of this world. When religion enters the domain of this world, it inevitably incorporates the fallibilities and shortcomings of this world.'[40]

The notion of continuity of revelation

Another theme in Shabestari's theory is that of the continuity of revelation. Following a Neoplatonic position concerning God and His relation with the world, Shabestari states that the dialogue between God and humans continues forever. In an approach reminiscent of Soroush's, Shabestari argues that although Muhammad was the last prophet sent by God to humanity, the relationship between God and humanity continues in other forms. In fact, Shabestari believes in the 'dynamics' of divine revelation. The notion of the continuity of revelation is compatible with Shabestari's idea that the Qur'ān has an 'interpretive' nature. It is also closely associated with his idea that religious experience is always an incomplete process. Shabestari argues that it is through the act of interpretation that revelation never comes to an end for the community of believers:

> The story of [our] understanding of God's word is that of a timeless, wrangling [*jedāl āmiz*], passionate, and two-sided conversation between God and man . . . The dialogue between man and God, the most incredible story in the universe, continues forever. This is how the interpretation of revelation is achieved and never comes to an end. Under these circumstances, as man is never negated vis-à-vis God, he will always remain one party in the dialogue and will always become the addressee of God's revelation.[41]

As the above passage shows, Shabestari argues that since human beings are the ultimate addressees of God's revelation, there is a perpetual dialogical interaction between God and humanity. That is, the relation between God and humans has not come to an end after the Prophet's death, and religion is open to be interpreted anew in every stage of history.

The sources of Shabestari's theory of revelation

This section deals with the issue of how various aspects of Shabestari's theory of revelation correspond to pre-modern and modern Muslim and non-Muslim scholars' views. I specifically compare Shabestari's theory with the ideas proposed by certain medieval Muslim theologians and mystics such as Muʿammar b. ʿIbad al-Salmi (d. 228/843) and Ibn ʿArabi, certain modern Muslim scholars such as Muhammad Iqbal, and some modern Christian scholars of religion such as Friedrich Schleiermacher (d. 1834), Barth, Tillich and George Tyrrell (d. 1909). I pay special attention in this section to the theme of 'experience' within both

Islamic and Western religious discourse to show how Shabestari (and by extension Soroush) have incorporated such a theme into their accounts of revelation. It should be noted that despite some similarities between Soroush's and Shabestari's theories, Shabestari differs from Soroush (and Rahman) in that he shows little interest in the medieval Islamic philosophical tradition.

The influence of the Muʿtazilis and certain medieval theologians

Shabestari's theory of revelation, as shown in the previous section, logically leads to the idea that the Qurʾān is created in history. The Qurʾān, for Shabestari, is neither the uncreated Word of God, nor was it created in the Preserved Tablet (*lawḥ al-maḥfūz*); rather, it was created in history. Shabestari's theory echoes some medieval Muʿtazili scholars' idea insofar as his theory relates to the *createdness* of the Qurʾān. As will be shown in this section, Shabestari's theory differs from the views of those medieval Muʿtazili scholars who admitted the existence of a pre-revealed Word of God, and is closer to the views of those who argued in favour of the creation of the Qurʾān at the time of its revelation to the Prophet.[42] In addition, his theory is close to the Muʿtazilis' views insofar as they both believe in the absolute oneness and absolute justness of God. Indeed, Shabestari seems to have appealed to the Muʿtazilis' emphasis on God's oneness (*tawḥīd*) and justice to argue in favour of the notion of the renewal of faith in various cultural epochs of history. It must be noted that despite some similarities between Shabestari's and the Muʿtazilis' views, the latter, unlike the former, did not often go so far as to argue that revelation is tantamount to the Prophet's human experience and that the Qurʾān is worded by the Prophet himself.

Shabestari's idea that the Qurʾān is made up of the words of the Prophet Muhammad is not absent in medieval *kalām* literature. Although there is no evidence showing that Shabestari has been influenced by particular medieval Muslim theologians, I see a number of similarities between his theory of revelation and that proposed by such theologians as Muʿammar b. ʿIbad al-Salmi. Central to Muʿammar's theory of revelation is the idea that God 'has no Word' and that 'there is no [such thing as] the Word of God'.[43] Shabestari comes close to Muʿammar in arguing too that there is no Word of God in the true sense of the term, since speech is, in its essence, the product of humans. Shabestari's idea that, despite its divine origin, the Qurʾān is the Prophet's human oration (*kalām-e insanī-e payāmbar*), had also been proposed by Muʿammar. Muʿammar stated that God endowed the Prophet with the capacity to utter His will through the spoken word. This is a special gift endowed by God to His Prophet. It follows that the Qurʾān 'is not the work of God',[44] but rather is a man-made work created by Muhammad; it is divine only 'in the sense that God endowed the Prophet with the power to produce it and also in the sense that it expresses the will and design of God'.[45] Central to Muʿammar's argument is the idea that the Qurʾān should be considered the words of the Prophet inspired by God, and thus the Prophet played a key role in producing the Qur'ān in human language. Both Mu'ammar and Shabestari therefore rule out any supernatural ground for linguistic phenomena, arguing that the language by which the Prophet expressed the Divine Will was chosen by himself. *Waḥy*, for both scholars, should be understood in the sense of giving the ability to the Prophet to form the wording of the Qur'ān.

A background on the theme of 'religious experience'

Since the nineteenth century, the notion of 'religious experience' has been used by many Western scholars of religion. It is often argued that the German theologian Schleiermacher was the earliest scholar to use such a term within Western religious scholarship for the purpose of freeing religious doctrines and practices from their dependence on ecclesiastical institutions.[46] The concept of religious experience, as understood by Schleiermacher, provided new grounds for defending religion against secular and scientific critiques.[47] It also gave priority to individualistic religious feeling in preference to doctrinal religions since, for Schleiermacher, 'not some body of divinely revealed information but the experience of the believers is the subject matter and criterion for theology'.[48] After Schleiermacher, the hermeneutic of experience was adopted by a number of scholars of the nineteenth and twentieth centuries such as William James (d. 1910), Rudolf Otto (d. 1937) and Ninian Smart (d. 2001). For Smart, 'a religious experience involves some kind of "perception" of the invisible world, or involves a perception that some visible person or thing is a manifestation of the invisible world'.[49] According to him, this experience is fundamental in shaping the great religions of the world:

> The factor of religious experience is even more crucial when we consider the events and the human lives from which the great religions have stemmed . . . We have records of the inaugural visions of some of the Old Testament prophets, of the experiences that told them something profoundly important about God and that spurred them on to teach men in his name. It was through such experiences that Mohammad began to preach the unity of Allah – a preaching that had an explosive impact upon the world from Central Asia to Spain.[50]

John Hick has also applied the notion of religious experience in his writings. Like Smart, Hick maintains that religious experience plays an important role in the foundation of all great religions of the world: 'On the basis of their own form of religious experience the Hebrew prophets thought of God as standing in a special covenant relationship with the people of Israel.'[51] Similarly, Muhammad, Hick continues, 'on the basis of his own experience, thought of God as the Qur'anic Revealer whose definite revelation was addressed to the people of seventh-century Arabia'.[52] According to this account, revelation is considered tantamount to the 'religious experience' of founders of religious traditions. In addition, by focusing on the subjective dimension of religious experience, Hick attempts to make a link between religions and the historical environments of their emergence.

While many modern Christian scholars of religion have adopted the term experience in their approach to religion, this notion has received little attention in contemporary Islamic scholarship. There have been a few contemporary Muslim scholars who have incorporated such a term when referring to religion or revelation. There are even some contemporary Muslim scholars who argue that it is unacceptable to speak about 'an experience of God' within the context of Islam.[53] Among contemporary Muslim scholars who have incorporated the concept of 'religious experience' in their approach to religion, one may point to the Muslim poet and philosopher Muhammad Iqbal. Iqbal began his project by focusing on the experiential dimensions of religion. For him, religion should be experienced in the form of an 'intuition' or 'feeling', as it 'aims at reaching the real significance of a special variety of human experience'.[54] Iqbal praises those Muslim theologians who 'moved to mystic experience' in order to find 'an independent content for religion'.[55] Building on this method, Iqbal argues that today's conflict between religion and science is 'due to the misapprehension that both interpret the same data of experience'.[56] Accordingly, he concludes that 'religion is not physics or chemistry seeking an explanation of Nature in terms of causation; it really aims at interpreting a totally different region of human experience – religious experience – the data of which cannot be reduced to the data of any other science'.[57]

The influence of modern Christian thought

In an approach reminiscent of those just discussed, both Soroush and Shabestari place an emphasis on 'feeling' as a crucial feature of religious faith. As discussed in the previous chapter, Soroush defines faith as a form of feeling in which one's heart is given to a divine source: 'This kind of faith is not just a mental assent or a dogmatic belief . . . [It] brings about an existential transformation in the life of the believer.'[58] This definition is close to Hick's description of religious experience as 'a transformation of the "information" generated at the interface between the Real and the human psyche'.[59] Along similar lines, Shabestari, as explained, considers faith (*imān*) the essence of religion, and uses this idea to distinguish between a perspective on religion that heavily focuses on its jurisprudential aspects (or *fiqh*), on the one hand, and religious experience, on the other: 'At the very beginning of monotheistic religions, faith comes into being. At this stage, believers do not express their faith as a principle of a definite theological system . . . What dominates their entire existence is faith.'[60] For both Soroush and Shabestari, faith dominates the entire existence of the founders of monotheistic religions. Revelation makes sense only in this context. In Islam, revelation is but the Prophet's experience of the divine, and the Qurʾān came into being as a result of such an experience.

It is possible to detect other influences of modern Christian theology in Shabestari's account of faith and experience. To distinguish religion from other worldly realms such as science, politics and societal matters, Shabestari draws on Karl Barth's idea about divinity. For Barth, God is 'wholly other' with respect to the world; God 'does not belong to the series of objects for which we have categories and words by means of which we draw the attention of others to them, and bring them into relation with them'.[61] God is 'wholly other' in relation to any this-worldly phenomenon with which human apprehension deals. In a similar vein, Shabestari states that the Word of God 'comes from beyond . . . and is wholly other (*be kolī dīgar*)'.[62] In this sense, Shabestari suggests that revelation must open an area or horizon for its addressees to which they do not ordinarily have access. For Shabestari, 'humans are limited by four dimensions: history, society, body and language . . . The role of divine revelation is to open another horizon other than these four dimensions.'[63]

Shabestari's idea that considers faith and experience to be the core of religiosity also echoes aspects of Paul Tillich's theological understanding of faith. For Tillich, 'faith is the experience of ultimacy'[64] and revelation is an 'ecstatic experience' that 'grounds a person's . . . ultimate concern'.[65] Belief, in Tillich's theory, is 'something that comes over man, that deeply stirs him, seizes and holds him'.[66] Tyrrell's understanding of faith and revelation also interests Shabestari, since it tends much more towards the primacy of religious experience. For Tyrrell, as Shabestari himself acknowledges, the essence of religion is religious experience, and 'revelation is understandable and conceivable only through the religious experience of the faithful'.[67] That is, the main feature of revelation is its experiential dimension; and this experience 'dominates the entire existence of its recipient, not only his cognitive faculty, but also his will, feeling and heart'.[68] This theory emphasises the reciprocity between man and God; for although man finds himself being addressed by God, he is also a partner in a conversation with God. Shabestari, in a fashion reminiscent of existential Christian theologies, sees the relation between man and God as an 'I-Thou relationship'.[69] Thus, through his openness to contemporary Christian theologies and by extending them outside the realm of Christianity, Shabestari proposes a novel notion of revelation, faith and the relation between God and man.

Muhammad Iqbal's influence

Shabestari's (and by extension Soroush's) understandings of revelation also correspond to various aspects of Muhammad Iqbal's thought – Iqbal being one of the few Muslim scholars to view revelation, and by extension religiosity, as an experience. Iqbal likens divine revelations to mystical inspiration, since in both cases their recipients go through an experiential stage: 'A prophet may be defined as a type of mystic consciousness in which "unitary experience" tends to overflow its boundaries and seeks opportunities of redirecting or refashioning the forces of collective life.'[70] For Iqbal, mysticism contains the same sense as prophetic consciousness. In regard to the revelation that he receives and communicates, the most significant contribution of the Prophet is that he enables humanity to experience the divine, and thus his personality should not be reduced to that of a mere politician or philosopher. Like Soroush, who sees religious experience as 'both the cause and reason for faith',[71] Iqbal links religion to a form of 'intuition' that exists above the realm of thought, thus viewing it as the highest form of experience.[72] Further, like Soroush, who sees prophecy as containing 'an element of mission which distinguishes it from the experiences of mystics',[73] Iqbal believes that prophets transform the human world in pragmatic ways through their religious experience. For Iqbal, prophets are 'more interested in remaking the world' and do not confine themselves to the level of 'repetition and intimacy with the divine'.[74]

In his theory of revelation, Shabestari, like Soroush, relies on Iqbal's understanding of prophecy. Shabestari draws the attention of his readers to the similarities he has found between the understanding of revelation found in Tillich's and Tyrrell's writings on the one side, and those of Iqbal on the other. He quotes Iqbal as having stated that 'the essence of religious knowledge [*maʿrefat-e dīnī*] is religious experience [*tajrobeh-e dīnī*]'.[75] What also interests Shabestari is Iqbal's idea that prophecy is a 'unitary experience' that dominates the very existence of the prophet.[76] Religious experience, in Shabestari's theory, gives one 'a new birth and a new life'; it transforms one's life and gives it 'a deeper meaning'.[77]

Iqbal has not addressed the area of hermeneutics in great detail in his work, but Shabestari finds the consequences of Iqbal's emphasis on the primacy of religious experience interesting. By claiming that religion is built on experience, and by focusing on the spiritual features of religion, Iqbal argues that the purpose of the Qurʾān 'is to awaken in man the higher consciousness of his manifold relations with God and the universe', and thus is 'not a legal code'.[78] That is, believers should not consider the Qurʾān to be a compendium of legalistic rules. For Iqbal, since the fundamental feature of religion is its experiential elements, and thus religiosity is highly individualistic and subjective, believers can reinterpret the Qurʾān in every age based on their own experience, which is unique to their era and context. According to Iqbal, this experiential approach to religion provides a practical mode for seekers of religious faith in the modern period not only because it results in bridging the gap between Islam and modernity, or between faith and reason, but also because the 'modern mind' requires 'a concrete living experience of God'.[79]

I have demonstrated the influences of Iqbal's idea on Soroush's and Shabestari's thought when it comes to be related to the notion of religious experience. What should also be taken into consideration is that by focusing on the experiential/subjective aspect of faith and religiosity, Iqbal, Soroush and Shabestari see religion in 'minimalist' (*hadaqalī*) terms, especially in relation to jurisprudence, and thus have distanced themselves from applying a legal-oriented approach to the Qurʾān. The notion of 'experience' is used by these scholars in their approaches to revelation and religiosity to reformulate a number of traditional doctrines. It is noteworthy that Hick, who makes a close connection between the religious experiences of prophets and the emergence of associated religions, has come to a similar conclusion. Hick believes that the epistemic validity of a religious tradition can only be a matter of hermeneutical effort, which is ultimately related to the individual experiences of believers. He writes:

> All human thoughts, beliefs, theories, conceptions, are generated by particular men and women, or group of men and women, living at a particular time and within a particular culture, with its particular presuppositions and modes of thought and its particular social and economic basis; and to say that thought is relative to those circumstances is simply to acknowledge that it takes different forms within different contexts.[80]

The theme of the continuity of revelation

Shabestari's position on the theme of the continuity of revelation reflects at least three lines of thought in both pre-modern and modern religious scholarship. Firstly, it echoes aspects of the views of some contemporary Muslim scholars on revelation, although there is no evidence showing the influence of the latter on the former. For instance, as stated in his theory of the expansion of prophetic experience, Soroush states that 'revelation continuously descends upon us, in the same way that it hailed Arabs [during Muhammad's time], as if the Prophet were chosen today'.[81] For Soroush, the relation between God and humanity is established in such a way that one can assert that 'it is as if God has composed a poem . . . in this world, from the beginning to the end of history, a long poem in which all creatures are letters and words which have come from the lips and mouth of God'.[82] Along similar lines, Muhammad Arkoun suggests that the interpretation of Qur'ānic revelations is a way through which a constant dialogue between God and believers is established, and that the act of interpretation itself becomes constantly transformed into a form of revelation: 'One could say that it is a revelation each time that a new vocabulary comes to radically change man's view of his condition, his being-in-the-world, his participation in the production of meaning.'[83]

Secondly, Shabestari's idea about the theme of the continuity of revelation echoes the major themes of Christian theology prevalent in the writings of Schleiermacher and Barth. For Schleiermacher, reading the Bible, in the way he prescribed, becomes a means of acquiring religious knowledge through participating in revelation.[84] In a similar vein, Barth argues that holy scriptures become 'revelation' for those who encounter God through the sacred texts.[85] In such approaches, rather than being portrayed as the mere passive recipients of revelation, readers of the holy scriptures could be considered as active participants in the revelatory process. Shabestari himself points to Tyrrell's idea that 'the religious experience through which revelation is conceptualized did not only exist in prophets . . . but the faithful have also an experience of encountering with God's spirit and thus *waḥy* continues forever'.[86] For Tyrrell, 'theology [in its nature] is a continuous interpretation of religious experience'.[87]

Thirdly, Shabestari's notion of the continuity of revelation is close to specific themes raised by certain Muslim mystics. Among such mystics, we may specifically point to Ibn ʿArabi. In his *Faith and Freedom*, Shabestari acknowledges that he appeals to Ibn ʿArabi's idea that 'the revelatory nature of a word is related to its influence on the person who hears it'.[88] If someone is influenced by the Qurʾānic words in the same way that the Prophet was influenced, these words become revelation for him/her.[89] For Ibn ʿArabi, 'the esoteric interpretation of the Qurʾān is itself a *waḥy*'.[90] Shabestari finds a number of similarities between this understanding of revelation and that proposed by Tyrrell and Tillich, arguing that they all believe in the continuous nature of revelation. All the scholars in question, for Shabestari, emphasise that revelation is not restricted to the prophets, and that the faithful can experience lesser forms of prophetic revelations.[91] The following passage from Ibn ʿArabi's *Futūḥat al-Makkiyya* (*The Meccan Revelations*) reflects this understanding of revelation:

> It [the Qurʾān] came down upon the heart of Muhammad, and it does not cease to come down upon the hearts of the faithful of his community up to the Day of the Resurrection. Its descent upon hearts is always new, for it is perpetual Revelation.[92]

Shabestari's hermeneutics

As discussed, Shabestari rejects the idea that the Prophet was a passive channel of communication between the divine realm and his human audience, as well as the view that the Qurʾān was equal to God's verbal inspiration revealed to Muhammad during the process of revelation. Central to his account is the idea that the revelation did not negate the human subjectivity of its immediate recipient, i.e. the Prophet Muhammad. Shabestari's account of revelation therefore, I suggest, consists of three main characteristics. First, revelation is a '*Blick*'. Second, revelation is the same as the religious experience of the Prophet, and thus faith, in its essence, has an experiential character. In other words, religion has an existential feature rooted in the human experience of the divine. Third, revelation has a continual character, in lesser forms, and did not simply come to an end with the Prophet's death. Therefore, unlike the traditional accounts, Shabestari's theory suggests that revelation actualised itself within history and by the Prophet's human subjectivity. His theory does not negate the meta-historical aspects of revelation insofar as its source is concerned, but still acknowledges its human dimension, since it emphasises that the Prophet's religious experience, like other human experiences, was intimately tied to the specific environment in which he lived. In sum, like the other two scholars whose ideas were explored in the previous chapters, Shabestari maintains that the Qurʾān operates on two levels: the divine and the human.

Furthermore, in line with his idea that the Qurʾān consists of the words of the Prophet, and that the text essentially reflects a human relation between the Prophet and his society, Shabestari suggests that modern hermeneutical approaches that are used to analyse other texts can be applied to the analysis of the Qurʾān. That is, unlike the ideas of some scholars who argue that certain hermeneutical approaches for the interpretation of the Bible or other non-religious texts cannot be applied to the Qur'ān,[93] Shabestari suggests that an interpreter of the Qur'ān can make use of approaches employed in modern linguistics and philosophy of language.[94] Shabestari argues that the verses of the Qur'ān 'do not speak by themselves' and are only disclosed through the act of interpretation.[95] The Qur'ān, like other texts, 'speaks by means of interpretation, and pours out what it is inside'.[96]

My analysis of Shabestari's account of revelation now becomes relevant to a broader formulation of what central features an interpreter of the Qur'ān must take into account when approaching the text. In what follows, I argue that there are two central hermeneutical approaches in Shabestari's writings, both of which are the inevitable results of his account of revelation.

Shabestari's first hermeneutic

In accordance with his theory that revelation is a *Blick* and that faith has an experiential character, Shabestari argues that revelation, and by extension its product, the Qur'ān, have an interpretive character. The Qur'ān, for Shabestari, was the prophetic reading of the world, meaning that it shows how the Prophet saw the world, and not how the world actually was. 'In this prophetic reading, the experience of the Divine is equal to an interpretive understanding (*fahm-e tafsīrī*) of the world', Shabestari states.[97] 'The Qur'ān', according to Shabestari, 'reveals the Prophet's "hermeneutical experiences" of the world.'[98] For Shabestari, 'the Prophet's reading of the world becomes sometimes deeper than a mere explanation of the world. In these stages the Prophet experiences God, describing Him (for instance) as "the light of the heavens and earths".'[99]

To demonstrate the Qur'ān's interpretive nature, Shabestari argues that the Qur'ānic verses describing God (such as Q 15:26; 4:16; 55:3; 84:6; 9:4; 96:6; 26:79; 3:145; 14:15; 67:2; 16:97; 7:182; 18:17; and 16:45, to mention a few) are not 'indicative sentences', but rather are 'interpretive statements' (*jomalāt-e tafsīrī*). Other Qur'ānic verses (such as Q 44:38–42; 28:16–18; 91:7; 16:45; 67:2; 10:100; 84:6; and 23:72, to mention a few) that describe the fate of human beings and historical events have also an interpretive nature. Such verses report the fate of human beings in the light of God's interaction with them. It reveals a particular worldview because the Prophet presents 'an interpretation of existence' that could be described as a 'monotheistic outlook'. For Shabestari, even the Qur'ānic verses that concern the resurrection of mankind reflect an interpretive understanding of human fate. The Qur'ān states that human beings will be resurrected in the afterlife like the trees that sprout in the spring (Q 30:19). Here, the Prophet, from his experiential perspective, saw human beings in the form of trees and plants sprouting in the spring. Shabestari states that the Qur'ān's use of narratives of people or individuals from past eras, such as the account of creation and the narrative of Adam and Eve, shows (such as Q 15:28–44; 17:61–64; 20:116–17; 38:71–85) that the text aims to prompt humanity to turn to the One God.[100] In such verses, God is understood as an active agent in the fate of all human communities. In sum, for Shabestari, the

Qur'ān has an interpretive nature: 'In the Qur'ān, the Prophet reveals his own perspectives (*bīnesh*) of the world and his worldview (*jahān-bīnī*).'[101]

If revelation, as a dialogue between God and humanity, continues endlessly, such that the scriptures 'become' revelation for believers who encounter God through the sacred texts, then the process of interpretation of the Qur'ān, i.e. the product of revelation, is also continuous. In fact, the concept of the continuity of revelation is closely associated with the notion of the continuous interpretation of God's Word. 'It is precisely through interpretation', as Campanini notes, 'that the revelation never comes to an end.'[102] That is, the process of Qur'ānic interpretation is never final, complete and absolute: 'Understanding the Word of God is not something that takes place once and for all times. Its understanding is tantamount to its continuity.'[103] Shabestari also asserts that 'a distinctive aspect of God's word is its perpetual interpretive feature. No interpretation of God's word is the ultimate understanding . . . There should always be an open path for new interpretations.'[104] Shabestari warns against any attempt that aims to emphasise finality of interpretation.

According to Shabestari, due to its experiential character, faith is in constant interaction with other human experiences; even the Prophet's religious experience did not take place in a vacuum, but rather was intimately related to his context and surrounding environment. Therefore, Shabestari emphasises a hermeneutical approach in which human subjectivity plays a crucial role in the process of interpretation. The practice of exegesis is related to how we experience ourselves and the world surrounding us: 'A Muslim can approach and experience revelation only with the aid of a particular understanding and experience of himself and the world . . . It is by combination of these that any religious thought is formulated.'[105] For Shabestari, any interpretation of the Qur'ān is deeply affected by the interpreter's preconceptions, preferences and prejudgements.

Shabestari's hermeneutical approach mirrors his understandings of revelation. Since in his theory of revelation Shabestari emphasises the two-sided relation between humans and God, and does not negate the human subjectivity of the recipient of the divine or revealed message, he draws on a hermeneutical approach that postulates a dialogue between the two sides of a message. Indeed, just as the Prophet's worldview shaped the content of the Qur'ān, the historical environment and the worldviews of different readers shape their individual interpretations of the Qur'ān. The act of interpretation, for Shabestari, has never been isolated from the episteme of the specific period in which it is shaped: 'In every period the intellectual foundations utilized by everyone who engages in understanding and interpreting God or the prophets are derived from the human sources of knowledge available in that period.'[106] There are a number of bodies of knowledge that are unavoidable means of interpretation in every historical era. Therefore, every form of religious thought and knowledge is subject to change, since each is shaped based on the prior knowledge and preconceived ideas of its constituter. Here, Shabestari's position becomes even closer to Soroush's, who argues that there has been always a close relation between our knowledge of nature and our religious knowledge, and the latter has been subject to contraction and expansion in different individuals and at various historical epochs.[107] This idea leads both Soroush and Shabestari to argue that one should distinguish between the Qur'ān and any human interpretation of it, which is contingent and fallible, and thus the corpus of interpretation must be open to revision and criticism.[108] It has also led Shabestari to challenge the applicability of pre-modern interpretive discourses in the modern context, as will be argued later.

In developing what I have identified as Shabestari's first hermeneutic, Shabestari has been strongly influenced by characteristics of the contemporary Subjectivity School of hermeneutics. As explored in the second chapter, the German scholar of hermeneutics Gadamer adopts the idea that readers arrive at the task of interpretation with a variety of presuppositions and personal knowledge.[109] Indeed, in the Gadamerian hermeneutic, which is adopted in some important respects by Shabestari, the relationship between a text and its reader is two-sided, rather than one-sided, in the sense that an object-centred notion of 'truth' is transferred to a subject-centred one.

Therefore, from a comparative perspective, Shabestari is closer to Soroush than to Fazlur Rahman because of the special role that Shabestari attributes to the Prophet's subjectivity during the event of revelation. Also, unlike Rahman, who advocates the possibility of gaining an objective meaning of the text by putting aside preconceived assumptions and presuppositions, Shabestari argues that it is not possible to remove one's biases from interpretation, and thus any understanding of the Qur'ān depends on the interpreter's subjectivity. Indeed, Shabestari does not seem to emphasise the need to put aside one's pre-knowledge, nor to subordinate one's *a priori* understanding in the process of interpretation, since he believes that one inevitably brings his/her own interests and prior knowledge to his/her interpretive methods.[110] This approach stems from how Shabestari believes the process of revelation took place. Not only do interpreters of the Qur'ān not have direct access to the essence of the Divine and God's will, but the Qur'ān itself is already an interpretation of the event of revelation experienced by the Prophet. By this, Shabestari 'means not only that the religious exegetes have formulated their own understanding of revelation but that Muhammad himself did so too'.[111] Indeed,

> The Prophet having interpreted and rendered the Qur'ān means that it is no longer necessary to tread warily and stealthily in the domain of *ijtihād*. It is no longer obligatory to apologize for entering one's subjectivity into the interpretive process since the Qur'ān itself, being but one interpretation, is no longer sacrosanct.[112]

Therefore, what I have identified as Shabestari's first hermeneutic approach is marked by two major characteristics. First, Shabestari regards the act of interpretation as subjective, shaped by the specific pre-knowledge and presuppositions of interpreters, as well as the intellectual norms, values and standards of the era in which they live. Second, the process of interpretation is never final and absolute, and thus as long as history continues, new interpretations of the Qur'ān will appear.

Every interpreter brings his/her unique experiences to the task of interpreting the text, which gives rise to and reflects his/her own understanding. In the following sections, after discussing the second hermeneutic of Shabestari, I explore how this method of interpretation applies to a number of socio-political themes.

Shabestari's second hermeneutic

As demonstrated, in Shabestari's theory there is a divine reality that stands behind Muhammad's *Blick* or worldview, meaning that the *Blick* which shaped the content of revelation is entirely sacred. The *Blick* consists of the core messages of religion: 'The core message of the *Blick* is that all natural events as well as all developments in human history and fate are "phenomena" indicating One Foundational Reality, God.'[113] The primary concern of the prophetic mission of Muhammad was to draw the attention of his audiences to the existence of One Creator God. That is, the main goal of prophecy in Islam was to promote the theme of the oneness of God. The specific rules and provisions found in the Qur'ān only came into existence as a result of the specific socio-political circumstances that Muhammad encountered during his mission. Indeed, while the specific rules and precepts of the Qur'ān belong to the realm of 'change', the general and broad principles of the Qur'ān such as the oneness of God, the belief in the afterlife, and some fundamental values such as justice and freedom, fall into the category of 'fixed and eternal' principles, since these elements are all closely related to the Prophet's worldview (*jahān-bīnī*).[114]

Shabestari maintains that the entirety of the Qur'ān illustrates an inner coherence, conveying a specific message. The separate historical events narrated throughout the text stipulate a particular message that binds them together. According to Shabestari, when the Qur'ān states that there is no inconsistency in its content (Q 4:82), it is actually referring to the fact that all phenomena of the world must be viewed as God's signs. Indeed, the religious message of the text can be understood under the rubric of *tawḥīd* (oneness of God).[115] In this context, Shabestari argues that the Qur'ān has a 'central meaning' (*maʿnā-ye markazī*) towards which other passages of the text converge.[116] The fixed and eternal features of the text are related to the central meaning it seeks to deliver, which are all related to the Prophet's *tawḥīdī* (monotheistic) worldview.[117] The specific commands or prohibitions that came into existence within the socio-political conditions that the Prophet confronted should all be interpreted in the light of this central meaning. Here, in a fashion reminiscent of Soroush's approach, Shabestari divides the content of the Qur'ān into fixed and variable categories, arguing that while the essential values of the Qur'ān remain eternal for all times and places, its accidental aspects are bound to a specific time and place, and thus are contingent. He states that 'there are no timeless commands/prohibitions in the revelatory words'.[118] For him, 'if there is a Qur'ānic verse about a specific issue, it does not mean that it should always be practised'.[119]

Shabestari's main conclusion, which has specific consequences in the context of contemporary Iranian political discourse is that the Qur'ān does not have a legislative function since it only establishes fundamental values (*arzesh-ha*) and not laws.[120] Here, Shabestari's idea is very close to Rahman's and Soroush's. Shabestari argues that the main objective of 'the Qur'ān and the Tradition is to provide us with the eternal sources of value not to instruct us specific forms and manners of life'.[121] The main purpose of the Qur'ān is only to show us the 'direction' (*jahat*), and Muslims should strive in every era to remain on the path proposed by the Qur'ān.[122] In other words, values are unchangeable and could be implemented in every time and place, while forms are changeable and time-bounded. For Shabestari, whatever exists in the Qur'ān and the Sunna concerning the accidental aspects of religion does not necessarily represent the best possible precept or rule for all times; rather, they represent the best possible solutions offered by the Prophet for the benefits of the people during the time of revelation.[123] Indeed, 'Qur'ānic verses should be understood in their historical context . . . Some Qur'ānic precepts were considered fair and just in the era of revelation, but may not be considered [just and fair] today.'[124]

Therefore, Shabestari's second hermeneutic revolves around one important idea: Qur'ānic precepts and provisions in the socio-legal realm must be approached in their historical contexts since they are the products of contextually specific social realities in Arabian society. In accordance with his idea that the Qur'ān is a narrative about how the Prophet read and saw the world, Shabestari suggests that the historical situation in which the Qur'ān emerged must be understood. For him, language is a means of expression and consists of five main elements: speakers, listeners, context, community and meaning.[125] Expanding this approach to the realm of Qur'ānic studies, he argues that interpreters of the Qur'ān must take the cultural norms of the revelatory context into serious consideration when engaging in the task of interpretation.[126]

Shabestari's hermeneutics in practice

This section demonstrates how Shabestari's account of revelation and his hermeneutical methods are used in his work to approach certain Islamic themes. I focus on three main themes: (1) Qur'ānic socio-legal precepts; (2) pluralism; and (3) some political discourses such as democracy and *shūra*.

First implication: *aḥkām* and traditional jurisprudence

The immediate implication of Shabestari's hermeneutics is that religious laws are contingent. Shabestari gives socio-political precepts found in the Qur'ān and in the Sharī'a literature a contingent nature in two steps. First, legal precepts of the Qur'ān (*aḥkām*) are contingent because they came into existence under specific circumstances that the Prophet and the nascent Muslim community confronted. Second, many socio-political stipulations of Islam grew out of the works of human interpreters of the Qur'ān and were shaped according to the interpreters' specific prejudgements and presuppositions. The discipline of *fiqh* is, in general, 'a human knowledge, originating from religious texts'.[127] Shabestari indeed denies the divinity of Islamic law, making a strong case for its changeability in the modern period, and calls for a fresh review of traditional jurisprudence in its entirety.[128] For Shabestari, the discipline of *fiqh* only answered certain questions that arose within the time it emerged, and thus is unable to address many problems that Muslim societies are confronting today. In other words, since religious ideas have always been dependent on the episteme of the periods in which they were shaped, traditional religious laws are incapable of serving as the basis for modern politics, economics and laws.

Much like Rahman and Soroush, Shabestari is critical of implementing some Qur'ānic provisions dealing with social issues in today's context since, for him, they were to a large extent the direct result of the accidents of the Prophet's life and had nothing to do with the essential features of the Qur'ān. Given that the context of today's society is different from that of the Prophet's time, and in general from that of the medieval and pre-modern periods, these socio-political provisions must undergo substantial revisions in this era. Furthermore, based on the premise that the task of interpretation is highly 'subjective' and is often shaped by the episteme of the specific period in which an interpreter lives or lived, Shabestari concludes that it is not necessary for today's interpreters of the Qur'ān to rely on an interpretive corpus of previous generations.[129]

In his writings, Shabestari gives a number of examples in order to illustrate how the socio-political provisions mentioned in the Qur'ān should undergo substantial revision in the modern period; and it is here that Shabestari applies his hermeneutical approaches. For instance, he asserts that the Qur'ān and the Prophet could not abolish the institution of slavery since it was one of the main cultural norms of Arabian society at the time of revelation, though Muhammad encouraged the emancipation of slaves. The Qur'ān also sought to improve the conditions of slaves at the time of its revelation. Therefore, it is important to interpret the Qur'ānic verses concerning slavery in the light of the prevailing conditions, and by examining their underlying objective, which includes improving the conditions of slaves and encouraging their emancipation. This leads Shabestari to conclude that interpreters of the Qur'ān should conceptualise the direction towards which the Qur'ān was moving, i.e. encouraging the emancipation of slaves. Here, his argument is very similar to Rahman's.[130] Shabestari applies a similar methodology for interpreting the Qur'ānic verses concerning retaliation (*qeṣāṣ*). In the case of a murder, *qeṣāṣ*, or taking the murderer's life, was the best method for resolving issues between the tribes to which the murderer and the murdered belonged. In tribal societies like Arabia, killing a member of a tribe often led to the rise of a series of battles between two tribes, as a result of which many people were killed. Therefore, the underlying logic behind the institution of *qeṣāṣ* was to prevent people from becoming involved in larger warfare. Given that today's context is different from that of the Prophet's tribal society, Shabestari concludes that *qeṣāṣ* cannot be implemented as punishment for murder in today's world.[131] In fact, what must be taken into consideration in this case is the eternal value that the Qur'ān attempted to establish, i.e. the prohibition against the excessive and violent practice, not a particular law. This mirrors his idea that values are unchangeable but laws are changeable.[132]

In terms of the issue of women's rights, Shabestari argues that *fuqaha* and *mufassirīn* of previous generations interpreted the Qur'ānic verses dealing with such issues in line with the dominant political and cultural norms of their times. Interpreters of previous eras sought to discover some eternal laws from the Book and the Sunna and never thought that these laws could undergo substantial revisions in another era.[133] Leaning on his idea that the task of interpretation is, in general, related to other modes of knowledge, and that the discipline of *tafsīr* is a contextually based one, Shabestari challenges the applicability of the corpus of the *tafsīr* literature produced in past generations in the modern period.

Shabestari's approach to the status of women in the Qur'ān centres around two major assumptions, both of which have their roots in his theory of revelation and his methods of interpretation. His approach is first based on the idea that most Qur'ānic precepts in regard to women were consistent with the current norms of the time, since the Qur'ān is a historically contextual book. The Qur'ānic precepts concerning the social arena are the products of particular socio-cultural conditions and naturally include the statements about the superiority of men's rights over women's.[134]

Second, Shabestari's approach focuses on the progressive nature of the Qur'ānic rulings in seventh-century Arabia, arguing for the continuation of that progress in our era. Although the Qur'ān does not acknowledge equality between men and women in relation to their social rights, it sought to improve the conditions of women compared to their situation in the pre-Islamic era. In this sense, the Prophet gave the 'direction' (*jahat*) and Muslims of every era should now strive to be faithful to it, rather than deriving some eternal laws from the Qur'ān in relation to women's status.[135] Building on these two assumptions, Shabestari concludes that the Qur'ānic precepts about women must be viewed within the context of the Qur'ān's emergence and in terms of its progressive spirit.[136] For Shabestari, this 'progressive spirit' of the Qur'ānic rulings is one of the 'essential' aspects of the religion, and thus imitating an inherited practice in its literal form may thwart the 'direction' towards which the Qur'ān was moving.[137] The Qur'ān implemented the maximum possible reforms in relation to women's status in seventh-century Arabian society, and it was inconceivable that the Qur'ān could call for an absolute equality between men and women in the time of its emergence; but Muslims should now strive to remain in the 'direction' that the Prophet and the Qur'ān instigated. Unlike Rahman, Shabestari does not deal with different aspects of the discourses of women's rights, such as inheritance and testimony, and only argues that the prophetic reforms could be extended in a way that many inequalities imposed on women might become subject to change and modifications.[138]

Second implication: pluralist interpretation – one text, multiple interpretations

As discussed, Shabestari focuses on the experiential dimensions of religion in his work. Paralleling Soroush's theory of revelation, Shabestari argues that the experiential dimension of religion is so important that even the Qur᾽ān grew out of the Prophet Muhammad's personal experience of revelation. In this context, he defines faith as the 'experience of the absolute boundless essence through the experience of the limited' or 'the experience of divine address'.[139] Based on his/her religious experience, every individual is able to establish a direct connection with God.[140] By emphasising the subjective nature of religiosity, Shabestari distinguishes the very heart of religion from any form of collective movement. He argues that while manifestations of religion take place in the world through rituals, religious ceremonies are meaningful only when they entail an individual religious experience. Without religious experience, rituals are little more than cultural traditions, since they fail to address the very essence of religiosity.[141] For Shabestari, the believer is a person whose beliefs are shaped on the basis of his/her religious experiences (*tajrobeh-hāye imānī*).[142]

Shabestari's identification of faith as an experience is one of the core premises around which his philosophy of religious pluralism is constructed. His understanding of religiosity as an experience rooted in our individual subjectivity inevitably leads him to downplay certainty as an essential element of faith: 'Faith is not certainty.'[143] This idea opens the way for religious pluralism, since it does not consider faith based on absolute certainty but rather on a feeling and experience of the transcendent. In other words, faith rooted in religious experience practically leads to pluralism: 'Those who emphasize religious experience in their approach to religious studies, consider religiosity as the product of humankind's experiential encounter with the Ultimate Truth, and considering those experiences the source of their knowledge results in religious pluralism.'[144] Indeed, Shabestari suggests that pluralism is only possible when one recognises that the main feature of religion lies in its experiential content.

Although Shabestari's notion of experience is a significant element of his philosophy of religious pluralism, his discussion about the multiple possible interpretations of the Qur᾽ān is also based on his first hermeneutic. When one distinguishes between the Qur᾽ān and its human interpretation, or holds that humanity could never fathom God's true intentions, then one recognises there could be inherently many interpretations of the divine message. In addition, when one recognises that those engaging in the act of interpretation of the Qur᾽ānic text carry within themselves a variety of presuppositions and assumptions, then one must conclude that there exist many types of Qur᾽ānic interpretation. The implication of this idea is significant especially in the context of contemporary Iranian religious discourse. Conservative theologians and the clerical authorities in Iran such as Ayatollah Mesbah Yazdi tend to present a literalist interpretation of the Qur᾽ān, believing that any emphasis on the concept of 'multiple interpretations' is misleading: 'We should cut out the tongue of those who speak of multiple interpretations of the Qur'ān', says Mesbah Yazdi.[145] Along similar lines, the conservative religious scholar Ayatollah Javadi Amoli attacks the concept of the relative nature of 'truth', arguing that there is only one correct path in religion.[146] Another conservative figure also stated that 'nothing is dirtier than [the idea of] a pluralist reading of Islam'.[147] Iranian conservative scholars often argue that modern values and discourses should not influence the interpretive process, and they often dismiss the notion of a 'new reading of Islam' (*qerā'at-e jaded az dīn*). As a conservative theologian states:

> The Islam that we believe in is what has been interpreted by the Twelve Imams and, alongside them, by fourteen centuries of juridical work by the *ulama*. That is the interpretation that informs our understanding of Islam. If there are new interpretations that call for alterations to the teachings of Islam and the creation of a new Islam, we want nothing to do with it.[148]

Shabestari rejects this idea, arguing that the interpretive corpus passed down from previous eras reflects the views of their ages – views that are limited in belonging to a specific time and place, and thus having no 'absoluteness'. Shabestari's idea about the multiple interpretations of the Qur'ān is also a response to those who attempt to set up their own interpretation of Islam as the only authorised and acceptable one. For Shabestari, nobody is able to claim that he/she is in possession of the entire truth concerning the divine message. This argument therefore destabilises some clerical claims to ultimate authority because the clerical authorities, like other individuals who interpret the Qur'ān, approach the text with their own preferences and presuppositions. Shabestari then concludes:

> It is possible that there are various interpretations in a Muslim society . . . equal rights may be given to different interpretations . . . Even if the majorities in a democratic sense follow a particular interpretation, the rights of other interpretations insofar as they aim to replace [that particular] interpretation should remain protected.[149]

Shabestari emphasises the centrality of human interpretation in the reading of religious sources, or what Foody identifies as 'the necessity of individual interpretation'.[150] This emphasis on the significance of multiple interpretations of the text hinges on the issue of human subjectivity that Shabestari highlights in his work. Therefore, one of the most important results of Shabestari's hermeneutic approach is the democratisation of the interpretive process. It is naïve to assume that there is only one valid interpretation of the text. Shabestari aims to liberate the act of interpretation from the self-centred and autocratic claims of those who only accept their own account of religious scriptures. He identifies official and canonical readings of religion as hermeneutically naïve: 'The official reading (*qerāʿat-e rasmī*) of the faith is the source of crisis in our society.'[151] Shabestari considers an 'official' reading of the Qurʾān unacceptable, since it forces individuals to adhere to this monopolising discourse rather than leaving them free to find their own path towards God through establishing an individual communication with Him. In addition, the idea of a single official interpretation of religion is unacceptable because some *fuqahā* who offer such a notion are, too, conditioned by their preconceptions and pre-understandings: 'General knowledge, assumptions, interests and expectations of a *faqīh* – be they related to social and political matters or the knowledge of the world – have an impact on his interpretive method.'[152] As such, their interpretation – just as anyone else's – cannot be considered the official one.

Shabestari's emphasis on the idea that there can be many interpretations of the Qurʾān not only provides grounds for natural recognition of intra-religious differences, but also has political consequences. For Shabestari, faith and freedom are two sides of one coin; if the path of exegesis and production of new interpretations of the Qurʾān are refused by political authorities, then the communication between God and human is terminated.[153] Indeed, Shabestari's emphasis on the individual relation between human and God leads him to argue against the politicisation of religion.

Third implication: Shabestari's political ideas

Shabestari's political ideas are intimately connected to his account of faith and his hermeneutical approaches. For Shabestari, the proper task of revelation is to establish the fundamental values in relation to governance, and not to give details of how societies must be governed. This is why the Qurʾān, the product of revelation, does not specify a particular form of state and method of governance: 'In the Qurʾān there is no emphasis on the forms or the systems of government, but the emphasis is placed on the justness of governance.'[154] By applying his second hermeneutic, Shabestari argues that the form of governance belongs to the category of the accidental aspects of religion, while the final objective of governance, namely justness, belongs to the realm of the essential dimensions of Islam: 'Forms and systems [of government] have differed among various societies and tribes throughout history. What should always remain constant . . . in societies is one fundamental value: rulers should act according to justice.'[155]

The implication of this idea is that methods of governance must be derived from non-religious sources and should be formulated through philosophical reasoning, because the Qurʾān only guides us to establish a government that fulfils the criteria of justness.[156] Accordingly, it is the responsibility of human beings to discover an appropriate way of articulating political matters within society. People should establish a particular form of state capable of fulfilling humans' needs based on the norms and standards of their time. In fact, for Shabestari, the issue of governance is an entirely this-worldly matter.[157] His approach sets the foundation for a dissociation of religion from the realm of political power. In general, Shabestari sees religion in minimalist terms:

> [Muslims] should create the required knowledge [for development] themselves or receive it from developed countries. The intervention of the Holy Book and Traditions in the development of Muslim societies is just for establishing the final moral goals of the development, which should not be inconsistent with the principles of the moral values of the Book and Traditions.[158]

Shabestari criticises those who believe that *fiqh* is capable of providing the answers for all the problems of Muslims in the modern period. That is, religion does not provide for all worldly needs of humans, let alone their needs within the realm of political matters. Indeed, in contrast to the viewpoint of most Islamists, Shabestari emphasises that religion is not all-encompassing.[159]

Extending his second hermeneutic to the realm of politics, Shabestari argues that many socio-political issues that confront contemporary Muslim societies did not exist during the time of the Prophet Muhammad or in the medieval era, and thus are not addressed in the Qur'ān or in medieval Islamic sources. Even if some political issues are discussed in the Qur'ān, they are only responses to the socio-political conditions that existed during the time of revelation, and are not identically applicable in all times and places. For Shabestari, since there are fundamental differences between the time and context in which the Prophet lived and that of modern societies, not all of the socio-political precepts of the Qur'ān can be implemented in our era.[160]

Building on these political discourses, Shabestari critiques religious justifications of democracy, arguing that the principles of establishing a democratic state should not be based on the Qur'ān and the Sunna, but rather must rely on extra-religious values. In an approach reminiscent of that proposed by Soroush, Shabestari argues that modern political values such as human rights and democracy are products of modernity and they could not have come into being during pre-modern times, let alone during the era of revelation. For Shabestari, it is an apologetic approach to seek to discover the equivalent of these modern concepts in the Qur'ān and the Sunna or in other religious traditions that came into existence in pre-modern eras.[161] The discourse of human rights in the modern sense, Shabestari asserts, 'is non-religious although it is not anti-religious'.[162] For Shabestari, it is unacceptable to depict modern methods of governance as derived from the Qur'ānic principles of *shūrā*. In other words, the *shūrā* institution cannot be simply developed into a modern democratic system of governance. Democracy and human rights are systems of value in their own right and must be appreciated for their own sake. In short, Shabestari builds a non-religious point of departure for establishing a theory about appropriate forms of governance in today's world.

Since it is impossible to dissociate the Qur'ān from how Muhammad saw the world, and how he interacted with the prevalent norms, institutions and values of

Hijaz at the time of the revelation, equating *shūrā* with modern political concepts such as democracy and human rights is misleading, Shabestari argues.[163] Moreover, in order to emphasise the importance of incorporating extra-religious elements into methods of governance, and thus to avoid basing democracy on the institution of *shūrā*, Shabestari also argues that the examples of allegiance (*bey'at*) and consultation (*shūrā*) are not the only methods of governance mentioned in the Qur'ān. He writes:

> [Apart from the institutions of allegiance and consultation] the Qur'ān refers to different types of government with approval . . . The governments of David and Solomon are some examples . . . From the Qur'ānic perspective, these forms of government have been legitimate. The main principle of governance from the perspective of the Qur'ān is that of 'justness' (*'edālat*), and not selection (*entekhāb*), appointed leadership (*entesāb*), consultation and the like.[164]

This confirms Shabestari's idea that the Qur'ān is not concerned with determining a fixed form of governance, but rather with the value of justice and of just governance. This implies that it is up to the members of each society to choose the form of government that is appropriate to the context. Shabestari's identification of religion as an experience is another premise on which his political ideas are based. Given that religion has an essentially experiential dimension, it is highly individualistic. By highlighting the importance of an individual communication between humans and God, Shabestari argues that this relation cannot take place under a theocratic state. State intervention in the religious beliefs of individuals undermines the true essence of faith, i.e. religious experience. As Foody suggests, by defining religion as 'finding one's path toward the presence of God', Shabestari states that 'this movement takes place only in individual communication with God and never under the authority or trusteeship of others'.[165] The faith of an individual flourishes only under the condition that he is given freedom to choose, and without feeling any obligation towards the authority of others. The political implication of this idea is that personal liberty is an essential feature of an ideal form of state because it creates an environment under which religious experience is able to flourish.[166] It follows that no person or institution could claim a monopoly over speaking on behalf of God or intuiting His will, and thus Muslims might conduct their socio-political affairs without the interference and authorisation of any specific authorities, including clerical ones. In other words, Shabestari prioritises religious experience in order to invalidate any external authority over individuals. According to him, the state should not take on the responsibility of propagating religion; for if it takes on such a responsibility, 'it will promote one particular interpretation of religion', which is inconsistent with the essence of faith.[167]

To sum up, Shabestari's political theory has three characteristics which have their roots in his hermeneutics. First, the Qur'ān does not stipulate a timeless form of government, and only asks believers to establish governments based on the criterion of justice. Second, it is impossible to implement all political provisions found in the Qur'ān or other Islamic sources in today's society. Third, no one has a God-given right to lead a society. Therefore, Shabestari rejects the idea that only the *'ulamā* (religious scholars) are capable of governing Muslim societies, concluding that it is the right of all citizens to participate in the political affairs of their country.[168] Shabestari emphasises that religion has a special place in the public sphere of Muslim societies and it should not be confined to the individuals' private domains.[169] Indeed, Shabestari never prevents the *'ulamā* or religious elites from participating in political affairs of their societies.[170] He does not argue for establishing a form of state in which a decline in religious beliefs and practices of individuals takes place at all. However, he warns against any attempt that aims to politicise or institutionalise religion.[171] In sum, for Shabestari, politicising religion undermines the spiritual aspects of religion, because religion is shaped on the basis of religious experience, and thus there is an essentially individualistic element associated with it.

Conclusion

This chapter argues that Shabestari's theory of revelation is humanistic for two reasons: firstly, the Qur'ān grew out of Muhammad's experience of the divine, and secondly, the Qur'ān was worded by Muhammad himself. The Qur'ān is a prophetic reading of the world, based on Muhammad's particular worldview. This led Shabestari to emphasise the interpretive nature of the Qur'ān and to appreciate the significance of the socio-cultural milieu and the prevailing norms, standards and values of Hijazi society in his approach to Qur'ānic interpretation. By distinguishing the accidentals of Qur'ānic teachings – i.e. the Qur'ān's socio-legal precepts – from their universal and trans-historical aspects, Shabestari argues for more flexibility in Qur'ānic interpretation, and thus seeks to establish a relationship between these precepts and the changing needs and circumstances of Muslims today.

The significance of Shabestari's approach and discourses lies in the fact that he has broken with the mainstream interpretation of the Qur'ān that is prevalent among conservative circles in Iran. His religious and political reformist discourses are grounded in his approach to faith and in his hermeneutics. In particular, his idea that interpreters always bring prior knowledge and preconceived ideas into their interpretation of the Qur'ān leads him to argue in favour of the theme of multiple interpretations of the text. Indeed, although his hermeneutics are not applied towards developing an inter-religious type of pluralism (as in the case of Soroush), nevertheless, they are applied very well in the realm of intra-religious pluralism. Further, Shabestari's hermeneutic approaches function in the realm of political discourses since they oppose the idea of an official interpretation of the Qur'ān and institutionalising religion. This guides him to reject the idea that a group of individuals has an exclusive right to establish a religio-political authority based on its own interpretation of religion. In addition, due to the lack of a Qur'ānic basis for determining specific issues related to forms of political governance, Shabestari argues that these must be entrusted to humans. This implies that Muslims can be flexible in adopting extra-religious values and practices in order to open a space conducive to contemporary democratic norms and values.

Notes

1. Shabestari, *Naqdī bar Qerā'at-e Rasmī az Dīn* [*A Critique of the Official Reading of Religion*], pp. 340–1.
2. Goldberg, *Shi'i Theology in Iran*, p. 145.
3. Shabestari, *Naqdī bar Qerā'at-e Rasmī az Dīn*, pp. 321–2.
4. For investigation of this viewpoint in Shabestari's writings, see Tavassoli, *Christian Encounters with Iran*, p. 157.
5. Shabestari, *Naqdī bar Qerā'at-e Rasmī az Dīn*, p. 323.
6. Ibid., p. 324.
7. Amirpur, *New Thinking in Islam*, p. 189.
8. Shabestari, *Naqdī bar Qerā'at-e Rasmī az Dīn*, p. 324. See also Shabestari, 'Hermenūtīk va Tafsīr-e Dīnī az Jahān' [Hermeneutics and Religious Interpretation of the World].
9. Goldberg, *Shi'i Theology in Iran*, p. 136.
10. Shabestari, 'Hermenūtīk va Tafsīr-e Dīnī az Jahān'.
11. Jahanbakhsh, 'Introduction', p. xxxvi.
12. Shabestari, 'Qerā'at-e Nabavī az Jahān' [Prophetic Interpretation of the World].
13. Goldberg, *Shi'i Theology in Iran*, p. 136.
14. Shabestari, 'Qerā'at-e Nabavī az Jahān'.
15. Ibid.
16. Shabestari, 'Hermenūtīk va Tafsīr-e Dīnī az Jahān'.
17. Shabestari, *Ta'amolātī dar Qerā'at-e Ensānī az Dīn* [*Some Thoughts on the Human Reading of Religion*], p. 165.
18. Ibid.
19. Shabestari, 'Qerā'at-e Nabavī az Jahān'.
20. For discussion about this, see the previous chapter.
21. Shabestari, 'Qerā'at-e Nabavī az Jahān'.
22. Shabestari, *Naqdī bar Qerā'at-e Rasmī az Dīn*, pp. 324–5.
23. Ibid., p. 324.
24. Shabestari, *Imān va Azādī* [Faith and freedom], p. 54.
25. Ibid.
26. Shabestari, 'Hermenūtīk va Tafsīr-e Dīnī az Jahān'.
27. Ibid.
28. Shabestari, 'Qerā'at-e Nabavī az Jahān'.
29. Shabestari, 'Hermenūtīk va Tafsīr-e Dīnī az Jahān'.
30. Shabestari, *Ta'amolātī dar Qerā'at-e Ensānī az Dīn*, p. 166.
31. Shabestari, 'Qerā'at-e Nabavī az Jahān'.
32. Ibid.
33. There are some indications in his writings that suggest he is aware of an intimate link that exists between the Prophet's personality and the content of the Qur'ān (see Shabestari, 'Qerā'at-e Nabavī az Jahān') but, compared to Soroush and Rahman, he has not placed much value on the role of Muhammad's personality in his theory.
34. Jahanbakhsh, 'Introduction', p. xxxix.
35. Cited in Dahlen, *Islamic Law, Epistemology and Modernity*, p. 172.
36. Shabestari, 'Qerā'at-e Nabavī az Jahān'.
37. Ibid.
38. Ibid.
39. Ibid.
40. Shabestari, 'Cherā bāyad Andīsheh-e Dīnī ra Naqd Kard?' [Why should we Criticise Religious Knowledge?], p. 18.

41. Shabestari, *Hermenūtīk, Kitāb va Sonnat* [*Hermeneutics, The Book and the Tradition*], p. 260.
42. These two views on the createdness of the Qur'ān are explored in detail by Wolfson, *The Philosophy of Kalam*, pp. 264–80.
43. Ibid., pp. 277–8.
44. Ibid., p.276.
45. Ibid., p.278.
46. Proudfoot, *Religious Experience*, p. xiii.
47. See Sharf, 'Experience', p. 98.
48. Grenz and Olson, *20th Century Theology*, p. 46.
49. Smart, *The Religious Experience of Mankind*, p. 28.
50. Ibid., p. 22.
51. Hick, *An Interpretation of Religion*, p. 104.
52. Ibid.
53. For example, see Aslan, 'What Is Wrong with the Concept of Religious Experience', pp. 299–312.
54. Iqbal, *The Reconstruction of Religious Thought*, p. 26.
55. Ibid., p. 5.
56. Ibid., p. 25.
57. Ibid.
58. See Tavassoli, *Christian Encounters With* Iran, p. 145.
59. Hick, *An Interpretation of Religion*, p. 154.
60. Shabestari, *Hermenūtīk, Kitāb va Sonnat*, p. 184.
61. Barth, *Church Dogmatics*, p. 750.
62. Shabestari, *Naqdī bar Qerā'at-e Rasmī az Dīn*, pp. 324–5. See also Shabestari, *Imān va Azādī*, pp. 27–8. Shabestari himself says that 'Karl Barth and his followers have created the best literature with regard to the experience of being addressed by divinity' (Shabestari, *Imān va Azādī*, p. 31).
63. Shabestari, *Imān va Azādī*, p. 120.
64. Stenger, 'Faith and Religion', p. 93.
65. Ibid., p. 99.
66. Cited in Amirpur, *New Thinking in Islam*, p. 182.
67. Shabestari, *Imān va Azādī*, p. 59.
68. Ibid., pp. 58–9.
69. Shabestari, *Naqdī bar Qerā'at-e Rasmī az Dīn*, p. 404; Shabestari, *Imān va Azādī*, p. 27.
70. Iqbal, *The Reconstruction of Religious Thought*, p. 125.
71. Soroush, *The Expansion of Prophetic Experience*, p. 228.
72. Iqbal, *The Reconstruction of Religious Thought*, p. 127. For details, see Ahmed, 'Progressive Islam and Qur'anic Hermeneutics', pp. 84–6.
73. Soroush, *The Expansion of Prophetic Experience*, p. 6.
74. Moosa, 'The Human Person in Iqbal's Thought', p. 27.
75. Shabestari, *Imān va Azādī*, p. 60.
76. Ibid., p. 61.
77. Shabestari, *Naqdī bar Qerā'at-e Rasmī az Dīn*, pp. 403–4.
78. Iqbal, *The Reconstruction of Religious Thought*, p. 165.
79. Ibid., p. 90. Some of the consequences of Iqbal's emphasis on religious experience are pointed out in Shabestari's writings. For instance, see Shabestari, *Imān va Azādī*, pp. 61–2.
80. Hick, 'Christianity among the Religions of the World', p. 21.
81. Soroush, *Farbeh-tar az Ideolojy*, p. 78.
82. Soroush, 'Masīh dar Eslam'.
83. Arkoun, *Rethinking Islam*, p. 34. See also Arkoun, 'The notion of Revelation', p. 76.
84. For Schleiermacher's idea, see Schleiermacher, *Hermeneutics*.
85. See Tavassoli, *Christian Encounters with Iran*, p. 159.
86. Shabestari, *Imān va Azādī*, p. 59.
87. Ibid.
88. Ibid., p. 54.
89. Ibid., p. 56.

90. Ibid.
91. Ibid., pp. 56–7.
92. Cited in Chodkiewicz, *An Ocean without Shore*, p. 140.
93. For exploration of these ideas, see Introduction.
94. Shabestari, 'Qerā'at-e Nabavī az Jahān'.
95. Shabestari, *Hermenūtīk, Kitāb va Sonnat*, p. 37.
96. Ibid., p. 15.
97. Shabestari, 'Qerā'at-e Nabavī az Jahān'.
98. Ibid.
99. Ibid.
100. Ibid.
101. Ibid.
102. Campanini, *The Qur'an*, p. 69.
103. Shabestari, *Hermenūtīk, Kitāb va Sonnat*, p. 260.
104. Cited in Ghobadzadeh, *Religious Secularity*, p. 69.
105. Shabestari, *Hermenūtīk, Kitāb va Sonnat*, p. 161.
106. Cited in Vahdat, 'Post-Revolutionary Islamic Discourses on Modernity in Iran', p. 202.
107. Soroush, *Qabz va Basṭ*, pp. 88–9.
108. For Shabestari's emphasis on this idea, see Shabestari, *Hermenūtīk, Kitāb va Sonnat*, p. 169.
109. Gadamer, *Truth and Method*, p. 271.
110. Shabestari, *Hermenūtīk, Kitāb va Sonnat*, pp. 291–2; Shabestari, *Naqdī bar Qerā'at-e Rasmī az Dīn*, pp. 45–6.
111. Amirpur, *New Thinking in Islam*, p. 189.
112. Madaninejad, 'New Theology in the Islamic Republic of Iran', p. 141.
113. Cited in Jahanbakhsh, 'Introduction', p. xxxvii.
114. Shabestari, 'Qerā'at-e Nabavī az Jahān'. See also Vahdat, 'Post-Revolutionary Islamic Modernity in Iran', p. 203.
115. Shabestari, 'Qerā'at-e Nabavī az Jahān'.
116. Shabestari, *Hermenūtīk, Kitāb va Sonnat*, p. 28.
117. According to Shabestari, these fixed and eternal features are constituters of the principle of *tawḥīd* (*moqavemāt-e tawḥīd*) 'in a way that if monotheism appears in every society and culture, they inevitably emerge'. Shabestari, *Naqdī bar Qerā'at-e Rasmī az Dīn*, p. 271.
118. Shabestari, 'Rāhe Doshvare Mardom Sālāri' [The Difficult Path to Democracy].
119. Shabestari, ''Amal be āye-ī dar Qur'ān hamīshegī nīst' [Practising a Qur'ānic Verse is not Eternal].
120. Ibid., p. 114.
121. Shabestari, *Hermenūtīk, Kitāb va Sonnat*, p. 59. See also Sadri, 'Sacral Defense of Secularism', p. 268.
122. Shabestari, *Ta'amolātī dar Qerā'at-e Ensānī az Dīn*, p. 167.
123. Shabestari, *Naqdī bar Qerā'at-e Rasmī az Dīn*, pp. 267–8.
124. Shabestari, 'Kāre Tafsīr-e Qur'ān Pāyān-nāpazīr Ast' [the Task of Interpretation of the Qur'ān is endless].
125. Shabestari, 'Qerā'at-e Nabavī az Jahān'.
126. Shabestari, *Naqdī bar Qerā'at-e Rasmī az Dīn*, p. 376.
127. Shabestari, *Hermenūtīk, Kitāb va Sonnat*, p. 51.
128. Shabestari, *Ta'amolātī dar Qerā'at-e Ensānī az Dīn*, p. 177.
129. Shabestari, *Imān va Azādī*, p. 105.
130. Shabestari, *Naqdī bar Qerā'at-e Rasmī az Dīn*, p. 59.
131. Ibid., pp. 243–4. See also Shabestari, ''Amal be āye-ī dar Koran hamīshegī nīst'.
132. Shabestari, *Hermeneutics, Kitāb and Sonnat*, p. 85.
133. Shabestari, *Naqdī bar Qerā'at-e Rasmī az Dīn*, p. 507.
134. Ibid., pp. 508–9.
135. Ibid., p. 509.
136. Ibid., p. 509.
137. Shabestari, *Ta'amolātī dar Qerā'at-e Ensānī az Dīn*, p. 167.
138. Shabestari, *Naqdī bar Qerā'at-e Rasmī az Dīn*, pp. 509–10; Shabestari, *Imān va Azādī*, p. 88.

139. Shabestari, *Imān va Azādī*, p. 23.
140. Shabestari, 'Islam is a religion, not a political agenda'.
141. This idea is similar to Soroush's. We recall that Soroush argues that religious ceremonies and rituals are parts of accidental aspects of religion.
142. Shabestari, *Imān va Azādī*, pp. 118–19.
143. Ibid., p. 37.
144. Shabestari, *Naqdī bar Qerā'at-e Rasmī az Dīn*, p. 383.
145. Cited in Ghamari-Tabrizi, *Islam and Dissent in Post-Revolutionary* Iran, p. 217. Shabestari himself refers to this statement in one of his books: Shabestari, *Naqdī bar Qerā'at-e Rasmī az Dīn*, pp. 245–6.
146. Javadi Amoli, 'Ayatollah Allameh Javadi Amoli va Pluralism-e Dīnī', pp. 352–3.
147. Bayat, *Making Islam Democratic*, p. 113.
148. Cited in Kamrava, *Iran's Intellectual Revolution*, p. 93.
149. Shabestari, *Naqdī bar Qerā'at-e Rasmī az Dīn*, p. 78.
150. Foody, 'The Limits of Religion', p. 189.
151. Shabestari, *Naqdī bar Qerā'at-e Rasmī az Dīn*, p. 11.
152. Shabestari, *Hermenūtīk, Kitāb va Sonnat*, p. 39.
153. Ibid., p. 302.
154. Ibid., p. 60. See also Ibid., pp. 86–7.
155. Shabestari, *Hermenūtīk, Kitāb va Sonnat*, p. 60.
156. Shabestari, *Ta'amolātī dar Qerā'at-e Ensānī az Dīn*, pp. 137–52; Shabestari, *Naqdī bar Qerā'at-e Rasmī az Dīn*, pp. 191–206.
157. Shabestari, *Hermenūtīk, Kitāb va Sonnat*, pp. 60, 69; Ghobadzadeh, *Religious Secularity*, p. 71.
158. Shabestari, *Imān va Azādī* , p. 89.
159. Shabestari, 'Islam is a religion, not a political agenda'.
160. Shabestari, *Hermenūtīk, Kitāb va Sonnat*, p. 59; Shabestari, *Naqdī bar Qerā'at-e Rasmī az Dīn*, pp. 276–7.
161. Shabestari, *Naqdī bar Qerā'at-e Rasmī az Dīn*, pp. 191–206; Shabestari, *Ta'amolātī dar Qerā'at-e Ensānī az Dīn*, pp. 137–52.
162. Shabestari, 'Ḥuqūq-e Bashar Eslāmī nemishavad vali Mosalmānān bāyad ān rā bepazirand' [Human Rights is not Islamic, but Muslims must accept it].
163. Shabestari, 'Qerā'at-e Nabavī az Jahān'.
164. Shabestari, *Hermenūtīk, Kitāb va Sonnat*, p. 60.
165. This idea is also noted by Foody, 'Interiorizing Islam', p. 615.
166. For details, see Ghobadzadeh, *Religious Secularity*, p. 68; Vahdat, 'Post-Revolutionary Islamic Modernity in Iran', pp. 215–16.
167. Shabestari, *Naqdī bar Qerā'at-e Rasmī az Dīn*, pp. 143–51.
168. Shabestari, *Imān va Azādī*, pp. 75–6.
169. Shabestari indeed rejects the notion of a sharp distinction between religion and politics.
170. See Rajaee, *Islamism and modernism*, p. 225.
171. Shabestari, 'Islam is a religion, not a political agenda'.

6

Nasr Hamid Abu Zayd: Revelation as a Linguistic Manifestation of the Communicative Interaction between God and the Prophet

Nasr Hamid Abu Zayd is another contemporary scholar who has challenged various aspects of traditional theories of revelation and traditional methods of Qurʾānic exegesis. This chapter aims to explore whether, and to what extent, his understanding of revelation and the nature of the Qurʾān influences his broader approach to the interpretation of the Qurʾān both on a theoretical and a practical level. On the theoretical level, I discuss the development of his approaches to Qurʾānic exegesis, and on the practical level, I explore how his hermeneutics function in relation to certain texts or themes of the Qurʾān. With regard to the practical level of analysis, I first examine how the notion of context is related in Abu Zayd's work to the issue of the mutability and immutability of the socio-legal rulings of the Qurʾān (*aḥkām*). I then outline three examples or themes that appear in his writings. These themes are similar to those presented in the fourth chapter: (1) the discourse of women's rights; (2) issues related to governance, and in particular the case of *shūrā*; and (3) religious pluralism. In addition to the aforementioned examples, I ask how Abu Zayd uses his contextual approaches to re-examine the standard Muslim theological position on Jesus' death and crucifixion.

Abu Zayd's account of revelation

Revelation as an act of communication

Central to Abu Zayd's account of revelation is the idea that revelation is a form of communicative interaction between God and humans. Revelation is a form of inspiration that prophets, including Muhammad, received from God when they found themselves in communication with Him: '*Waḥy* represents a temporary channel of communication between God and man where only the voice of man is explicit eternalisation of God's message.'[1] It was through such a process of communication, or channel, that the Word of God was revealed to the Prophet Muhammad.[2] The process of revelation included 'all the possible elements of communication: argument, discussion, persuasion, challenge and dialogue'.[3] Abu Zayd asserts that the act of communication between God and humankind is established within three stages, as shown in the following schema:[4]

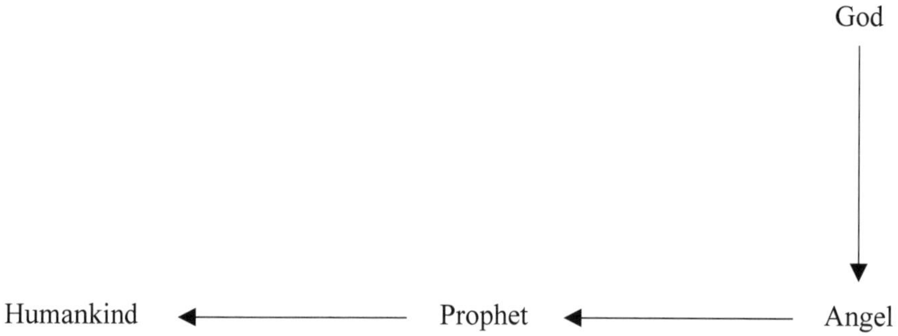

At the first communicative stage, represented here by a vertical line, God sent His message to the Angel Gabriel in the process of *tanzīl*. Abu Zayd says that 'the state of the original sacred text is a metaphysical one about which we can know nothing'.[5] That is, God should not be considered a subject of investigation, because He exists in a sphere beyond human knowledge.[6] Abu Zayd does not express the distinction between *waḥy* and *tanzīl* in detail; but here he seems to agree with Toshihiko Izutsu (who significantly influences his theory of revelation) that the term *tanzīl* cannot be used in reference to an occurrence of communicative interaction in which a human being is involved, whereas the term *waḥy* can be used for a communication in which one human, at least, is involved.[7]

At the second and third communicative stages, represented in the above diagram by the horizontal line, Gabriel transmits God's message to Muhammad, the first human addressee of revelation, whose main job is to convey God's message to humanity. Therefore, through the communication between God and man, revelation becomes something public when transmitted to humanity. As a result, revelation is not a communication between or among two or even three parties. Rather, it involves a 'four-person-relation' between God, Gabriel, Muhammad and humanity.[8] Like any other communicative interaction, revelation is not only dependent upon its initiator, but also upon those who receive it. Indeed, Abu Zayd approaches revelation no longer from the perspective of God, but from that of its human recipients. This approach, as will be discussed, has significant implications for various features of Abu Zayd's hermeneutics.

Abu Zayd gives a number of examples in his *Mafhūm al-naṣṣ* (the Concept of the Text) in order to show that the term *waḥy* (and its verbal forms such as *awḥā* and *yūḥī*) are used to refer to different forms of communicative interaction, either between parties occupying the same existential position or between those belonging to different existential levels. He asserts that the Qur'ān uses the term *waḥy* when referring to the tale of Zakariyya. According to the Qur'ān (Q 19:10–11), Zakariyya was told not to speak to anyone for three days except by 'signs' (as a means of communication): 'Then, he came out unto his people from the sanctuary and signified (*awḥā*) to them: Glorify (your Lord) morning and evening.'[9] The Qur'ān also uses the term *yūḥī* to describe the communication that takes place among the demons

(Q 6:112; 6:121). Abu Zayd further asserts that the term *waḥy* was even used in pre-Islamic poems to refer to a mode of communication. For example, a pre-Islamic poet, ʿAlqama, used the verbal form *yūḥī* to describe the 'speech' of a male ostrich to his nestlings.[10] Like the case of Zakariyya, the term *waḥy* is used in ʿAlqama's poem to refer to a kind of communicative interaction between two parties occupying the same existential position.

There are, however, some cases in which the term *waḥy* is used to refer to communication between two parties that belong to different existential levels, i.e. humans and superhuman beings. For example, the Qurʾān uses the term *yūḥī* to describe the communication that takes place between demons and unbelievers (Q 6:121).[11] The term *awḥā* is also used in the Qurʾān to refer to God's communication with ordinary human beings such as Moses' mother (Q 20:38; 28:7) and the disciples of Jesus (Q 5:111) as well as His communication with animals such as the bee (Q 16:68). In addition, Abu Zayd refers to the example of the communicative relation between poets and the *jinn* in pre-Islamic Arab legends. Arab poets of the pre-Islamic era are said in *jāhilī* legends to have communicated with the *jinn* and been inspired by them. For instance, Aʿsha, a pre-Islamic poet, wrote in one poem about his relation with a *jinn* whose name was Mishal: 'I am not an inexperienced debutante in the art of poetry, but my situation is like this: Mishal bestows upon me the word; then, I begin to be able to speak.'[12] Abu Zayd draws an important conclusion from these examples, which is later applied in his hermeneutics. The culture of pre-Islamic Arabia made it easier for the Qurʾānic revelation to be accepted by the Arabs because the idea that human beings can communicate with supernatural beings was strongly rooted in the cultural environment of Arabian society.[13] Indeed, owing to the fact that the pre-Islamic Arabs were already accustomed to the idea of communicative interactions between the poet and superhuman beings such as the *jinn*, they could grasp the verisimilitude of the communication between the Prophet and the angel. This is why, according to Abu Zayd, the Arabs did not reject the phenomenon of the Qurʾānic revelation; rather, they objected to the content of revelation.[14]

The comparison between revelation and soothsaying

As discussed in the third and fourth chapters, Rahman and Soroush compared revelation to poetry and mystical experiences in order to explain its nature. Along similar lines of thinking but with some differences, Abu Zayd compares prophecy with poetry and soothsaying. Soothsayers (the *kāhin*) had important positions in pre-Islamic Arab society, interpreting dreams and predicting the future. They were believed to have been in communication with supernatural realms and beings, and in particular with the *jinn*.[15] This shows that the Qurʾānic revelation took place in an environment where the notion of communication with the supernatural realm was an acceptable norm. Abu Zayd states that 'revelation was not a rupture with the past in its epistemological and cultural dimensions, rather it was a continuation'.[16] Revelation, however, differs from soothsaying in that the communication between God and His Prophet was established because the Prophet was selected by God, and bestowed a special personality by Him. However, the communication between the *kāhin* and supernatural beings was established because of the former's personal attempt to distance himself from this-worldly obstacles. This is why such a communication had many shortcomings that were not found in the Prophet's communicative interactions with God.[17] Therefore, while prophecy in Islam was the continuation of the past tradition (pre-Islamic culture) and came into being within a particular cultural milieu, it was nevertheless a point of departure from the past tradition because it was initiated by God. That is, in the same way that Rahman and Soroush compare revelation with poetry or mysticism, but believe that the former is superior to the latter, Abu Zayd compares revelation with soothsaying, arguing that the former does not suffer the same shortcomings as the latter.

The consequences of viewing revelation as an act of communication

Abu Zayd's identification of revelation as a communication with humanity brings with it important consequences. Firstly, 'given that humans constitute the ultimate recipients of the revelation, it would be inconceivable to imagine that it would address them except through their particular linguistic system'.[18] Revelation in the second stage (when revealed from Gabriel to Muhammad) had a linguistic nature. This linguistic structure must be known to the receiver of revelation and thus should consist of a human language. Abu Zayd reasons that if the recipient of revelation does not know the message sent by the transmitter, then he cannot understand the content of revelation, and thus is not able to reveal it to his immediate audience(s). This is why 'revelation took place through the use of language (Arabic)'.[19] 'When He [God] revealed the Qur'ān to the Messenger, God, the Elevated and Praised, chose the specific linguistic system of the first recipient.'[20] Indeed, when revelation enters the realm of humans, it should take a human linguistic form which is understandable to the first human addressee (the Prophet Muhammad) as well as the immediate human audiences of the revelation (the residents of Mecca and Medina): 'God [via the process of revelation] wanted to communicate to human beings. If God spoke God-language, human beings would understand nothing.'[21] It is in this sense that Abu Zayd considers the Qur'ān, the product of revelation, a 'linguistic text' (*naṣṣ lughawī*).[22]

The reason why revelation was transmitted in a clear human language, Abu Zayd observes, is also found in the Qur'ān itself. By referring to the Qur'ānic verse 14:4, Abu Zayd argues that God always communicates to His prophets in their own languages, making it possible for humans to comprehend the will of God as uttered in their language.[23] I add that the Qur'ān stresses that it is 'an Arabic recitation' (Q 12:2) and 'an Arabic decree' (Q 13:37), composed in the 'Arabic tongue'

(Q 26:195; 46:12 and 16:103), which made it easy for Muhammad to comprehend (Q 19:97 and 44:58).

The second consequence of Abu Zayd's identifying revelation as a form of communication is that the Qur'ān, in this way, becomes the product of a communicative process, and thus it must be seen as a created product, and one deeply connected to humanity and its particular context.[24] In his lecture at Leiden University in 2000, Abu Zayd argued that *waḥy* was only the channel of communication through which the Sacred Scriptures, including the Qur'ān, came into existence, and thus 'cannot be considered identical to the Qur'ān [itself]'.[25] *Waḥy* and the Qur'ān belong to two different existential positions. Abu Zayd asserts elsewhere that the Qur'ān 'as we have it today in the (form of) *muṣḥaf* does not reflect the dynamic process by which it came into being through various forms of communication'.[26] What Abu Zayd emphasises here is that the Qur'ān is the result of the communicative process between God and the Prophet, which lasted for twenty-three years (*waḥy*) and included a multiplicity of discourses in the form of verses, passages and short chapters.

The communicative character of *waḥy* emphasised in Abu Zayd's writings also points to the anthropological or human aspect of the revelation, and consequently of the Qur'ān. As Campanini maintains, 'communication involves the descent of the Qur'ān in history as the divine word that intervenes in human affairs'.[27] In fact, the entrance of the Qur'ān into history stems from the idea that God and humanity have been placed in direct communication. The final point that has to be emphasised is that the communication between God and the Prophet in the process of revelation resulted in the formation of the Qur'ān as a 'human text'. According to Abu Zayd, the communicative process of revelation transfers the Qur'ān from the existential level of a pure divine text (*al-naṣṣ al-khām al-muqadas*) to that of a human text (*al-naṣṣ al-insānī*).[28] Abu Zayd argues that the revelation of the divine text transforms it from its metaphysical status (incomprehensible to humans) to that of a humanly comprehensible text: 'The divine text became a human text at the moment it was revealed to Muhammad.'[29] Once the Qur'ān changed into a 'human text', Abu Zayd continues, it became subject to the rules of human understanding and interpretation, and thus it must be treated as any other human text.[30]

Abu Zayd emphasises that from the very moment of revelation (when the Prophet recited the divine text), the Qur'ān entered human history and became a text like any other text. His distinction between a divine text and a human text is not dissimilar to that proposed by the Syrian scholar Muhammad Shahrour (b. 1938).[31] In both Abu Zayd's and Shahrour's accounts, the moment of revelation represents what Charles Hirschkind refers to as 'the total secularization of the text'.[32] Secularisation here implies the transformation of the text from its transcendent position to a this-worldly level which is graspable by human reason. That is, the text is 'humanized'. Therefore, although Abu Zayd's account does not involve a total rejection of what I have referred to as a traditional theory of revelation, it is still 'humanistic' and can be situated within a reform theology discourse, as will be demonstrated in the next section.

Abu Zayd's account: traditional or humanistic? An analysis

What distinguishes Abu Zayd from Soroush and Shabestari is that he does not seek to explain the revelation in terms of the Prophet's human experiences as such. His approach is also different from Rahman's and Soroush's theories since the concept of revelation in Abu Zayd's writings is not normally dealt with as part of a discussion of Muhammad's personality. In fact, Abu Zayd does not place significant emphasis on the Prophet's feelings in the formation of revelation. He does not believe in the idea that Muhammad's power of imagination made the angel of revelation appear in his psyche. Abu Zayd seems to have rejected the idea that the angel was in some sense a product of Muhammad's imagination. Therefore, Abu Zayd does not, in general, challenge traditional theories which say that within the process of revelation three parties were initially involved; namely God, as the source of revelation, the Angel Gabriel, as the intermediary figure, and the Prophet, as recipient of revelation. As he has acknowledged, 'I believe the Qur'ān to be a divine text revealed from God to the Prophet Muhammad through mediation of the archangel Gabriel.'[33]

Katharina Völker gives the impression that Abu Zayd believes that 'Muhammad received non-verbal inspirations' and then used 'his fallible and limited human language abilities to clothe the messages into human words'.[34] While this statement is more in line with Soroush's and Shabestari's understandings of revelation, it is hardly true in the case of Abu Zayd's theory. I agree more with Hildebrandt and Kermani that revelation, in Abu Zayd's theory, was transmitted to the Prophet verbally and that the Prophet did not make any contribution to the wording of the Qur'ān.[35] Like Hildebrandt and Kermani, Saeed notes that in Abu Zayd's theory 'the cultural code of the text has been initiated solely by the author (God) and that the Prophet played no role whatsoever in this'.[36] Language, for Abu Zayd, is synonymous with a cognitive understanding which precedes feeling in the event of revelation. Here, Abu Zayd is indebted to Gadamer's idea that every form of understanding and knowledge shares a linguistic nature. Extending this to the realm of revelation, Abu Zayd opposes some scholars' idea that the Qur'ān was revealed to Muhammad not in certain phrases of words, but rather in the form of ideas and feelings which the Prophet then poured out in his native Arabic tongue. This is why Abu Zayd was more concerned with developing a theory, according to which 'the Prophet did not *experience* insofar as he *thought* revelation . . . [A theory] in which thought is placed above feeling, [and] rationality over intuition.'[37] As discussed, for Abu Zayd revelation itself included a specific linguistic system adapted to the language spoken by the Prophet. That is, the Prophet could grasp God's message only when it was made linguistically understandable to him.

Therefore, Abu Zayd's theory still accords with the traditional one insofar as Muhammad's position and role as a passive recipient and transmitter of God's message is concerned. His approach to revelation and the Qur'ān is, however, humanistic insofar as it considers revelation a kind of communicative interaction between God and His Prophet. Abu Zayd depicts *waḥy* as a time-bound and context-based phenomenon highlighting the historicity of revelation or its 'occurrence in time' (*al-ḥudūth fi zamān*).[38] He concludes that the Qur'ān is the product of an intercommunicative process; it is 'the outcome of dialoguing, debating, augmenting, accepting and rejecting'.[39] His theory becomes more humanistic when he distinguishes between the Qur'ān and the Word of God. God's Word 'is impossible to be confined', as the Qur'ān itself confirms (Q 18:109; 31:37), whereas 'the Qur'ān as a text is limited in space'.[40] Language is a human construct and thus cannot encompass all aspects of the divine message. In other words, the divine message should not be reduced to the Qur'ān. Leaning on the ideas of some Mu'tazili figures, Abu Zayd notes that the Qur'ān 'only represents a specific manifestation of the Word of God' rather than being the exact Word of God.[41] Abu Zayd's idea stands in sharp contrast to the traditional view that the Qur'ān was inscribed in the Preserved Tablet (*al-lawḥ al-maḥfūz*) before the creation of the universe.

The sources of Abu Zayd's ideas about revelation

In addition to his debt to pre-modern scholarship, Abu Zayd has been consistently influenced by contemporary Muslim and non-Muslim scholars in developing his theory of revelation. As Abu Zayd himself states, 'it would be more appropriate to consider me a critical continuation of the Islamic rationalism, both classical and modern, in the present context'.[42] In what follows, I first discuss the influence of the ideas of pre-modern Muslim thinkers (specifically the Mu'tazilis) and modern Muslim scholars (specifically contemporary Egyptian scholars such as Hasan Hanafi) on various aspects of Abu Zayd's account of revelation. Then I examine the extent to which Abu Zayd's understanding of revelation has its roots in contemporary Western scholarship.

The influence of traditional Muslim scholarship on the discourse of language?

Many pre-modern Muslim scholars have emphasised that one of the main features of revelation is its linguistic framework, and thus have referred to the importance of the Arabic language in the development of any interpretive method. The Arabic lexicon *al-Qāmūs al-Muḥīt* cites an unnamed classical scholar who expresses in religious terms the importance of mastering the Arabic language: 'Our duty to learn languages is like that of memorizing prayers . . . No religion is understood except by the study of languages.'[43] In a similar vein, the classical grammarian Abu 'Amr b. al-'Ala (d. 154/770) states that 'the knowledge of the Arabic language is the religion itself'.[44] This view of the Arabic language has had a far-reaching influence on the debates among some pre-modern Muslim scholars about rendering the Qur'ān in non-Arabic languages.[45] Many pre-modern Muslim interpreters of the Qur'ān had questioned why the Qur'ān was revealed in the Arabic language. For instance, in his interpretation of Q 12:2, al-Baydawi (d. 716/1316) states:

> Perhaps you will understand: this is the reason why God sent down the Book in the Arabic form. The meaning is: We have sent it down to you as something that is composed in your own language or can be recited in your own language, so that you will be able to understand it and grasp its meaning.[46]

While it is true that both Abu Zayd and the aforementioned scholars emphasise the importance of language in any approach to the revelation and Qur'ān, the former insists that the Arabic language does not have divine characteristics since all languages are human inventions. For him, the reason why the Qur'ān was revealed in Arabic is not related to the sanctity of the Arabic language; rather, it is because revelation inevitably requires a human language when entering history – a language that is understandable to its first recipient.[47]

The influence of the Mu'tazilis

Abu Zayd's account of revelation echoes several aspects of the views expressed by the medieval Mu'tazilis. In the same way that the Mu'tazilis divided the attributes of God into those of essence and those of action, Abu Zayd considered the Qur'ān to be an attribute of God's action by which he considered it to be created.[48] Some Mu'tazili figures considered *waḥy* an act of communication that consisted of a clear human language. Abd al-Jabbar, a prominent Mu'tazili theologian and jurist, stated that 'God's speech must be communicative and understandable for human beings; therefore, God must speak in an accepted human language'.[49] He reasons that 'speech cannot be meaningful unless it is formed in accordance with some linguistic convention', and concludes that 'a valid verbal form is necessary for speech'.[50] Vishanoff's analysis of *al-Mughni* shows that Abd al-Jabbar's aim is to construct 'a religious epistemology capable of explaining how it is possible for an eternal and utterly transcendent God to reveal . . . [His Message] through the medium of human language'.[51] In a similar vein, Peters states that 'for Abd al-Jabbar revelation is speech; it is not the self-revealing of a divine being, not some form of emanation or incarnation, but pure information and exhortation expressed in human language'.[52]

Although there is little explicit evidence that Abu Zayd has drawn from Abd al-Jabbar in presenting his views here, I assume that this idea about the linguistic structure of revelation inspired Abu Zayd to think of the nature of revelation being expressed in human language. Both Abu Zayd's and Abd al-Jabbar's theories are somehow removed from the medieval philosophical Islamic tradition, which views revelation as occurring through a process of emanation and by the involvement the Prophet's faculty of imagination.[53] Further, both theories of revelation are grounded in the idea that the Qur'ān was not revealed to the Prophet in the form of ideas and feelings that were impressed upon his heart, but rather in clear human language. In addition to these similarities between Abu Zayd's and certain Muʿtazili ideas, the former's notion of the Qur'ān as a historical phenomenon echoes the latter's idea that the Qur'ān is a concrete manifestation of God's speech in the human world.[54] The final similarity between the two accounts is their emphasis on the idea that humankind is the ultimate addressee of revelation. Abu Zayd writes:

> Contrary to [dominant] religious thought that focuses its attention on the revealer of the text – God in this case – and makes it the departure point for its conclusions, we place the receiver – meaning human in his historical and social situation – at the center of our focus, making him the point of departure.[55]

Abu Zayd emphasises here that the revelation is not for God, but for humankind. Indeed, from Abu Zayd's humanistic perspective, revelation, like any other communicative interaction, is dependent upon those who receive it, meaning that revelation is not primarily for God, but for humankind. Such an idea is reminiscent of Abd al-Jabbar's approach to revelation: 'When God performs an act, He must do it because of some benefit He finds in the act concerned. This cannot be His own benefit; hence, it must be the benefit of other beings.'[56] Abd al-Jabbar concludes that 'in any form revelation must be for the benefit of mankind'.[57] It must be noted, however, that Abu Zayd places high emphasis in his hermeneutics on the role of the human interpreter of a given text in contributing to its meaning, rather than simply discovering the author's original intention. This view is different from that of the Muʿtazilis, who were not totally removed from an author-centred approach. It is in this sense that Abd al-Jabbar states that 'words have no reference apart from the intention' of their author.[58] The importance of the role of the interpreter in the process of interpretation, and the idea that the interpreter is not entirely passive but also actively takes part in the production of meaning, is indeed a contemporary hermeneutic approach, and as discussed in other chapters, it does not have a strong precedent in the classical Islamic hermeneutics, which is rather focused on methods of discovering God's intention. This is where Abu Zayd's view reflects mostly the ideas of some contemporary Egyptian scholars and Gadamer, as will be explored later.

The influence of contemporary Egyptian scholarship

Abu Zayd was also strongly influenced by modern Egyptian scholars in developing his account of revelation. In an approach reminiscent of that presented by Amin al-Khuli (d. 1966) and Taha Husayn (d. 1973), Abu Zayd emphasises that the language and content of revelation include elements of the pre-Islamic Arab culture. Al-Khuli argued that understanding the Qur'ān requires gaining knowledge of the intellectual milieu of the Arabs during the pre-Islamic era.[59] Husayn studied pre-Islamic literature to gain an appropriate perspective of the culture of that era and to examine those aspects of the Arabian pre-Islamic cultural milieu presented in the Qur'ānic revelations. For example, he considers the Qur'ānic story of Abraham as an oral narrative that existed in pre-Islamic Arab culture, having found its way into the Qur'ānic revelations.[60] In addition – similar to Abu Zayd – Husayn rejected the idea that Arabic is a sacred language. He called for applying a 'true scientific investigation' to study Arabic literature and the Qur'ān.[61] He states that 'if Arabic literature is to enjoy an existence suitable to the present day, the study of it should receive the same recognition, and should be conducted . . . accorded to the study of . . . any other recognized science'.[62] This idea echoes Abu Zayd's approach to the Qur'ān, in which the linguistic analysis of the text – i.e. in a scientific and non-sacred way – is given priority.

In addition to Husayn and al-Khuli, Abu Zayd's ideas about revelation reflect the strong influence of Hasan Hanafi (d. 1935), who was one of his teachers at the University of Cairo, though Abu Zayd does not often acknowledge his debt to his teacher.[63] Various aspects of Abu Zayd's humanistic hermeneutics had already been stressed by Hanafi. For example, Abu Zayd's distinction between a divine text and a human text is similar to that proposed by Hanafi, who coined the term 'original (pure) divine text' (*al-naṣṣ al-khām al-muqaddas*).[64] For Hanafi, the Qur'ān became comprehensible to human intellects when it descended from the metaphysical realm into the worldly realm. It was only within this process that the Qur'ān became expressible in a clear human language (Arabic), and thus adapted to the social conditions of the time. Hanafi's ideas here are also similar to Abu Zayd's view that 'when we talk about God communicating with humanity, what we have in the Qur'ān is human language'.[65] Like Abu Zayd, Hanafi considered *waḥy* a phenomenon, existing not outside history but inside it and conditioned by it. For Hanafi, many Qur'ānic verses came into existence in harmony with the needs and requirements of the nascent Muslim community.[66]

Hanafi appears even closer to Abu Zayd when the former asserts that the Qur'ān should be treated like any other text in the practice of exegesis – an approach that opens up a flexible space for a variety of different interpretations of the Qur'ān. This idea is the consequence of emphasising the notion of humans' inability to directly access the divine: 'The Qur'ān is considered to be like any other text. It is subject to interpretation as a legal code, a literary work, a philosophical text, a historical document, etc. . . . All texts are subject to the same rules of interpretation.'[67] In this respect, both Abu Zayd's and Hanafi's approaches represent the idea that revelation is not for God, but for man – an idea which is in line with a human-centric approach to the text. Hanafi indicates:

> God continues to be a value in our awareness. But it is no less true that humankind too is a value. God has been acquired for always, but humankind, land, freedom, democracy, liberation, development and progress are aims, goals to be reached, needs to be satisfied.[68]

The influence of contemporary linguists

Abu Zayd's methodology in developing his theory of revelation is heavily influenced by Roman Jakobson's and Yuri Lotman's theory of literary communication between two parties. In his *Mafhūm al-Naṣṣ*, Abu Zayd clearly acknowledges his debt to the linguistic analysis of literary texts presented by these scholars.[69] According to Jakobson, in every communication there must be a common code between the sender and receiver because it is only in this way that the latter understands the former. In addition, the message transmitted from the addresser to the addressee requires a context in order to be operative. Jakobson writes:

> The ADDRESSER sends a MESSAGE to the ADDRESSEE. To be operative the message requires a CONTEXT referred to ('referent' in another, somewhat ambiguous, nomenclature), seizable by the addressee, and either verbal or capable of being verbalized; a CODE fully or at least partially common to the addresser and addressee (or in other words, to the encoder and decoder of the message); and, finally, a CONTACT, a physical channel and psychological connection between the addresser and the addressee, enabling both of them to enter and stay in communication.[70]

The model proposed by Lotman is similar to that presented by Jakobson. Lotman uses a model of encoded broadcasting which centres around the idea that the transmitted message can be understood only when the sender uses a code that the receiver is able to decode. The communication between the sender and receiver is first mute for those who are not included within the process. They might only be aware that a communicative interaction takes place between two parties, but do not understand its content. The content is only revealed to the third party when the receiver speaks about it. Lotman considers art 'a special means of communication' in which 'a language organized in a particular manner' is used. This situates art as a 'text' which conveys 'different information to different readers in proportion to each one's comprehension'.[71]

Central to the theories of literary communication presented by both Jakobson and Lotman is the idea that the information contained in a message can only be understood if the sender transmits it in a code known to the recipient. Expanding these models to his account of revelation, Abu Zayd considers revelation as consisting of a message, an addresser, an addressee, a contact, a code and a context, all of which are closely linked together. Revelation, for Abu Zayd, consists of 'a communicative relationship between the sender [*mursil*] and receiver [*mustaqbil*], based on a code [*shifra*] or linguistic system'.[72] Abu Zayd argues that there must be a common code between the two parties involved in every stage of revelation (that is, from God to the angel and from the angel to Muhammad). He further states that revelation requires a certain context. In an approach reminiscent of Lotman's view on art, Abu Zayd points out that the information conveyed to receivers varies according to the reader's personal as well as sociocultural horizons.

The influence of Toshihiko Izutsu

Among all the writings produced by non-Muslim scholars on the Islamic concept of revelation, Toshihiko Izutsu's works are those to which Abu Zayd's ideas are most indebted. In an interview with Morteza Karimi-Niya, the translator of *Mafhūm al-Naṣṣ* into Farsi, Abu Zayd asserts that he had been significantly influenced by Izutsu's linguistic approach to understanding revelation.[73] For both Izutsu and Abu Zayd, revelation essentially means that God 'speaks'. Izutsu states that 'revelation means in Islam that God "spoke"' and that 'Islam arose when God spoke'.[74] In a similar vein, Abu Zayd argues that 'the idea of prophecy means that God speaks to a human agent'.[75] Like Abu Zayd, Izutsu considers the divine revelation a linguistic phenomenon which took place in a clear, humanly understandable language. Izutsu writes:

> He [God] revealed Himself through language and that not in some mysterious non-human language, but in a clear humanly understandable language . . . It is no wonder, then, that Islam should have been from the very beginning extremely language conscious . . . The whole Islamic culture made its start with the historic fact that man was addressed by God in a language which he himself spoke.[76]

An examination of Izutsu's book entitled *God and Man in the Qur'an* discloses other themes that appeared in Abu Zayd's account of revelation. Abu Zayd's investigation of the term *waḥy* in its pre-Islamic context is a reflection of Izutsu's examination of this term in pre-Islamic poetry.[77] In addition, Abu Zayd's idea that *waḥy* cannot be considered identical with the Qur'ān reflects Izutsu's distinction between *waḥy* and the Qur'ān.[78] Further, Abu Zayd's understanding of the term *tanzīl* is not unlike that of Izutsu, who considers *tanzīl* 'a theological mystery' or 'something essentially mysterious' which 'does not allow of analysis'.[79] Another similarity between Abu Zayd's and Izutsu's accounts of revelation is that Izutsu argues that revelation is not a relation between two or even three parties, but is a four-party relation involving God, Gabriel, Muhammad and humankind: 'Revelation does not aim at the personal salvation of Muhammad. God docs not speak to Muhammad in order simply to speak to him. The Divine words should go beyond Muhammad: they must be transmitted to others.'[80] Izutsu, like Abu Zayd, argues that it is only by virtue of transmitting the revelation to humanity that Muhammad is called *rasūl* (messenger); otherwise, he would have remained a mere *nabī*.[81]

Abu Zayd's hermeneutics

My analysis of Abu Zayd's theory of revelation now becomes relevant to a broader formulation of what issues an interpreter of the Qur'ān must take into account when approaching the text. Abu Zayd himself is aware that differing views about the nature of the text (*māhiyyat al-naṣṣ*) play a significant role in one's understanding of the text.[82] Considering revelation as a form of communication consisting of a clear human language is the central premise on which Abu Zayd's interpretive approach towards the Qurʾānic text is based. Abu Zayd asserts that the 'horizontal, communicative and humanistic dimension is in the "structure" of the Qurʾān, not outside it. The invitation to "rethink the Qurʾān" flows from this communicative dimension.'[83]

The human characteristics of the Qurʾān – in particular, the human language that God used in revelation – and the importance of the specific context in which the Qurʾān was revealed, are closely related to the communicative character of the revelation. In Abu Zayd's opinion, the 'stagnation in Islamic thought' is due to the fact that Muslims have overemphasised 'the divine dimension of the Qurʾān at the expense of acknowledging its human characteristics'.[84] Abu Zayd argues that Muslims have generally failed to recognise that 'the Qurʾān is both human and divine'.[85] Thus, he states that 'in order to make Islamic thought relevant, the human dimension of the Qurʾān needs to be reconsidered'.[86] In what follows, I shall discuss how Abu Zayd's account of revelation led him to develop hermeneutic approaches towards interpreting the Qurʾān. But first, I examine Abu Zayd's views on the relation between language and socio-cultural issues in society.

The relationship between language, history and culture

As shown, Abu Zayd has been strongly influenced by some Western linguistic theories. In the previous two chapters, it was shown that both Soroush and Shabestari have been influenced by Gadamer's notion of preconceptions and the role of interpreters in the task of interpretation. I now make a comparison between Abu Zayd's understanding of language and Gadamer's, and argue that Abu Zayd follows Gadamer's ideas too. Gadamer places 'the nature of language at the center of' his philosophical hermeneutics.[87] For Gadamer, language is not only a means of communication or expression since every form of understanding takes place through the medium of language. Accordingly, language, for Gadamer, is not only 'one of man's possessions in the world'; rather, the 'world [of man] is linguistic in nature'.[88] That is, 'in all our knowledge of ourselves and in all knowledge of the world, we are always already encompassed by the language that is our own'.[89] As such, 'learning to speak does not mean learning to use a preexistent tool for designating a world already somehow familiar to us; it means acquiring a familiarity and acquaintance with the world itself and how it confronts us'.[90] In this way, language has two main characteristics: firstly, it is essentially a human construct; and secondly, it shapes all our understandings, meaning that thinking is only possible in language and that language mirrors our worldview and thought.

In light of Gadamer's theory of language, Abu Zayd's theory of revelation and its link with his hermeneutic approaches becomes clearer. Abu Zayd's ideas about the nature of the Qurʾān, as argued, do not initially involve making a link between the revelation and the historical or cultural milieu of its emergence; rather, Abu Zayd begins with the idea that revelation is essentially a linguistic phenomenon. From Abu Zayd's perspective, the Qurʾān was not revealed to the Prophet's heart, and then expressed through his own words; rather, it was revealed through the medium of language itself.

Leaning on Gadamer's all-encompassing approach to language, Abu Zayd states that language reflects 'the way human beings conceive, conceptualize and symbolize reality'.[91] For Abu Zayd, language is a human product: 'Language is a human invention because relating sound to meaning is a social convention.'[92] Language develops in keeping with those who speak it. Accordingly, for Abu Zayd, language does not emerge in a vacuum, but reflects the socio-cultural framework of any given society: 'Language has a cultural, social and political context . . . Human beings, living throughout the world in specific places at specific times, leave their mark on language.'[93] Therefore, 'it is impossible to speak of a language apart from its [associated] culture'.[94] This means that all languages are socio-culturally produced, and there is an organic link between language, culture and history.

It is important to note that Abu Zayd's idea about the intimate relationship between language and culture also echoes Graham Ward's account concerning the reciprocity between linguistic forms for expression of our thoughts and our metaphysical outlook, which is shaped by the cultural environment in which we live. Ward states that 'different languages encode different symbolic worldviews – different construals of time, space, objects, subjects and their connectedness'.[95] Along similar lines, Achrati argues that 'the presence or absence of copula in a language is often a reflection of the elemental assumptions about life and existence that are embedded in a given culture'.[96]

This idea results in an important conclusion: the Arabic language of the Qurʾān is not divine. For Abu Zayd, the reason the Qurʾān was revealed in Arabic is not related to the sanctity of the Arabic language; rather, it is because God adjusted the language of revelation to accord with that of the first addressee(s) of His message. Abu Zayd insists that the linguistic structure of revelation is, as in any other communicative interactions, 'culturally and historically determined'.[97] To put it differently, God had to speak to humans in their own language, which was itself limited by their cultural values and standards. Although Abu Zayd does not go so far as to assert that Muhammad himself formulated the language of the text (in a way that Soroush and Shabestari assert), nevertheless he imputes a strongly human character to revelation: the language of revelation is essentially human, and it is linked to the socio-historical elements of the society in which revelation takes place. Abu Zayd's approach to language sharply contrasts with that of most classical Muslim scholars, who considered the sanctity of the Arabic language an essential feature of religion because they regarded it as a God-given language.[98] Abu Zayd believes in the human createdness of all languages, including the languages of the Sacred Scriptures.

The first hermeneutic: the Qur'ān within its context

The Qur'ān as a cultural product

By making a link between language and culture, Abu Zayd concludes that the Qur'ān is 'a product of culture' (*muntaj al-thaqāfī*).[99] To clarify Abu Zayd's idea, I have organised his method of argumentation as follows: (1) At the moment of revealing the Qur'ān, God chose a clear human language as the code of revelation; and (2) A language does not exist in isolation from its culture. Therefore, the Qur'ān is closely related to its cultural context. For Abu Zayd, the relation between language and culture is pertinent not only to the Qur'ān, but to all Sacred Scriptures:

> In the last analysis, religious texts are only linguistic texts, in the sense that they belong to a determined cultural structure; they are produced in accordance with the laws governing the culture of their birth and the language of which is, rightly, the principal semiotic system.[100]

Abu Zayd emphasises here that Sacred Scriptures are not only linguistic texts, but also cultural texts. In the case of Islam, when God revealed His divine message to the Prophet Muhammad, He not only adapted it to the human language of its recipient(s), but also adjusted it to their cultural norms and values. That is, the cultural circumstances of the pre-Islamic Arabian society in which the revelation emerged had an important role in shaping the Qur'ān: 'The Qur'ān was a cultural production, in the sense that pre-Islamic culture and concepts are re-articulated via the specific language structure.'[101] Abu Zayd insists that the Qur'ān is in a mutual relationship with pre-Islamic practices, norms and culture.[102] Here, his approach is close to Izutsu. As Izutsu points out, some Qur'ānic terms such as *hādī* (guide) and *ṣirāt al-mustaqīm* (straight path) were frequently used in pre-Islamic times among the Arabs. While the Qur'ān uses such terms with absolute religious connotations, pre-Islamic Arabs used them for 'the most material aspect of human life', such as finding ways in deserts.[103] Abu Zayd emphasises that pre-Islamic Arabs' understanding of the concept of *waḥy* also sheds light on how the Qur'ānic use of the term must be understood. As discussed, the term *waḥy* refers to various forms of communicative interactions in the Qur'ān, as it did in the pre-Islamic Arab cultural environment. The main corollary of this argument is that the importance of the cultural norms of pre-Islamic times must be taken into serious consideration by commentators on the Qur'ān as part of their interpretations: '[A]ny genuine hermeneutics has to take into consideration the pre-Islamic culture as the key context without which ideological interpretation will always prevail.'[104]

The Qur'ān in its socio-historical context

Abu Zayd's argument for considering the Qur'ān a 'historical text' is as follows: (1) At the moment of revealing the Qur'ān, God chose a clear human language as the code of revelation; and (2) Language is a product of society and has a socio-historical context. Therefore, the Qur'ān is closely related to its socio-historical context.

For Abu Zayd, the Qur'ān is not only a 'human text' (*naṣṣ al-insānī*), a 'linguistic text' (*naṣṣ al-lughawī*) and a 'product of culture' (*muntaj al-thaqāfī*)[105] but also a 'historical text' (*naṣṣ al-tārīkhī*).[106] Historical contexts have always played a crucial role in the missions of prophets, and consequently in the formation of all Sacred Scriptures: 'We [should] look at religious figures against their historical background, against the needs of their time, judging them according to the norms of their time and not that of today.'[107] Abu Zayd emphasises that God's message was revealed in accordance with the historical situation of His community.[108] This idea is in line with the ideas of some reformist Muslim scholars who consider the needs of the direct recipient audiences of the Qur'ān essential in shaping the text.[109] The Qur'ān represents, for Abu Zayd, a gradual response to the Prophet's concerns, as well as the needs of his community in a particular time and space, rather than the product of a single and complete act of revelation. This is because revelation, by its nature, involved a process of dialogue between God and man, with humanity as the ultimate target of revelation. The Qur'ānic discourse reflects the relationship between the text and the realities of the early Muslim community.[110] As such, a responsible hermeneutics must incorporate contextualisation. Taking the socio-historical elements of the Qur'ān into consideration is a precondition for what Abu Zayd refers to as a 'defreezing' of the text. Abu Zayd criticised many Qur'ānic commentators for not being 'aware of the historical background [of the Qur'ān] . . . That is a simplistic way of reading the Qur'an, but not a historically correct one.'[111] This is the main reason why such scholars, according to Abu Zayd, often 'quote texts and explain Qur'ānic passages literally'.[112]

To sum up, it has been argued that by making a close connection between the Qur'ān and both the language in which it was shaped and the socio-cultural and historical circumstances of the society in which it emerged, Abu Zayd links the Qur'ān to its immediate context. In other words, since the Qur'ān was transmitted in the Arabic language, and since this language was connected to the cultural and socio-historical milieu in which the Qur'ān appeared, the message of the text should be understood in light of the socio-historical context of its emergence – i.e. seventh-century Arabian society and the psychology of the immediate addressees of the revelation. Therefore, I disagree with Yusuf Rahman's idea that Abu Zayd regarded linguistic analysis of the Qur'ān as the only proper tool to be employed in the task of Qur'ānic interpretation,[113] and also with Esack's observation that Abu Zayd's 'emphasis on the Arabicity of the text places him firmly in the camp of Arabists rather than students of Islam'.[114] As demonstrated, Abu Zayd considers a variety of approaches relevant to the analysis of the Qur'ān, one of which was the linguistic analysis of the text; but he never 'reduces the text to only one of its aspects', as Yusuf Rahman claims.[115] This is because Abu Zayd does not separate language from the socio-cultural realities of society.

The second hermeneutic

A key point of departure for understanding what I consider Abu Zayd's second hermeneutic is the idea that 'the Qur'ān is a fixed religious text that is definitely fixed from the standpoint of the literal wording, but once it has been subjected to *human reason* it becomes a "notion" (*mafhūm*), which loses its fixed nature and gains countless new meanings'.[116] The concept of human reason emphasised here by Abu Zayd is of particular significance and is to be examined in detail. For Abu Zayd, the moment of revelation signified the historical emergence of the Qur'ān as a human text. Abu Zayd says:

> The Qur'ānic text changed from the very first moment – that is, when the Prophet recited it at the moment of its revelation – from its existence as a divine text, and became something understandable, a human text, because it changed from revelation (*tanzīl*) to interpretation (*ta'wīl*). The Prophet's understanding of the text is one of the first phases of movement resulting from the text's connection with the human intellect.[117]

Abu Zayd deliberately uses the term *ta'wīl* here instead of the more common term *tafsīr*, in order to emphasise the share of human reason and intellect (*'aql*) in the act of interpretation.[118] He emphasises that the encounter of the divine text with the Prophet's reason was the first human attempt to understand and interpret it in a certain time and place. This was in fact the first of many encounters between the divine text and the human reason that took shape within the following eras. From the moment of its revelation, the divine text was shaped, and continues to be reshaped, through the operation of human reason: 'The meaning of the text is renewed through contact with human activity.'[119] Given that there are many encounters between the text and human interpreters in the course of history, Abu Zayd insists that the first understanding of the text by the Prophet is not fixed and absolute; rather, it is 'relative' (*nisbī*) and 'changeable' (*mutaghayyir*). He writes:

> A claim that the Prophet's understanding is sacred leads to a form of polytheism, because it equates the Absolute with the relative, and the constant with the temporary; and, more specifically, because it equates the divine intent with the human understanding of this intent . . . This is a claim that leads to an idolization of a conferral of sainthood upon the Prophet, by concealing the fact that he was a human, and by failing to present clearly enough the fact that he was merely a prophet.[120]

This way of considering the relative modes of humans' understanding of the Qur'ānic text lays the foundation of Abu Zayd's hermeneutic. It leads him to distinguish between the Qur'ān and any human interpretation of it, and between religion and religious thought (*al-dīn va al-fikr al-dīnī*) – an argument reminiscent of Soroush's and Shabestari's hermeneutics. Abu Zayd states that 'in this historical phenomenon of the exchange of cultural influences we have to make distinction between the Qur'ān, as a given fact, and Islam'.[121] Islam, unlike the Qur'ān, Abu Zayd emphasises, is 'the result of the interpretation and experiences of real people, it has grown historically'.[122] It follows that 'any form of interpretation is constructed in a particular time, under particular circumstances and it is not forever', thus meaning there is nothing sacred about the corpus of interpretation.[123] Abu Zayd writes:

> One cannot find the meaning of a religion in the text but in the interaction between the text and the historical process, in the interaction between the believer(s)/the communities with their holy texts. Of course that does not mean that one cannot speak of religion in a normative sense. But this normative sense is historically determined, and is, thus, changeable. It is normative according to the specific milieu paradigm; any paradigm-change leads to norms-change.[124]

Therefore, in addition to placing an emphasis on the idea that the act of interpretation is inherently plural and relative, Abu Zayd attempts to examine the conditions under which the corpus of existing interpretation was shaped in the course of Islamic history. In this context, Abu Zayd refers to the famous statement of Imam Ali in which he described the Qur'ān as silent and as a text which 'does not speak [by itself], but humans speak it out'.[125] A specific socio-historical context not only influenced the formation of the Qur'ān, as Abu Zayd's first hermeneutic emphasises, but also its interpretation. Abu Zayd insists that any understanding of the text depends on the cultural and intellectual horizons of the reader.[126] Each interpretation is therefore the result of a certain relationship between the text and its interpreter, and is not identical to an interpretation shaped in another era or under another socio-cultural context.

Here, Abu Zayd emphasises the important role that one's interests and prior knowledge play in the practice of interpretation, and thus distances himself from an author-centred hermeneutic. Unlike Rahman, he does not seek to uncover God's intention through the act of interpretation, nor the transcendental objectivity of the text. For Abu Zayd, God's intentions can never be 'understood by human beings. Human knowledge of God ['s intention] is inevitably subjective.'[127] Indeed, as Kermani puts it, central in Abu Zayd's approach is the idea that 'the information in the divine message varies according to whoever receives it'.[128] Even the earliest receivers of the divine message – i.e. the Prophet and the nascent Muslim community – interpreted it according to their own 'horizon' of understanding, and thus their interpretive discourse was not absolute and should not be considered a model to be emulated by all later Muslims. As such, 'The Qur'ān does not only plant meanings . . . but builds them in the hearer of the verse, and the only way it can build . . . is by engaging the subjectivity of the hearer.'[129] I attribute the difference between Abu Zayd's and Rahman's hermeneutic approaches to their different understandings of revelation, and especially the former's emphasis on the importance of the Prophet's subjectivity in the reception of God's message. Abu Zayd places an emphasis on the Prophet's subjectivity in his theory of revelation, but in a way different from Soroush and Shabestari. For Abu Zayd, the Prophet's understanding of the divine text is, too, non-absolute and relative, and thus we should distinguish the Qur᾽ān as revealed to the Prophet from the Prophet's understandings of the text. It follows from this that it is natural that any interpreter who engages with the Qur᾽ān does so in a relative manner, and brings certain preconceived ideas or prior knowledge when interpreting the text. Like Soroush's and Shabestari's hermeneutics, Abu Zayd's second hermeneutic approach is Gadamerian too, insofar as it emphasises the relativity of the truth of any interpretation, underscoring its contextual nature.

In sum, for Abu Zayd, the human interpretation of the Qur᾽ān must be differentiated from the Qur᾽ān itself. Human understanding of the text is never absolute; it is relative and dependent upon the socio-cultural horizons of the interpreter and his interests/prior knowledge. This stems from the idea that the moment of revelation was 'a break in the historical formation of the Qur᾽ān as a human text'.[130] This view also suggests that the Qur᾽ān is basically a human text which must be treated and interpreted as any other texts produced by humans. This implies that in the practice of exegesis, no sacred hermeneutic is required.

The third hermeneutic: the Qur᾽ān within today's context

Abu Zayd's idea is not limited to historicising the Qur᾽ān by situating it in the cultural and historical context of its formation. Because God and humankind are placed in direct communication through revelation, God's message must go beyond the first community of believers and has to be transmitted to ensuing generations of Muslims. The dialogue between man and God continues endlessly. This is because the encounter of the divine text with the Prophet's reason was only the first human attempt to understand it. From the moment of its revelation, the divine text was shaped and continues to be reshaped through the operation of human reason.[131] The Qur᾽ān, according to Abu Zayd, has to be taken as a 'living phenomenon':

> The Qur᾽ān is a living phenomenon, like the music played by the orchestra, whereas the muṣḥaf, the written text, is analogous to the musical note; it is silent. A humanistic hermeneutics of the Qur᾽ān must take seriously the living phenomenon and stop reducing the Qur᾽ān to the status of solely a text.[132]

Due to the contextual nature of interpretation, the message of the text conveyed to a twentieth-century reader could be different to that conveyed to an eighth- or ninth-century reader: 'If the information conveyed by the text varies according to the reader's personal as well as his cultural and social horizons', then 'the message conveyed by the Qur᾽ān to a twentieth-century reader must vary from the information conveyed to a Muslim in the seventh, eighth or eleventh century'.[133] The contextual understanding of the Qur᾽ān helps an interpreter to move from a literal reading to the core of its message, which the text is able to carry for today's context. As Abu Zayd asserts, 'it enables the interpreter to . . . efficiently extract the historical . . . and temporal, which carry no significance in the present context. In other words, the contemporary interpreter can distinguish between circumstances and principles.'[134] This entails differentiating between the historic and universal, or the accidental and the essential elements in the message of the Qur'ān – a view that is reminiscent of those of the other three scholars surveyed in this book.[135] It should be emphasised that although in the pre-modern period a large number of Muslim theologians and philologists provided a range of ideas about language and meaning, as Saeed notes, they often relied on the literal meaning of the Qur'ān:

> Historically, many Muslim commentators on the Qur'ān have relied heavily on a rather literal reading of the text, examining each word in the text and identifying its literal meaning, or, at sentence level, giving the sentence a direct word-for-word interpretation, seeking to remain faithful to the literal meaning of each word and true to the syntactic and semantic features of the language.[136]

Like many pre-modern commentators, one of the main characteristics of contemporary religious discourse was that of identifying words and things 'too closely, the result [of which] is the loss of that symbolic character of the text that allows the bypassing of literal meaning in favor of interpretive flexibility'.[137] Abu Zayd suggests that an interpreter has to distinguish between the sense (*ma'nā*) and the significance (*maghza*) of the words:

> The sense is the meaning of the texts at the moment they were written down. To limit oneself to this type of meaning means to fix the text at a certain point in time, so that it . . . has no value except as historical evidence. But, the meaning of a religious text . . . [should] continue to evolve . . . The *ma'nā* is endowed with a certain stability, while the *maghza* is fluid, varying according to the readers' perspectives.[138]

For Abu Zayd, there are three main differences between the sense and the significance of the Qur'ān. Firstly, although the sense of the Qur'ānic text is fixed and constant, its significance is changeable and dynamic. Secondly, the significance must relate to the sense because this relation determines the direction of the significance. Thirdly, while the sense represents the historical signification of the text within the context of its emergence, its significance has a contemporary importance. The differentiation between the sense and the significance of the Qur'ān makes the text and its interpretation relevant to the present.[139] Abu Zayd believes that the process of interpretation must move between these two directions, namely the present situation and the time in which the Qur'ān was revealed, like the movement of a pendulum.[140]

Returning again to the issue of situating Abu Zayd within a Western hermeneutic milieu, a similar distinction to the one that Abu Zayd draws between meaning and significance had already been employed by E. D. Hirsch (b. 1928), on whose ideas Abu Zayd drew. As already stated, Abu Zayd's hermeneutic is not an author-oriented one, and thus he can be considered Gadamerian in his approach. However, Hirsch himself belongs to the Objectivity School, and, like Betti, he believes that uncovering an objective meaning of a text (i.e. one which is essentially related to its author's intention) can be achieved by the task of interpretation.[141] For Hirsch, 'meaning' signifies the original intent of the author, and it is fixed, whereas 'significance' implies a relation between the 'meaning' and the person who interprets the text in a particular context.[142] Abu Zayd does not exactly incorporate this view into his hermeneutic approach. The term 'meaning' (*maʿnā*) in Abu Zayd's hermeneutic, as Yusuf Rahman noted, does not refer to that 'imposed by the author, but the historical meaning as understood by the first addressees of the text'.[143] That is, Abu Zayd remains more Gadamerian in his approach, since he does not seek to identify the author's intention, but rather seeks to identify how the text was conceptualised by the first community of believers. Abu Zayd uses Hirsch's hermeneutic only insofar as it enables him to argue that the text may convey different meanings to different people according to the context in which they live.

A summary of Abu Zayd's three hermeneutics

Given that revelation is a communicative act between God and man, God's speech manifests itself in human language. Since language is a human construction and is not isolated from the socio-cultural norms of societies, interpreters of the Qurʾān must consider it a historical text as well as a product of a particular culture. In the process of interpretation, the commentator should take its context into consideration. Because the ultimate target of revelation is humanity, the interpreter must also relate the text to his own time and place. To do so, he/she must distinguish between the 'historic and universal', or 'the accidental and the essential in the message of the Qurʾān'. Finally, it is important for the interpreter to be aware of his own subjectivity. Awareness of this frees the interpreter from making claims to finality, and allows him to distinguish between the text and his own interpretation.

The implications of Abu Zayd's hermeneutics

In what follows, I demonstrate how Abu Zayd has used his account of revelation and hermeneutics in his writings to interpret various themes of the Qurʾān. Similar to the hermeneutics of other scholars surveyed in this book, one of the consequences of Abu Zayd's hermeneutics involves his rejection of the application of many Qurʾānic socio-legal precepts in the present context. According to Abu Zayd, some Qurʾānic legal stipulations such as the penalty for robbery were the product of pre-Islamic times. Some penalties originated from Roman law or were adopted from the Jewish tradition:[144] 'The Qurʾān adopted particular forms of punishment from pre-Islamic cultures in order to have credibility with the contemporary civilization.'[145] Therefore, these 'legal stipulations are expressed in discourse style, and these reveal a context of engagement with human needs in specific times'.[146] Having applied his hermeneutics, Abu Zayd emphasises that many legal stipulations of the Qur'ān that found their way into the body of Sharīʿa literature emerged only in accordance with the human needs of a particular context, and were therefore time-bounded. The contingent nature of these legal statements should be identified, and one should not claim their universal and timeless validity. Inasmuch as today's context differs from that of the Prophet's time, a flexible interpretation of the Qur'ānic passages dealing with legal matters is required. Abu Zayd writes:

> In our modern times of human rights and respect for the integrity of the human body, the amputation of body parts or execution cannot be divinely sanctioned religious punishments. Other aspects of sharia, such as those dealing with the rights of religious minorities, women's rights and human rights in general, also need to be revised and reconsidered.[147]

According to Abu Zayd, those Qur'ānic verses which seem to contain legal connotations and are considered the basis of Sharīʿa only comprise five-hundred verses, or 16 per cent of the entire Qur'ān. Therefore, the Sharīʿa was also built upon three other sources, i.e. the Sunna (prophetic traditions), the *ijmāʿ* (consensus) and the *ijtihād* (independent reasoning).[148] Abu Zayd concludes that Sharīʿa in its integrity 'is a man-made production and there is nothing divine about it'.[149] Given that religion must be distinguished from its human understanding (as Abu Zayd's second hermeneutic asserts), he concludes, '[T]o claim that the body of Shariʿa literature is binding for all Muslim communities . . . is simply to ascribe divinity to the human historical production of thought.'[150] In what follows, I demonstrate in detail how Abu Zayd's method of interpretation applies in practice to a number of other themes such as women's rights, issues relating to governance and religious pluralism.

Gender issues

In order to assess Abu Zayd's interpretive approach, it is useful to analyse how he applies it to questions such as that concerning what the Qur'ān has to say about women's status. The starting point, Abu Zayd asserts, is to consider 'the status of women and their position in the society before the Qur'ān, not just a comparison between Qur'ānic discourse and our legitimate wishful thinking concerning a woman's status'.[151] The Qur'ānic discourse of women's status emerged in an absolutely patriarchal environment.[152] Because the Qur'ān is a cultural product and God had to adapt and adjust his message to the cultural horizons of the first recipients of revelation, the discourse of patriarchy found its way into God's revelation. It is in such an environment that the addressees of the Qur'ānic discourse on matters of marriage and divorce were naturally males who received permission to marry and divorce, and also marry their female relatives.[153] As for polygamy, Abu Zayd asserts that it 'was a popular practice in human societies before Islam, so it is a great mistake and gross academic error to think of polygamy as part of the Islamic revelation, [only] stipulated by the Qur'ān'.[154] The next step is to examine the historical condition in which the Qur'ān legalises polygamy. Polygamy, according to Abu Zayd, was merely a solution to the social problem that resulted after the battle of Uhud, which saw many Muslims martyred and left many children orphans, at which point the Qur'ān allowed Muslims of the time to practise polygamy. Abu Zayd writes:

> The Qur'ānic verse taken as to have stipulated polygamy is basically addressing the issue of orphans, who needed protection and custody after losing their parent(s) in the battle of Uhud (3 AH/625 CE), when Muslims were seriously defeated and 10% of the army . . . were killed leaving behind their children. The historical context, as well as the textual context, reveals that the permission given was to marry an orphan's mother (widow) or a female orphan, in case of fear of failing to provide protection properly, especially if any of them inherited some fortune.[155]

Abu Zayd emphasises here that the Qur'ān is not against polygamy, but that polygamy was not made a law either; rather, it was only a practical solution to a historical problem, namely the problem of orphans. An interpreter should reinterpret the Qur'ānic legislation on polygamy for the present context. 'Given current social circumstances', Abu Zayd asserts, 'polygamy is insulting to women as well as the children born into the family.'[156] We must render polygamy as forbidden to be practised in the present context.[157] Abu Zayd adds that in the historical context of the Qur'ān's emergence, men were considered *qawwamūn* (literally translated as guardian) to women because men were the major providers of family income. God considered some people to be superior depending on their socio-economic position and financial contribution to the household.[158] Therefore, the idea that men are *qawwamūn* to women (mentioned in Q 4:34) should not be understood outside the context of the emergence of the Qur'ān. Abu Zayd argues that the pronoun used in the related Qur'ānic verse could refer either to men or women; it does not refer to an inherent superiority of one gender over another, but rather is based on certain qualities that both genders could possess within different socio-economic contexts. In order to understand the verse in the present context, we must move from what the verse meant for the immediate addressees of revelation (or what Abu Zayd identifies as the 'sense' of the verse). This opens the possibility of new interpretation for Abu Zayd: 'In our social structure, women can be considered *qawwamūn*.'[159]

Abu Zayd argues that similar methodology should be applied in regard to women's inheritance. For him, although the Qur'ān specifies that women should receive half an inheritance compared to that of men, this was revealed at a time when women were not allowed to inherit at all. The pre-Islamic cultural norms of Arabian society unjustly did not allow women to inherit because the eldest son received everything; but as women are now considered equal to men, they should inherit equally today.[160] As a result, for Abu Zayd, following an approach not dissimilar to that of Shabestari, what is concealed beneath the Qur'ānic verse concerning inheritance is the progress towards which the Qur'ān is moving. While a literal reading of the Qur'ān leads one to conclude that women only have the right to inherit half the amount that men do, the context in which such a provision came into being reveals that the Qur'ān was actually moving towards improving women's status within the cultural context of Arabian society. The conclusion that Abu Zayd draws about women's issues is that the position of women could be 'reinterpreted according to what it reveals by its historical and contextual significance in order to unfold its implication and, therefore, to foster the basic principle of equality'.[161] The position of women expressed in the Qur'ān, in general, is relatively and historically speaking progressive; the misunderstanding of some Qur'ānic concepts that relate to women's status is caused by the de-contextualisation of these verses: 'If we recognize that, we are in a better position to enunciate that . . . equality in intermarriage is possible.'[162]

Therefore, Abu Zayd's ideas about the discourses of women's rights are premised on two main assumptions: (1) the position of women expressed in the Qur'ān is relatively progressive considering their status in the pre-Islamic era; and (2) much of the gender inequality found in the Qur'ān or other primary sources of Islam was closely intimated to the historical and cultural circumstances in which women were naturally considered inferior to men. Abu Zayd concludes that if commentators move beyond the literal meaning of the Qur'ānic verses dealing with discourses of women's rights and the meaning understood by the first addressees of revelation (*ma'nā* of verses), and thereafter interpret such verses in their proper social and historical contexts, they would then be able to promote the theme of gender equality.

A political case: the *shūrā*

Abu Zayd is aware of the fact that the Sharī'a also deals with political issues. Like other parts of the Sharī'a literature, those dealing with political matters merely present human efforts that came into existence in accordance with specific needs of pre-modern Muslim societies, and thus they should be considered time-bound principles. Given that the pre-modern era was very different from the socio-political context of the contemporary world, most political precepts found in the body of Islamic law can no longer be implemented in today's societies.[163] Abu Zayd confirms that in the political arena there is not one form and type of government for all times. As such, 'there is no obligation to establish a theocratic state claimed as

Islamic. Such a demand is nothing but an ideological call to establish an unquestionable theo-political authority.'[164]

Applying his hermeneutics to the political arena, Abu Zayd asserts that the Qur'ān does not introduce any particular political system since it 'is not in itself a book of law'.[165] In an approach not dissimilar to that presented by Soroush and Shabestari, Abu Zayd regarded the issue of governance an entirely worldly matter, stating that political stipulations for governing Muslim societies in today's world could not be derived from the Qur'ān. For Abu Zayd, any political theory that focuses on establishing a particular form of state based on the Qur'ān would inevitably weaken the spiritual and ethical dimension of Islam. Abu Zayd adds that because responsible hermeneutics must always consider the socio-historical circumstances in which a given text emerged, it is impossible to derive a comprehensive modern political system from the Qur'ān for today's context:

> The Qur'ān has emerged in a traditional environment . . . Today, people in Europe, the Middle East and many other Islamic societies live in modern or modernizing environments that are very different from that of the time of the Qur'ān's emergence. These societies are characterized by a diversity of outlooks, identities and interests.[166]

Government, for Abu Zayd, should be contextually dependent on the times and the circumstances in which it finds itself. Some Qur'ānic verses state that the head of the community must consult with the people (Q 42:38; 3:159), but these Qur'ānic verses which deal with the issue of *shūrā*, Abu Zayd asserts, could not be used for today's political regulations of Muslim societies. Abu Zayd asserts that the principle of *shūrā* does not resemble a modern system of democracy due to the context in which it came into being: 'In a traditional environment', the *shūrā* 'implies something very specific, namely consulting vertically, from the top down, but not too far down'.[167] It would also be difficult to expect *shūrā* to fulfil the needs of today's Muslim societies. Indeed, given that the Qur'ān's precepts came into being as gradual responses to the Prophet's concerns and the needs of his community in a particular time and space, and given too that there existed a close relation between the Qur'ānic discourse and the reality of the nascent Muslim community, *shūrā* 'is not democratically structured' and 'cannot be developed into something democratic because it is traditional'.[168] When the Qur'ān speaks of *shūrā*, it is referring to an institution already in existence in Arabian society, and not to a democratic practice as conceived in today's context. The *shūrā* was a historical concept pre-dating Islam, and involved discussions among tribal elders concerning the management of the affairs of their society:

> This practice [*shūrā*] was not introduced by Islam . . . What I would observe in contextualizing the Qur'ān in this instance would be that in the pre-Islamic context the heads of tribes used to meet in specific places called *dar al-Nadwa*, places of congress.[169]

For Abu Zayd, equating democracy with *shūrā* would essentially divorce revelation from the context of its appearance. This means that, unlike Rahman, Abu Zayd has managed to apply his contextualist method in the political arena, especially in relation to matters of democracy. By making a distinction between *shūrā* and democracy, Abu Zayd moves beyond seeking theological justifications for promoting democracy. In order to develop a democratic system in a given Muslim country, he argues that:

> The *shūrā* doesn't give us much help since we no longer live within a tribal unit. The organization of political life, the social system and the structure of the state . . . are to be arranged in terms of our experiences, our reason and the will of the citizenry.[170]

For Abu Zayd, if the Qur'ānic verses on political matters are understood within the specific time and context in which they emerged, one would conclude that the 'form of government . . . is open to Muslims to choose for themselves'.[171] Central in this political theory is the idea that developing a democratic system of governance for Muslim-majority societies should not be merely based on certain Islamic principles such as *shūrā*. That is, it is theoretically required that Muslims turn to extra-religious reasoning to incorporate some democratic norms in their methods of governance. It should be noted that Abu Zayd, like Soroush and Shabestari, defended the notion of separation between state and religion only to the extent that it ensures the protection of religion from any type of political misuse, and thus he was not interested in confining religion to the private realms of individuals. Abu Zayd indeed argued against the idea that religion should be relegated to the private domain of individuals, or relegated 'religion to a backseat in society'.[172]

The case of religious pluralism

Abu Zayd's ideas about the holy scriptures of Judaism and Christianity stem from his account of revelation and his hermeneutics. Having considered revelation as a communicative act, he argued that the Jewish and the Christian holy scriptures were revealed through the same channel as the Qur'ān[173] and that those scriptures were, like the Qur'ān, products of God's revelation to His prophets in specific cultural and historical circumstances. In this sense, there is no difference between the Qur'ān and previous holy scriptures because they are all manifestations of God's Word in human language:

> A distinction must be made between the absolute Word of God and the Qur'ān. The Word of God in the Qur'ān can be best described as a manifestation of the Word of God. Therefore, there are other manifestations of the Word of God. God does not speak only Arabic. God speaks no specific language as we understand language. So if God has no specific language, this opens up a space for other Scriptures to be recognized as manifestations of God's Word as well.[174]

As discussed in the fourth chapter, the hostile relation between Jewish communities of Arabia and the Muslim community during the time when Muhammad resided in Medina had a great influence on the attitudes that Muslims in the course of Islamic history have held towards Jews.[175] Abu Zayd does not deny the fact that the early relationship between Muslim and Jewish communities involved mutual polemic or dispute, and that these interactions even reached, at different stages, the level of harsh condemnation.[176] What Abu Zayd refutes is the interpretation of literalist scholars about those Qurʾānic verses dealing with the Jews. The literalists, according to him, often ignore the fact that the Qurʾānic discourses about the Jews correspond to the various historical stages and formative experiences of the nascent community of believers, and that they were shaped in a context in which Islam was being organised as a distinct religion. As such, the literalists' tendency to extend early disputes and polemics to today's context is invalid. Abu Zayd states that:

> Not being able to appreciate the 'discourse' structure [or to see the Qurʾān as a communicative discourse] it is likely to extend the discourse to be addressing all the Jewish people till the present . . . It is not only a question of contextualization, which is pivotal in discourse analysis, but more than that it is what the discourse tells about the context and how . . . [c]onservatives will apply the principal of 'abrogation' to historicize 'togetherness' as abrogated and will universalize 'hostility' as the abrogate.[177]

In order to establish legal regulations, jurists often developed the doctrine of abrogation, according to which the historically later revelations are considered the final rule.[178] By dealing with the Qurʾān as communicative discourse, however, one goes far beyond jurists' outlook, which 'needs [a] certain mode of fixation'.[179] Therefore, by applying Abu Zayd's first hermeneutic, it is possible to contextualise the hostile statements directed at Jews as occurring at a time when Muhammad was waging outright war to ensure the triumph of the nascent community over its enemies.

The same hermeneutic approach should be applied to understanding the disputes with the Christians. The issue of the human nature of Jesus attested in the Qurʾān is incompatible with the church dogma that Jesus is of divine nature. However, the notion of the crucifixion of Jesus can be reinterpreted in the context in which the related Qurʾānic verses came into existence. Pre-modern Muslim commentators have interpreted the relevant Qurʾānic passages about the crucifixion and death of Jesus (such as Q 4:157) in a way that suggests Jesus was neither crucified nor killed. They agreed that someone else was substituted for Jesus on the cross and that God rescued Jesus in a miraculous way.[180] Abu Zayd's hermeneutic provides a new insight into the verses concerning the death and crucifixion of Jesus. From Abu Zayd's perspective, the actual fact of the crucifixion is not itself a matter which the Qurʾān seeks to accept or deny. What is of particular importance is the attribution of Jesus's death to the Jews, who were boasting that they had killed the

Prophet of God.[181] In other words, the context in which the issue of crucifixion came into existence involved a dispute against the Jews in defence of Christ, and thus the Qur'ān's position should not be viewed here as a polemic launched against a Christian dogma. Unlike the issue of the nature of Jesus, which is dealt with in different contexts, the issue of crucifixion arises only

> in the context of responding to the Jewish claim. [T]he discourse structure suggests it was denying the capability of the Jews to have done this depending on their own power, and by implication telling Muhammad that their implicit threat to slay him, as they slew Jesus, is not feasible, as God will not permit it.[182]

The implication of this idea is that nothing would be compromised in Islamic theology if Muslims adopted the view that Jesus was crucified. More importantly, this interpretation entails that the Qur'ān does not criticise a Christian theology or dogma, thereby encouraging Muslims and Christians to arrive at mutual understanding about the issue of Jesus's death.

Following an approach not dissimilar to Soroush's and Shabestari's, Abu Zayd's second hermeneutic provides an insight into the acceptance of a plurality of exegeses, and involves a rejection of claims that link Islam or the Qur'ān to a single valid or official interpretation. According to Abu Zayd, the main mistake of Islamists is that they often identify religious thought with religion itself, and consider their interpretations of the primary texts of religion, including the Qur'ān, tantamount to the religion itself. In this way, they disregard their own subjectivity when approaching the interpretation of the Qur'ān.[183] The context in which Abu Zayd discusses multiple interpretations can be better understood when one conceptualises how contemporary Egyptian Islamists highlight the existence of one 'true' Islam. As an Egyptian Islamist stated:

> There is no progressive Islam or reactionary Islam, revolutionary Islam or political Islam or social Islam, Islam for kings or Islam for the masses. There is one single Islam, one single book revealed by God to His messenger in order to convey it to people.[184]

By applying his hermeneutical approach which distinguishes between religion *(dīn)* and religious thought (*al-fikr al-dīnī)*, Abu Zayd dismisses Islamists' agendas. For him, any insistence on the existence of a single Islam results in an understanding of religion that has an unchanging and fixed nature. What is more problematic is when one's interpretation of religion is regarded as 'official', and exempt from criticism. In fact, the identification of religion with religious thought, according to Abu Zayd, 'eventually leads to the appointment of certain groups of people who claim to have a monopoly on comprehension, explanation, commentary and interpretation, and thus feel that they alone are entitled to speak on behalf of God'.[185] It is in this context that *rijāl al-dīn* (men of religion) and the *ulama*, according to Abu Zayd, should be free of arrogance since their approach to holy texts inevitably involves the natural bias of humans.[186] Abu Zayd emphasises that the conflation of religion and religious thought leads contemporary religious discourse to speak on behalf of God, pretending to know His will and His intentions. This mirrors Abu Zayd's approach, which departs from an author-centred hermeneutic. Abu Zayd strongly rejects the creation of a form of 'priesthood' or a 'sacred power' which claims to 'understand true Islam'. This would only confine the power of interpretation and neglect the plurality of meaning which the text is able to deliver. For Abu Zayd, if one is 'sincere in freeing religious thought from power manipulation, whether political, social or religious, [one] need[s] to construct open democratic hermeneutics'.[187] When religion turns into an institution in which certain groups of people are able to monopolise the interpretation of its central text, Abu Zayd asserts, it will lose its spiritual character. As a result, the inevitable consequence stemming from the distinction between religion and religious thought is that there must be an intellectual tolerance towards those who do not share other exegetes' specific interpretations of religion.

Conclusion

This chapter has argued that Abu Zayd's view of *waḥy* as a form of communication expressed in a clear human language is the central premise on which his Qur'ānic hermeneutics are based. The Qur'ān is a linguistic text in a comprehensible human language; and because each language is closely connected to the historical and cultural horizons of those who speak it, the Qur'ān is also a context-bounded document – that is, it is a socially and culturally conditioned text. As such, a responsible hermeneutic must study the Qur'ān in relation to the socio-cultural conditions of the Hijaz at the time of its revelation.

Abu Zayd's approach represents an important step in relating the Qur'ān to the contemporary needs of Muslim societies. As shown by the examples found in his writings, strongly connected to his hermeneutics is the idea that there is a need to move away from a literal reading of the Qur'ānic verses dealing with socio-legal issues. His hermeneutics provide a solid theoretical foundation for improving women's rights. In addition, his ideas stand in sharp contrast with any effort to politicise religion, since they ensure the protection of the natural plurality of different human understandings of sacred scriptures. Abu Zayd's hermeneutics provide the foundation not only for an intra-religious pluralism, as it is in the case of Shabestari, but also for an inter-religious pluralism. What is significant in terms of the application of Abu Zayd's hermeneutics in practice is his theological position on the theme of Jesus's death or crucifixion – a theme that places him in sharp contrast to the mainstream pre-modern and most modern interpretations which hold that Jesus was neither crucified nor killed. This shows how Abu Zayd is able not only to arrive at a flexible interpretation of the Qur'ān that safeguards democratic values, gender equality and religious pluralism, but also to rethink a theological position that has long been taken for granted in Islamic interpretive discourse.

Notes

1. Abu Zayd, 'The Qur'ān: God and Man in Communication'.
2. Ibid.
3. Abu Zayd, 'The Others in the Qur'an', p. 287.
4. This schema is derived from Abu Zayd, *Mafhūm al-Naṣṣ* [The Concept of the Text], p. 57.
5. Abu Zayd, *Naqd al-Khiṭāb al-Dīnī* [The Critique of Religious Discourse], p. 93.
6. Abu Zayd, *The Voice of an Exile*, p. 57.
7. Izutsu, *God and Man in the Qur'ān*, pp. 165–6. As argued in the second chapter, the general tendency to treat *tanzīl* as interchangeable with *waḥy* is highly problematic.
8. Abu Zayd, *Mafhūm al-Naṣṣ*, p. 57. See also Sukidi, 'Naṣr Hāmid Abū Zayd and the Quest for a Humanistic Hermeneutics', pp. 185, 202.
9. Abu Zayd, *Mafhūm al-Naṣṣ*, p. 32.
10. Ibid., p. 32. See also Izutsu, *God and Man in the* Qur'ān, p. 171 and discussions in the first chapter of this book.
11. Abu Zayd, *Mafhūm al-Naṣṣ*, p. 38.
12. Ibid., p. 34.
13. Ibid., p. 39.
14. Ibid., p. 34.
15. For details of Arabs' views towards revelation, see Saeed, *Interpreting the* Qur'an, pp. 28–9.
16. Abu Zayd, *Mafhūm al-Naṣṣ*, p. 37.
17. Ibid., pp. 37–8.
18. Cited in Saeed, *Reading the Qur'ān in the Twenty-First Century*, p. 56.
19. Abu Zayd, *The Voice of an Exile*, p. 57.
20. Abu Zayd, *Mafhūm al-Naṣṣ*, p. 24.
21. Abu Zayd, *The Voice of an Exile*, p. 97.
22. Abu Zayd, *Mafhūm al-Naṣṣ*, p. 9.
23. Abu Zayd, *The Voice of an Exile*, p. 57.
24. Abu Zayd, 'The Others in the Qur'an', p. 287.
25. Abu Zayd, 'The Qur'ān: God and Man in Communication'.
26. Abu Zayd, 'The Others in the Qur'an', p. 288.
27. Campanini, *The Qur'an*, p. 58.
28. Abu Zayd, *Naqd al-Khiṭāb al-Dīnī*, p. 126.
29. Abu Zayd, *The Voice of an Exile*, p. 97.
30. Abu Zayd, *Naqd al-Khiṭāb al-Dīnī*, p. 126.
31. For similarities between Abu Zayd's and Shahrour's approach, see Browers, 'Islam and Political Sinn', p. 60.
32. Hirschkind, 'Heresy or Hermeneutics', p. 467. See also Campanini, *The Qur'an*, p. 59.
33. Abu Zayd, *The Voice of an* Exile, p. 57. See also Abu Zayd, *Mafhūm al-Naṣṣ*, pp. 56–7.
34. Völker, 'Two Accounts of Qur'anic Revelation', pp. 280–1.
35. These accounts are reported in Ibid., p. 281.
36. Saeed, *Interpreting the Qur'an*, p. 24.
37. Ahmed, *Reform and Modernity in Islam*, p. 64. This idea was also presented by Sayyid Ahmad Khan.
38. Abu Zayd, *al-Naṣṣ, al-Sulṭa, al-Haqīqa* [The Text, The Authority, The Truth], p. 71.
39. Abu Zayd, *Rethinking the Qur'ān*, p. 63.
40. Abu Zayd, 'The Qur'ān: God and Man in Communication'.
41. Ibid.
42. Cited in 'Islam and Political Sinn', p. 59.
43. al-Firuzabadi, *al-Qāmūs al-Mūhīt*, p. 7.
44. Cited in Lahoud, *Political Thought in Islam*, p. 71.
45. As already stated, Ibn Qutayba held that the Qur'ān could not be translated into any other language as Arabic itself was a sacred language. Abu Zayd emphasised this idea: Abu Zayd, 'The Translation of the Qur'an', p. 101
46. Gatje, *The Qur'ān and its Exegesis*, p. 53.

47. Abu Zayd, 'The Qur'ān: God and Man in Communication'.
48. See Campanini, 'The Mu'tazila in Islamic History and Thought', p. 48.
49. Peters, *God's Created Speech*, p. 418.
50. Vishanoff, *The Formation of Islamic Hermeneutics*, p. 134.
51. Ibid., p. 133.
52. Peters, *God's Created Speech*, p. 418.
53. I disagree with Yusuf Rahman, who considers Abu Zayd's theory of revelation in line with philosophers' discussion of prophecy and revelation. Rahman, *The hermeneutical Theory of Nasr Hamid Abu* Zayd, p. 136.
54. For such ideas of the Mu'tazilis, see *Reading the Qur'ān in the Twenty-First Century*, p. 84.
55. Abu Zayd, *Naqd al-Khiṭāb al-Dīnī*, p. 60.
56. Translation is in Peters, *God's Created Speech*, p. 417.
57. Ibid., p. 418.
58. Vishanoff, *The Formation of Islamic Hermeneutics*, p. 134.
59. On al-Khuli's ideas, especially his ideas about applying a literary approach to the realm of Qur'ānic studies, see Rahman, 'The Qur'ān in Egypt: Nasr Abu Zayd's Literary Approach', pp. 48–58.
60. Husayn, *Fi al-Shi'r al-Jāhilī* [on Jahili Poems], pp. 33–5 (this book was first published in 1926). Abu Zayd mentions such an idea in one of his papers, acknowledging his debt to Taha Husayn: Abu Zayd, 'The dilemma of literary approach to the Qur'an', p. 21.
61. Adams, *Islam and Modernism in Egypt*, p. 257.
62. Ibid.
63. Campanini emphasises that Hanafi was Abu Zayd's teacher at the University of Cairo: *The Qur'an: Modern Muslim Interpretations*, p. 57.
64. For such influence and the use of this term in Hanafi's works, see the Farsi translation of *Naqd al-Khiṭāb al-Dīnī* and the comments made by translators: Nasr Hamid Abu Zayd, *Naqd Gofteman-e Dīnī*, p. 155.
65. Abu Zayd, *The Voice of an Exile*, p. 97.
66. Hanafi, *Qaḍāyā Mu'āṣirah*, p. 93.
67. Hanafi, 'Method of Thematic Interpretation of the Qur'an', p. 202. See also this chapter, Abu Zayd's second hermeneutic.
68. Hanafi, *Theologie ou Anthropologie*, pp. 234–5, translated by Campanini, *The Qur'an: Modern Muslim Interpretations*, p. 58.
69. Abu Zayd, *Mafhūm al-Naṣṣ*, pp. 25, 19. According to Navid Kermani, Abu Zayd translated two of Lotman's works into Arabic: Navid Kermani, 'From Revelation to Interpretation', p. 172.
70. Jakobson, 'Linguistics and Poetics', p. 353.
71. Lotman, *The Structure of the Artistic Text*, p. 6.
72. Abu Zayd, *Mafhūm al-Naṣṣ*, p. 24.
73. Abu Zayd, *Mafhūm al-Naṣṣ*, translated by Morteza Karimi-Niya, p. 500.
74. Izutsu, *God and Man*, p. 164.
75. Abu Zayd, 'The Others in the Qur'an', p. 283.
76. Izutsu, *God and Man*, p. 164.
77. For Izutsu's examination of this term in Arabs' poetry in pre-Islamic times, see Izutsu, *God and Man*, pp. 166–72.
78. Abu Zayd himself acknowledges his debt to Izutsu: Abu Zayd, 'The Qur'ān: God and Man in Communication'.
79. Izutsu, *God and Man*, p. 154.
80. Ibid., p. 192.
81. Ibid., p. 193.
82. Abu Zayd, *Mafhūm al-Naṣṣ*, p. 19.
83. Abu Zayd, *Rethinking the Qur'ān*, p. 63.
84. Abu Zayd, *The Voice of an Exile*, p. 57.
85. Ibid., p. 97.
86. Ibid., p. 57.
87. Gadamer, *Philosophical Hermeneutics*, p. 60.
88. Gadamer, *Truth and Method*, p. 401.

89. Gadamer, *Philosophical Hermeneutics*, p. 62.
90. Ibid., p. 63.
91. Abu Zayd, *The Voice of an Exile*, p. 98.
92. Abu Zayd, 'The dilemma of literary approach to the Qur'an', p. 36. See also Abu Zayd, 'Women in the Discourse of Crisis'.
93. Abu Zayd, *The Voice of an Exile*, p. 96.
94. Abu Zayd, *Mafhūm al-Naṣṣ*, p. 24.
95. Ward, 'In the daylight forever?', p. 161.
96. Achrati, 'Arabic, Qur'ānic Speech and Postmodern Language', p. 174.
97. Abu Zayd, 'The Qur'ān: God and Man in Communication'.
98. For example, Razi narrates a number of traditions which assert that 'Arabic letters were a divine behest and taught by God Himself'. Cited in Chejne, 'Arabic: Its Significance and Place in Arab-Muslim Society', p. 452. Along similar lines, al-Shafi'i states that Arabic, the language of the Qur'ān, was a God-given language and had a divine nature. Ibid., pp. 454–5. See also discussions about language in Chapter 3.
99. Abu Zayd, *Mafhūm al-Naṣṣ*, p. 24; Abu Zayd, *Reformation of Islamic Thought*, p. 97; Abu Zayd, *The Voice of an Exile*, p. 99.
100. Abu Zayd, *Naqd al-Khiṭāb al-Dīnī*, p. 63.
101. Abu Zayd, *Reformation of Islamic Thought*, p. 97.
102. Ibid., p. 99
103. Izutsu, *God and Man*, pp. 154–7.
104. Abu Zayd, *Reformation of Islamic Thought*, p. 97.
105. For these characteristics that Abu Zayd attributes to the text, see Abu Zayd, *Mafhūm al-Naṣṣ*, p. 24; Abu Zayd, *Reformation of Islamic Thought*, p. 97; Abu Zayd, *The Voice of an Exile*, p. 99.
106. Nasr Hamid Abu Zayd, 'Divine Attributes in the Qur'ān', p. 197.
107. Abu Zayd, 'The others in the Qur'an', p. 291.
108. Ibid., pp. 287–8.
109. For instance, Ebrahim Moosa argues that the Qur'ān without its direct audiences would cease to be the Qur'ān. Moosa, 'The Debts and Burdens of Critical Islam', pp. 111–27.
110. Abu Zayd, 'The Qur'ān: God and Man in Communication'.
111. Abu Zayd, 'The Others in the Qur'an', p. 294.
112. Ibid.
113. Rahman, 'The hermeneutical Theory of Nasr Hamid Abu Zayd', p. 175.
114. Esack, *The Qur'an: A Short Introduction*, p. 144.
115. Ibid.
116. Abu Zayd, *Naqd al-Khiṭāb al-Dīnī*, p. 93.
117. Ibid.
118. This is also noted by Kermani in 'From Revelation to Interpretation', p. 172.
119. Abu Zayd, *Mafhūm al-Naṣṣ*, p. 188.
120. Abu Zayd, *Naqd al-Khiṭāb al-Dīnī*, p. 93.
121. Abu Zayd, 'The Others in the Qur'an', p. 283.
122. Ibid., p. 282.
123. Ibid., p. 284.
124. Ibid.
125. Abu Zayd, *Rethinking the Qur'ān*, p. 12; Abu Zayd, *Naqd al-Khiṭāb al-Dīnī*, p. 95.
126. For analysis of this idea, see Kermani, 'From Revelation to Interpretation', pp. 171–2.
127. Cited in Amirpur, *New Thinking in Islam*, p. 40.
128. Kermani, 'From Revelation to Interpretation', p. 173.
129. Abu Zayd, *al-Tajdīd wa al-Taḥrīm wa al-Ta'wīl*, p. 198, cited in El-Desouky, 'Between Hermeneutic Provenance and Textuality', p. 29.
130. Sukidi, 'Naṣr Hāmid Abū Zayd and the Quest for a Humanistic Hermeneutics of the Qur'ān', p. 188.
131. Abu Zayd, *Mafhūm al-Naṣṣ*, p. 188.
132. Abu Zayd, *Rethinking the Qur'ān*, p. 13. See also Abu Zayd, *Rethinking the Qur'ān*, pp. 62–3.
133. Kermani, 'From Revelation to Interpretation', p. 173.

134. Abu Zayd, 'The Dilemma of Literary Approach to the Qur'an', p. 39.
135. Abu Zayd, *Reformation of Islamic Thought*, p. 97.
136. Saeed, *Reading the Qur'an in the Twenty-First Century*, p. 18.
137. Campanini, *The Qur'an*, p. 55.
138. Abu Zayd, *Naqd al-Khiṭāb al-Dīnī*, pp. 84–5.
139. Abu Zayd's approach partly echoes Fazlur Rahman's double movement theory, which states that one has to move from the present situation to the time in which the Qur'ān was revealed and then attempt to interpret the ramifications of the verses in the present socio-historical condition.
140. Abu Zayd, *Naqd al-Khiṭāb al-Dīnī*, p. 216.
141. Hirsch, *Validity in Interpretation*, p. 46.
142. Ibid., pp. 8, 216.
143. Rahman, 'The Hermeneutical Theory of Nasr Hamid Abu Zayd', p. 153.
144. Abu Zayd, *Reformation of Islamic Thought*, p. 95.
145. Abu Zayd, *The Voice of an Exile*, p. 166.
146. Abu Zayd, *Reformation of Islamic Thought*, p. 95.
147. Ibid. See also Abu Zayd, *Rethinking the Qur'ān*, p. 37.
148. Abu Zayd, *Reformation of Islamic Thought*, p. 94.
149. Ibid. See also Abu Zayd, *The Voice of an Exile*, p. 203. This is where Abu Zayd defines Sharī'a law as 'human law derived largely from the foundational texts of Islam'.
150. Abu Zayd, *Reformation of Islamic Thought*, p. 95.
151. Abu Zayd, 'Women in the Discourse of Crisis'.
152. Abu Zayd, *Rethinking the Qur'ān*, p. 26.
153. Ibid.
154. Abu Zayd, 'The Qur'anic Concept of Justice'; Abu Zayd, *The Voice of an Exile*, p. 172.
155. Abu Zayd, 'The Qur'anic Concept of Justice'; Abu Zayd, *The Voice of an Exile*, p. 173.
156. Abu Zayd, *The Voice of an Exile*, p. 174.
157. Abu Zayd's idea echoes the views of Muhammad Abduh, who considered polygamy connected to the issues concerning orphans, arguing that polygamy should not be practised in the modern context. For Muhammad Abduh's views on polygamy, see Gatje, *The Qur'ān and its Exegesis*, pp. 248–50.
158. Abu Zayd, *The Voice of an Exile*, p. 176.
159. Ibid.
160. Ibid, p. 177.
161. Abu Zayd, 'The Qur'anic Concept of Justice'.
162. Abu Zayd, *Rethinking the Qur'ān*, p. 26.
163. Abu Zayd, *Reformation of Islamic Thought*, p. 95.
164. Ibid.
165. Ibid.
166. Ibid.
167. Ibid., p. 96.
168. Ibid.
169. Ibid.
170. Cited in Amirpur, *New Thinking in Islam*, p. 60.
171. Abu Zayd, *The Voice of an Exile*, p. 183.
172. Ibid. See also Akbar, 'The Political Discourses of three Contemporary Muslim Scholars', pp. 397–8.
173. Abu Zayd, *Rethinking the Qur'ān*, pp. 32–3.
174. Abu Zayd, *The Voice of an Exile*, p. 96.
175. For an example of literalists' understanding of the Qur'ānic verses dealing with Jews, see Nettler, *Past Trials and Present Tribulations*.
176. Abu Zayd, *The Voice of an Exile*, p. 29.
177. Abu Zayd, *Rethinking the Qur'ān*, p. 30.
178. Abu Zayd, *Reformation of Islamic Thought*, p. 94.
179. Abu Zayd, *Rethinking the Qur'ān*, p. 25.
180. For a comprehensive study on how pre-modern commentators interpreted the related verses, see Saeed, *Reading the Qur'an in the Twenty-First Century*, pp. 132–40.

181. Abu Zayd, *Rethinking the Qur'ān*, p. 34.
182. Ibid., pp. 34–5.
183. Abu Zayd, *Naqd al-Khiṭāb al-Dīnī*, p. 29.
184. Cited in Mansour, 'The Unpredictability of the Past', p. 230.
185. Abu Zayd, *Naqd al-Khiṭāb al-Dīnī*, p. 81.
186. Ibid., p. 30.
187. Abu Zayd, *Rethinking the Qur'ān*, p. 11.

7

Conclusion

This book has explored the discourses of four contemporary Muslim scholars, namely Fazlur Rahman, Abdolkarim Soroush, Muhammad Mujtahed Shabestari and Nasr Hamid Abu Zayd, as a means of providing insight into new directions in contemporary Islamic thought that aim to pose various challenges to traditional theories of revelation. It has examined the extent to which the theory of revelation presented by each of the scholars in question facilitates greater flexibility in Qur'ānic interpretation at both a theoretical and a practical level, seeking to establish a relationship between various Qur'ānic themes and the changing needs and circumstances of Muslims today. Indeed, the book has examined the extent to which the reform project of each of these four scholars is based on their understandings of revelation, or what I called a reform theology discourse from the very outset.

The findings of this book stand in sharp contrast with two common assumptions often found in Qur'ānic studies: 1) accepting or rejecting a traditional theory of revelation does not necessarily influence an interpreter's hermeneutic approach; and 2) one's understanding of revelation and one's approach to the interpretation of the Qur'ān are to be distinguished from one another. Rather, by referring to four contemporary discourses, I have argued that these two elements can go hand in hand; and although adhering to a particular understanding of revelation may not necessarily influence the entire range of views that a scholar might hold, it does influence, in certain important respects, one's approach to interpreting the Qur'ān. In other words, there might be an intimate relation between a scholar's theory of revelation and his or her Qur'ānic hermeneutics, and these combined views might in turn influence his or her ideas about issues pertaining to the socio-political arena. Thus, the book has argued that the accounts of revelation proposed by Rahman, Soroush, Shabestari and Abu Zayd are not only limited to providing a theological understanding of God's relation to the Prophet, but that they also have broader implications in the realm of Qur'ānic interpretation and in the discussions centred on socio-political issues, such as the discourse of women's rights, religious pluralism, democracy and human rights. To put it another way, this study has paid specific attention to reformism and has presented various aspects of contemporary reform projects within Islamic tradition based on new understandings of the nature of revelation and the Qur'ān. The case studies presented in this book represent an attempt made by Muslim scholars to demonstrate that a reform project within the realm of theology – i.e. understandings of revelation – should precede a reform project which is only limited to socio-political precepts of Islam, or to the Sharīʿa.

In the following sections I reconstruct the four levels of analysis through which the works of the scholars in question were examined, in order to make the contribution of this book clearer. I also engage with the discourses of these scholars at each level of analysis from a comparative perspective in order to demonstrate my results.

Accounts of revelation

When considering the works of Rahman, Soroush, Shabestari and Abu Zayd, it can be concluded that the manner in which these scholars present their theories of revelation is radically different from the mainstream Muslim understanding. The book has demonstrated that the approaches of the scholars in question to understanding the phenomenon of revelation and the nature of the Qurʾān are humanistic and historical. Rahman, Soroush, Shabestari and Abu Zayd all believe that revelation operates at two levels and in relation to two realms: the divine and human. As such, the conclusion that I have drawn from an analysis of these four discourses is the following: what they all have in common is the idea that the Qurʾān is not entirely a supernatural production, but is a quasi-natural product of the Prophet's mind in its encounter with the socio-cultural realities of his society, implying that the Qurʾān should also be considered a human text. Indeed, reformulating traditional views of revelation, the projects of the scholars in question are oriented around an emphasis on the human aspects of the Qurʾān, since each argues that revelation is not only dependent upon its initiator (God), but also dependent on the person who receives it (the Prophet), as well as on the cultural conditions of the community to which the text was originally revealed. This idea, as argued, provided these scholars with the foundation to approach the Qurʾān from a historical-contextual perspective.

It should be noted that the scholars in question retain a sense of proportion as believers and have never questioned all meta-historical aspects of revelation and the Qurʾān. Even with his radical approach to understanding the nature of revelation, the Iranian scholar Abdolkarim Soroush consistently emphasised in his work that the revelation originated in a transcendent realm and that God was the ultimate source of the Qurʾān. Soroush shows a deep appreciation of the Prophet's personality in his writings and regards Muhammad's religious experience as a guide for humans. For all the scholars surveyed in this book, the Qurʾān remains an unquestionably authentic, truthful and sincere document untouched by corruption of any kind. As such, there has been no argument in their writings against the authenticity and credibility of the Qurʾān or its reliable transmission per se. Therefore, issues related to the textual integrity of the Qurʾān and the process of canonisation have not been, by and large, approached by these scholars.

From a comparative perspective, Soroush presents the most radical approach to revelation among the scholars surveyed in this book. Like Rahman, he weakens the kinds of meta-historical and supernatural assumptions found in traditional theories of revelation by neglecting the externality of the angelic figure vis-à-vis the Prophet and by arguing against the physical nature of the angel. While Rahman does not explicitly say that the Qurʾān contains the Prophet's own words, Soroush states that the Prophet did indeed formulate the Qurʾān in his own words. Soroush's approach is even more humanistic than Shabestari's because the latter does not, by and large, emphasise the role of Muhammad's personality in shaping the content of revelation. Abu Zayd's approach is less humanistic than those of the other three scholars surveyed in this study. While in his view the Qurʾān is to be seen as a linguistic, historical and human text that came into being as a result of a communicative interaction between God and His Prophet, there is no emphasis in Abu Zayd's theory upon the idea that the Qurʾān was worded by the Prophet himself. In addition, Abu Zayd does not seem to have challenged the traditional theory that the content of revelation was revealed to the Prophet verbally, or was auditory in nature, nor that Gabriel played a significant role in transmitting God's message to His Prophet.

The roots of each scholar's account of revelation

This book has contributed to the project of discovering the foundations of each of these four scholars' ideas about revelation. The theories of revelation developed by the scholars surveyed in the book are based on the ideas of certain Muslim and non-Muslim scholars from the pre-modern and modern periods. As argued, Rahman's and Soroush's theories of revelation are an extension of the ideas of a number of Muslim philosophers such as al-Farabi, Ibn Sina and Mulla Sadra, and those of certain Muslim reformers such as Shah Wali Allah. Whereas Rahman and Soroush recover arguments from certain discourses in the realm of Islamic philosophy, Shabestari and Abu Zayd show little interest in the Islamic philosophical traditions as such. Shabestari's approach is close to certain humanistic discourses in classical Islamic theology in which the Qurʾān is considered the human words of the Prophet and not God's direct speech. Shabestari, however, is close to Soroush when he incorporates the language of religious experience into his theory of revelation. Both Shabestari and Soroush are heavily influenced by Western theological discourses that consider the nature of revelation tantamount to the religious experiences of prophets. Abu Zayd recovers aspects of the Muʿtazili theology, especially the ideas of Abd al-Jabbar. Indeed, with regard to the question of how the theory of revelation presented by each of these scholars is related to the Muʿtazili theology, my conclusion is that Abu Zayd's account is the closest. Abu Zayd does not go so far as to explicitly state that the Qurʾān contains Muhammad's own words, but rather remains confined in stating that the Qurʾān, though it is not God's literal Word, contains the humanisation of God's Word. In addition, Abu Zayd can be viewed as an example of a Muslim scholar who reformulated various aspects of traditional theories of revelation as a result of incorporating certain ideas of contemporary non-Muslim scholars such as those developed by the linguist scholar Jakobson, and those developed by Izutsu.

Hermeneutic approaches: theoretical level

In terms of the practice of exegesis, despite some differences, all the scholars surveyed in this book share a great deal in common. As a result of reformulating various themes of traditional theories of revelation, each promoted or followed a contextualisation method, according to which the context in which the Qur'ān emerged influenced its content. Central to their project is the idea that the Qur'ān stands in a close relationship with the socio-historical context of its emergence – a view that sharply contrasts with the ideas of those scholars who maintain that the Qur'ān is a 'timeless' text whose divine status necessitates that we consider it independent of all historical and temporal constraints. This emphasis on the context led them to maintain that any hermeneutics of the Qur'ān should take fully into account the culture, history and context of the Arabian Peninsula at the time when the revelation emerged.

It should be noted that although pre-modern commentators on the Qur'ān were aware of the importance of context in approaches to interpreting the Qur'ān and developed the discipline of occasions of revelation, their understanding of the notion of context was too restrictive to be considered as a basis for liberal interpretations of Qur'ān – such as those presented in this book. Traditional Qur'ānic studies often confined the significance of context to the legal sphere, i.e. for developing laws and injunctions. In addition, the fact that the socio-legal precepts of the Qur'ān emerged in a specific context did not often lead them to reject the universality of these precepts and their functionality in all times and contexts. It can be stated with certainty that there was no humanistic element attached to the discipline of occasion of revelation in traditional Qur'ānic studies.

From a comparative perspective, while Rahman, Soroush and Shabestari begin their hermeneutic approaches by each somehow arguing that the revelation reflects the interconnection between Muhammad's mind and his worldview (or that of his society) as well as the reactions of his listeners and his immediate social situation, Abu Zayd's point of departure involves emphasising the linguistic nature of revelation. However, Abu Zayd arrives at a similar conclusion to that reached by the other three scholars by following this idea.

On the theoretical level, this book argued that each scholar's theory of revelation is reflected in, and influenced by, his understanding of the Qur'ān and his practice of exegesis. Strongly related to the notion of context in the works of Rahman, Soroush, Shabestari and Abu Zayd is their departing from what I have termed a 'legal-oriented hermeneutic' – a way of viewing or approaching the Qur'ān primarily as a legal document that contains specific legal prescriptions – and also their stance in regard to the issue of the mutability and immutability of Qur'ānic teachings. In fact, an emphasis on the importance of context in the writings of the scholars in question led to a discussion about which aspects of the Qur'ān are universal (and should therefore be accepted as unchangeable), and which are merely particular to the context of the revelation (and thus are subject to change). Their humanistic view of the

Qur'ān is a point of departure that allows them to argue that the spirit of the text or its universality should take precedence over its accidental aspects.

Qur'ānic exegetes have long focused on discovering the most appropriate ways to comprehend God's intentions and purposes, and thus there were no major discussions about the connections between the subject of interpretation (Qur'ān), the interpreters' interests or prior knowledge, and the audiences to which an interpretive discourse is addressed. This 'God-centric' approach is transformed into what I refer to as a 'human-centric' approach – an approach which places human beings at the centre of religious understanding – in the writings of Soroush, Shabestari and Abu Zayd. In this way, the notion of context is related to another broad theme in the writings of Soroush, Shabestari and Abu Zayd: namely, that the Qur'ān has been interpreted by a diverse community of faith in different socio-historical contexts and in the light of a variety of pre-understandings, preconceptions and assumptions, each of which played a significant role in the creation of a given interpretive discourse. In Rahman's project, little attention is given to the interpreter's *pretext*, since his work is mainly oriented around developing an appropriate method for discovering what he refers to as the 'underlying unity' or 'transcendent objectivity' of the text. Soroush, Shabestari and Abu Zayd distance themselves from such an objective understanding. In Soroush's and Shabestari's theories, since the Qur'ān itself is considered as having an interpretive-subjective nature, mediated by the Prophet's human experiences, it is natural that one would bring forth his or her subjectivity and pre-understandings in the process of interpreting the Qur'ān. Abu Zayd's emphasis on Muhammad's subjectivity in revelation, too, inevitably opens up a space for refuting a commonly supposed notion of an objective, or what is often referred to as an 'innocent', interpretation of the Qur'ān.

At this level of analysis, this study has contributed to situate the hermeneutics of the scholars in question within a Western milieu. I argued that while Soroush's, Shabestari's and Abu Zayd's hermeneutical approaches are more Gadamerian, Rahman's hermeneutical approach is closer to the Objectivity School of Betti. While Abu Zayd refers to Hirsch's hermeneutic in his writings, this does not mean that his approach departs from Gadamer's at all. Abu Zayd's emphasis on the linguistic nature of revelation places him even closer to Gadamer in terms of their hermeneutic approaches.

Hermeneutic approaches functioning in practice

By analysing in detail several themes found in the works of Rahman, Soroush, Shabestari and Abu Zayd, this book examined some of the consequences that follow from the practical application of their hermeneutical approaches. In this way, the book contributed to demonstrating the strengths and limitations of the practical application of their hermeneutics. In addition, it brought forth new discourses in Islamic scholarship about gender issues, religious pluralism and democracy.

The contextualist methods proposed by the scholars in question have the capability of promoting gender equality. Indeed, these scholars provide us with a theoretical-theological argumentation for promoting gender equality. The quest for advancing women's rights in their works is based on taking the historical aspect of the revelation into serious consideration. From a comparative perspective, the contribution of Soroush and Shabestari in applying their hermeneutical approaches to the realm of gender issues is more limited than that of Rahman and Abu Zayd. While Rahman and Abu Zayd have extended their ideas in this realm to issues such as polygamy, testimony, inheritance and men's authority over women, Soroush and Shabestari have mainly emphasised how pre-modern interpretations of the Qur'ānic verses about gender issues were preconditioned by the beliefs, values and presuppositions associated with the socio-political context in which they emerged, and how such exegetical discourses reflected the hierarchical views of male–female relations in those eras. Unlike Rahman and Abu Zayd, Soroush and Shabestari have occasionally contextualised certain Qur'ānic themes on gender issues, and have not dealt with such a topic in a comprehensive way.

In terms of his ideas concerning the political arena, Rahman has not applied his contextualist approach. Although he acknowledges that democracy is of crucial importance for the future of Muslim-majority countries, by equating *shūrā* with democracy, his views are in line with those of mainstream liberal or modernist scholars. In this way, Rahman suggests that it is necessary to rely on the Islamic principle of *shūrā* to advance democracy in Muslim-majority societies. Rahman's approach is indeed oriented around a desire to find a Qur'ānic reference to fit his preconceived idea that democracy is necessary within an Islamic context. By contrast, Soroush, Shabestari and Abu Zayd have identified the epistemic limits of the era of revelation, acknowledging that the modern concept of democracy could not have emerged in seventh-century Arabian society. By applying their contextualist method to the political arena, they avoid approaching modern political concepts or themes anachronistically – that is, projecting our current views, which have been shaped by the specific conditions of our era, into the past.

Accordingly, central to the political discourses of Soroush, Shabestari and Abu Zayd is the idea that modern political notions such as human rights and democracy are not extractable from religious sources, including the Qur'ān. In the political arena, Soroush, Shabestari and Abu Zayd bring forth a new discourse for Muslim politics in today's context: the need to recognise the extra-theological values of an emerging model of democracy in the Muslim world. According to this discourse, Muslims can flexibly turn to some or most elements of modern Western democratic norms without claiming that these had already existed at the time of the Prophet Muhammad and without necessarily indicating that they are inherently 'Islamic'. This lays the foundation of a conceptual framework which highlights the idea that Muslim communities can turn towards a less religious approach to methods of governance, without necessarily emphasising that they should abandon basic Islamic values.

The last implication of the methods involving contextualisation presented by the scholars in question is related to the development of a framework of religious pluralism. As argued, we can distinguish between two forms of religious pluralism: inter-religious and intra-religious pluralisms. Among all the scholars whose ideas were examined in this book, Soroush presents the most comprehensive approach to the philosophy of religious pluralism. Soroush's theory of prophetic experience results in a pluralist perspective on religions, since, for him, the existence of various religious traditions is an inevitable manifestation of the different socio-historical conditions within which different religions emerged. Soroush's emphasis on the human side of revelation and its experiential character leads him to defend a deontological theory of religious truth. Soroush's theory also opens up a space in which it is possible to conduct a variety of different readings of the Qurʾān, since it acknowledges our human epistemic limits in regard to the interpretation of the Qurʾān. The most important consequence of this idea is that no single interpretation should be seen as solely reflecting the Truth, and thus no one should seek to impose or inflict his or her understanding of the Truth on others. Such approaches to religious pluralism are, by and large, absent in Rahman's writings. While Shabestari has applied his hermeneutics to the realm of intra-religious pluralism – a significant theme that emerged in response to the views held within traditional clerical circles of Iran – he has not presented a comprehensive approach in defence of inter-religious pluralism. For Shabestari, the idea of the exclusive validity of one interpretation is to be refuted, and it is hermeneutically naïve to believe that one single official interpretation of a religion exists. Abu Zayd uses the notion of an epistemological inaccessibility of humans to fathom God's intention to argue for a variety of interpretations of the Qurʾān. By applying his hermeneutic approaches, Abu Zayd has also contextualised some of the Qurʾān's apparently hostile statements about the Jews, as well as some Islam–Christian theological disputes such as that concerning the death and crucifixion of Jesus.

Final remarks

The main conclusion of this book is that the projects of Rahman, Soroush, Shabestari and Abu Zayd are not simply limited to the articulation of new theories of revelation as such, but extend to their applications in the socio-political realm. By exploring the works of these scholars, this study concludes that the important consequences of a humanistic approach to understanding revelation are not necessarily confined to the realm of speculation about God–human relations, but are also relevant to the area of scriptural exegesis and in approaching Qurʾānic socio-political precepts. The book has demonstrated that Rahman, Soroush, Shabestari and Abu Zayd are part of a distinctive group of contemporary Muslim scholars who call for new hermeneutical stances which are themselves based on the re-examination of various elements of traditional theories of revelation.

It should be noted that there has been a large amount of critique of the ideas of Rahman, Soroush, Shabestari and Abu Zayd, especially from Muslim scholars. Their ideas have often been confronted with considerable hostility, in some cases even prosecution. These scholars have also been accused of rejecting the sanctity of the Qur᾽ān. Their theories of revelation were subject to strong criticism from many Muslim scholars, who attacked them for considering the Qur᾽ān a historically contingent text.[1] Religious scholars and clergy understood these scholars' call for plurality in the interpretation of the Qur᾽ān as an attack on their monopoly over religious authority. Also, the fact that scholars such as Soroush, Shabestari and Abu Zayd heavily relied on concepts from Western philosophy and literary studies served as an additional reason to refute their hermeneutical theories.[2]

However, it can be stated with certainty that Rahman, Soroush, Shabestari and Abu Zayd have opened up a new horizon in contemporary Islamic discourse and initiated a notable scholarly debate within theological circles in both Islamic and Western countries. Despite the opposition they have faced in their homelands, their discourses may continue to provide a fertile space for further debates, and in this way might serve as an inspiration for a younger generation of Muslim scholars, whether in their own countries or in an international context.

Notes

1. See Akbar, 'Towards a Humanistic Approach to the Quran', pp. 94–5.
2. See Johanna Pink, 'Striving for a new Exegesis of the Qur᾽ān', pp. 788–9.

Bibliography

Primary Sources

Abu Zayd, Nasr Hamid, *Naqd al-Khiṭāb al-Dīnī* [The Critique of Religious Discourse] (Cairo: Dar al-Thaqafah al-Jadidah, 1992).

Abu Zayd, Nasr Hamid, *al-Naṣṣ, al-Sulṭa, al-Ḥaqīqa: al-Fikr al-dīnī bayna irādat al-maʿrifa wa irādat al-haymana* [the Text, the Authority, the Truth: Religious Thought between Knowledge and the Desire for Hegemony] (Beirut: al-Markaz al-Thaqafi al-ʿArabi, 1995).

Abu Zayd, Nasr Hamid, 'Women in the Discourse of Crisis', Dossier Articles International Fundamentalism 1997, http://www.wluml.org/node/280.

Abu Zayd, Nasr Hamid, *Mafhūm al-naṣṣ: Dirāsa fī ʿulūm al-Qurʾān, Mafhūm al-naṣṣ* [The Concept of the Text: Studies on the Qurʾānic Sciences] (Beirut: al-Markaz al-Thaqafi al-ʿArabi, 1998).

Abu Zayd, Nasr Hamid, 'Divine Attributes in the Qurʾan: Some Poetic Aspects', in John Cooper, Ronald L. Nettler and Mohamed Mahmoud (eds), *Islam and Modernity: Muslim Intellectuals Respond* (London: I. B. Tauris, 2000), pp. 190–211.

Abu Zayd, Nasr Hamid, 'The dilemma of literary approach to the Qurʾan', *Journal of Comparative Poetics*, 23, 2003, 8–47.

Abu Zayd, Nasr Hamid, *Rethinking the Qurʾān: Towards a Humanistic Hermeneutics* (Amsterdam: Amsterdam University Press, 2004).

Abu Zayd, Nasr Hamid and Esther R. Nelson, *The Voice of an Exile: Reflections on Islam* (London: Praeger, 2004).

Abu Zayd, Nasr Hamid, *Naqd-e Goftemān Dīnī* [The Critique of Religious Discourse], trans. Hasan Yusefi Eshkevari, Muhammad Javaher Kalam (Tehran: Yadavaran, 2005).

Abu Zayd, Nasr Hamid, *Reformation of Islamic Thought: A Critical Historical Analysis* (Amsterdam: Amsterdam University Press, 2006).

Abu Zayd, Nasr Hamid, 'The others in the Qurʾan: A Hermeneutical Approach', *Philosophy and Social Criticism*, 36(3–4), 2010, 281–94.

Abu Zayd, Nasr Hamid, 'The Translation of the Qurʾan: An Impossible Task', in Mehran Kamrava, (ed.), *Innovation in Islam: Traditions and Contributions* (Berkeley: University of California Press, 2011), pp. 98–110.

Abu Zayd, Nasr Hamid, 'The Qurʾān: God and Man in Communication', inaugural Lecture for the Cleveringa Chair at Leiden University, http://www.let.leidenuniv.nl/forum/01_1/onderzoek/lecture.pdf.

Abu Zayd, Nasr Hamid, 'The Qur'anic Concept of Justice', 2001, http://them.polylog.org/3/fan-en.htm.

Rahman, Fazlur, *Avicenna's Psychology* (London: Oxford University Press, 1952).

Rahman, Fazlur, 'The thinker of Crisis: Shah Waliyullah', *Pakistan Quarterly*, 6(2), 1956, 1–5.

Rahman, Fazlur, *Prophecy in Islam: Philosophy and Orthodoxy* (Chicago: University of Chicago Press, 1958).

Rahman, Fazlur, 'Concepts Sunnah, Ijtihad and Ijma in the Early Period', *Islamic Studies*, 1(1), 1962, 5–21.

Rahman, Fazlur, 'The Impact of Modernity on Islam', *Journal of Islamic Studies*, 5(2), 1966, 112–28.

Rahman, Fazlur, 'Islamic Modernism: Its Scope, Method and Alternatives', *International Journal of Middle East Studies*, 1(4), 1970, 317–33.

Rahman, Fazlur, *The Philosophy of Mulla Sadra* (Albany: State University of New York Press, 1975).

Rahman, Fazlur, 'Some Islamic Issues in the Ayyub Khan Era', in Donald P. Little (ed.), *Essays on Islamic Civilization, Presented to Niyazi Berkes* (Leiden: Brill, 1976), 284–302.

Rahman, Fazlur, 'Divine Revelation and the Prophet', *Hamdard Islamicus*, 1(2), 1978, 66–72.

Rahman, Fazlur, 'Islam: Challenges and Opportunities', in Alford T. Welch and Pierre Cachia (eds), *Islam: Past Influence and Present Challenge* (New York: State University of New York Press, 1979), pp. 315–30.

Rahman, Fazlur, 'Islam: Legacy and Contemporary Challenge', in Cyriac K. Pullapilly (ed.), *Islam in the Contemporary World* (Notre Dame: Cross Road Books, 1980), pp. 402–15.

Rahman, Fazlur, *The Major Themes of the Qur'ān* (Chicago: Bibliotheca Islamica, 1980).

Rahman, Fazlur, *Islam & Modernity: Transformation of an Intellectual Tradition* (Chicago: University of Chicago Press, 1982).

Rahman, Fazlur, 'The Islamic Concept of State', in John J. Donohue and John L. Esposito (eds), *Islam in Transition: Muslim Perspectives* (Oxford: Oxford University Press, 1982), pp. 261–71.

Rahman, Fazlur, 'The Status of Women in Islam: A Modernist Interpretation', in Hanna Papanek and Gail Minault (eds), *Separate Worlds: Studies of Purdah in South Asia* (Delhi: Chanakya, 1982), pp. 285–310.

Rahman, Fazlur, 'Law and Ethics in Islam', in Richard G. Hovannisian (ed.), *Ethics in Islam: Ninth Giorgio Levi Della Vida Biennial Conference* (Malibu: Undena, 1985), pp. 3–15.

Rahman, Fazlur, 'My Belief-in-Action', in Phillip L. Berman (ed.), *The Courage of Conviction* (Santa Barbara: Dodd, Mead & Company, 1985), pp. 153–9.

Rahman, Fazlur, 'Interpreting the Qur'an', *Inquiry*, 3, 1986, 45–9.

Rahman, Fazlur, 'Islam and Political Action: Politics in the Service of Religion', in Nigel Biggar, Jamie S. Scott and William Schweiker (eds), *Cities of Gods: Faith, Politics and Pluralism in Judaism, Christianity and Islam* (New York: Greenwood Press, 1986), pp. 153–65.

Rahman, Fazlur, 'Non-Muslim Minorities in an Islamic State', *Journal Institute of Muslim Minority Affairs*, 7(1), 1986, 13–24.

Rahman, Fazlur, 'Translating the Qur'an', *Religion and Literature*, 20(1), 1988, 23–30.

Rahman, Fazlur, 'Muhammad and the Qur'an', in Andre LaCocque (ed.), *Commitment and Commemoration: Jews, Christians and Muslims in Dialogue* (Chicago: Exploration Press, 1994), pp. 9–15.

Rahman, Fazlur, 'Islam's Origin and Ideals', in Nimat Hafez Barazangi, M. Raquibuz Zaman and Omar Afzal (eds), *Islamic Identity and the Struggle for Justice* (Gainesville: University Press of Florida, 1996), pp. 11–18.

Rahman, Fazlur, *Islam*, 2nd edn (Chicago: University of Chicago Press, 2002).

Rahman, Fazlur, de Boer, ''Akl' in P. Bearman et al. (eds), *Encyclopedia of Islam*, 2nd edn (Leiden: Brill) http://dx.doi.org.ezp.lib.unimelb.edu.au/10.1163/1573-3912_islam_COM_0038.

Shabestari, Muhammad Mojtahed, 'Cherā bāyad Andīsheh-e Dīnī ra Naqd Kard?' [Why should we Criticize Religious Knowledge?] *Kiyan*, 18, 1994, 16–21.

Shabestari, Muhammad Mojtahed, *Imān va Āzādī* [*Faith and Freedom*] (Tehran: Tarh-e No, 1997).

Shabestari, Muhammad Mojtahed, *Hermenūtīk, Kitāb va Sonnat* [Hermeneutics, The Book and the Tradition] (Tehran, Tarh-e No, 2000).

Shabestari, Muhammad Mojtahed, 'Rāhe Doshvār-e Mardom-sālāri' [The Difficult Path to Democracy] *Aftab*, 22, 2003. http://ensani.ir/fa/content/92242/default.aspx.

Shabestari, Muhammad Mojtahed, *Ta'amolātī dar Qerā'at-e Ensānī az Dīn* [Some Thoughts on the Human Reading of Religion] (Tehran: Tarh-e No, 2004).

Shabestari, Muhammad Mojtahed, *Naqdī bar Qerā'at-e Rasmī az Dīn: Boḥran-hā, Chālesh-hā va Rāh-e ḥal-hā* [*A Critique of the Official Reading of Religion: Crises, Challenges and Solutions*] (Tehran: Tarh-e No, 2005).

Shabestari, Muhammad Mojtahed, 'Hermenūtīk va Tafsīr-e Dīnī az Jahān' [Hermeneutics and Religious Interpretation of the World], 2007, http://www.rahesabz.net/story/34350.

Shabestari, Muhammad Mojtahed, ''Amal be āyeh-ī dar Qur'ān hamīshegī nīst' [Practising a Qur'ānic Verse is not Eternal], 2008, http://zamaaneh.com/seraj/2008/12/post_11.html.

Shabestari, Muhammad Mojtahed, 'Islam is a religion, not a political agenda', 2008, https://en. qantara.de/content/interview-with-mohammad-mojtahed-shabestari-part-1-islam-is-a-religion-not-a-political-0.

Shabestari, Muhammad Mojtahed, 'Ḥuqūq-e Bashar Eslamī nemīshavad valī Mosalmānān bayad ān ra bepazirand' [Human Rights is not Islamic, but Muslims must accept it], 2017, http://mohammadmojtahedshabestari.com

Shabestari, Muhammad Mojtahed, 'Gherāʾat-e Nabavī az Jahān' [Prophetic Interpretation of the World], 2008, http://mohammadmojtahedshabestari.com

Soroush, Abdolkarim, *Farbeh-tar az Ideolojy* [Loftier than Ideology] (Tehran: Sirat, 1994).

Soroush, Abdolkarim, *Qabz va Basṭ-e Teʾorīk-e Sharīʿat* [*The Theoretical Contraction and Expansion of the Sharīʿat*] (Tehran, Sirat, 1995).

Soroush, Abdolkarim, 'A Conversation with Abdolkarim Soroush', conducted by Faisal Bodi, *Q-News International (British Muslim Weekly)*, 220–1, June 1996.

Soroush, Abdolkarim, *Ṣirāṭ-hāye Mostaqīm* [*The Straight Paths*] (Tehran: Sirat, 1998).

Soroush, Abdolkarim, 'The Evolution and Devolution of Religious Knowledge', in Charles Kurzman (ed.), *Liberal Islam: A Sourcebook* (New York: Oxford University Press, 1998), pp. 244–51.

Soroush, Abdolkarim, *Basṭ-e Tajrobeh Nabavī* (Tehran: Sirat, 1999).

Soroush, Abdolkarim, 'The Prophet's Mission and Identity Crisis', *Kiyan*, 49, 1999.

Soroush, Abdolkarim, *Reason, freedom and democracy in Islam: Essential Writings of Abdolkarim Soroush*, edited and translated Mahmoud Sadri and Ahmad Sadri (Oxford: Oxford University Press, 2000).

Soroush, Abdolkarim, 'Contraction and Expansion of Women's Rights: An Interview with Dr Abdulkarim Soroush', 2000, www.Seraj.org 2000.

Soroush, Abdolkarim, *Nesbat-e ʿilm va Dīn* [The Relation between Science and Religion], in *Sonnat va sekuralism* [The Tradition and Secularism] (Tehran: Sirat, 2009), pp. 109–27.

Soroush, Abdolkarim, 'The Word of Muhammad: An Interview with Abdolkarim Soroush by Michel Hoebink', 2007, http://www.drsoroush.com/English/Interviews/E-INT-The%20Word%20of%20Mohammad.html.

Soroush, Abdolkarim, 'I am a Neo-Muʿtazilite', 2008, http://www.drsoroush.com/English/Interviews/E-INT-Neo-Mutazilite_July2008.html.

Soroush, Abdolkarim, *The Expansion of Prophetic Experience: Essays on Historicity, Contingency and Plurality in Religion*, trans. Nilou Mobasser (Leiden: Brill, 2009).

Soroush, Abdolkarim, 'The Changeable and Unchangeable', in Kari Vogt, Lena Larsen and Christian Moe (eds), *New Directions in Islamic Thought: Exploring Reform and Muslim Tradition* (London: I. B. Tauris, 2009), pp. 9–15.

Soroush, Abdolkarim, 'Masīh dar Eslam' [Jesus in Islam], 2010, http://www.drsoroush.com/Persian/By_DrSoroush/P-NWS-13880901-MasihDarIslam.html.

Soroush, Abdolkarim, 'Muhammad: Rāvī-e Ruʾyā-hāye Rasūlāneh' [Muhammad: the Narrator of Prophetic Dreams', 2013, http://drsoroush.com/fa/%d9%85%d8%ad%d9%85%d9%91%d8%af%d8%b5-%d8%b1%d8%a7%d9%88%db%8c-%d8%b1%d9%88%db%8c%d8%a7%d9%87%d8%a7%db%8c-%d8%b1%d8%b3%d9%88%d9%84%d8%a7%d9%86%d9%87/

Soroush, Abdolkarim, 'Taʿabīr-e Maʿād dar Ruʾyā-hāye Rasūlāneh' [Interpretation of Resurrection in the theory of Prophetic Visions], 2015, https://www.youtube.com/watch?v=ZE8VE-BkoLw.

Secondary Sources

Adams, Charles C., *Islam and Modernism in Egypt: A Study of the Modern Reform Movement Inaugurated by Muhammad Abduh* (London: Oxford University Press, 1933).

Adamson, Peter, 'al-Kindi and the Reception of Greek Philosophy', in Peter Adamson, Richard C. Taylor (eds), *The Cambridge Companion to Arabic Philosophy* (Cambridge: Cambridge University Press, 2010), pp. 32–51.

Ahmad, Anzaruddin, 'Applying Hermeneutics to the Qurʾan: A Recritique', in Noritah Omar, Washima Che Dan, Jason Sanjeev Ganesan and Rosli Talif (eds), *Critical Perspectives on Literature and Culture in the New World Order* (Newcastle: Cambridge Scholars Publishing, 2010), pp. 81–100.

Ahmad b. Faris, Abu al-Husayn, *Muʿjam Maqayis al-Lugha*, 6 vols (Beirut: Dar al-Fikr, 1979), http://www.waqfeya.com/book.php?bid=3144.

Ahmed, Achrati, 'Arabic, Qurʾānic Speech and Postmodern Language: What the Qurʾān Simply Says', *Arabica*, 55(2), 2008, 161–203.

Ahmed, Safdar, 'Progressive Islam and Qurʾanic Hermeneutics: The Reification of Religion and Theories of Religious Experience', in Lily Zubaidah Rahim (ed.), *Muslim Secular Democracy: Voices from Within* (New York: Palgrave Macmillan, 2013), pp. 77–92.

Ahmed, Safdar, *Reform and Modernity in Islam: The Philosophical, Cultural and Political Discourses among Muslim Reformers* (London: I. B. Tauris, 2013).

Akbar, Ali, 'The Political Discourses of three Contemporary Muslim Scholars: Secular, Nonsecular, or Pseudosecular?', *Digest of Middle East Studies*, 25(2), 2016, 393–408.

Akbar, Ali, 'From Revelation to Interpretation: Abu Zayd's Approach', *Islamic Quarterly*, 60(2), 2016, 159–86.

Akbar, Ali, 'A Contemporary Muslim Scholar's Approach to Revelation: Moḥammad Moǧtahed Šabestarī's Reform Project', *Arabica*, 63(6), 2016, 656–80.

Akbar, Ali, 'ʿAbdolkarim Soroush's Approach to "Experience" as a Basis for His Reform Project', *Islam and Christian–Muslim Relations*, 28(3), 2017, 313–31.

Akbar, Ali, 'Towards a Humanistic Approach to the Quran: New Direction in Contemporary Islamic Thought', *Culture and Religion*, 20(1), 2019, 82–103.

Ali, Kecia, *Imam Shafiʿi: Scholar and Saint* (Oxford: Oneworld, 2011).

Aliabadi, Ali M., 'Abdolkarim Soroush and the Discourse of Islamic Revivalism', PhD thesis (The New School University, 2005).

Amirpur, Katajun, 'The Expansion of Prophetic Experience: Abdolkarīm Sorūš's New Approach to Qurʾānic Revelation', *Die Welt des Islams*, 51(3–4), 2011, 409–37.

Amirpur, Katajun, *New Thinking in Islam: The Jihad for Democracy, Freedom and Women's Rights*, trans. Eric Ormsby (London: Gingko Library, 2015).
Andrea, Tor, *Muhammad: The Man and His Faith* (London: George Allen and Unwin Publishing, 1936).
An-Naim, Abdullahi Ahmed, *Toward an Islamic Reformation: Civil Liberties, Human Rights and International Law* (Syracuse: Syracuse University Press, 1990).
Arkoun, Muhammad, *Rethinking Islam: Common Questions, Uncommon Answers*, trans. Robert D. Lee (Oxford: Westview Press, 1994).
Arkoun, Muhammad, 'The notion of Revelation: From Ahl al-Kitāb to the Societies of the Book', *Die Welt des Islams*, 28(1), 1988, 62–89.
Arkoun, Muhammad, *The Unthought in Contemporary Islamic Thought* (London: Saqi, 2002).
Armajani, Jon, *Dynamic Islam: Liberal Muslim Perspectives in a Transnational Age* (Dallas: University Press of America, 2004).
Aslan, Adnan, 'What Is Wrong with the Concept of Religious Experience', *Islam and Christian–Muslim Relations*, 14(3), 2003, 299–312.
Atiyeh, George N., *Al-Kindi: The Philosopher of the Arabs* (New Delhi: Kitab Bhavan, 2006).
Barlas, Asma, *Believing Women in Islam: Unreading Patriarchal Interpretations of the Quran* (Austin: University of Texas Press, 2002).
Barlas, Asma, 'Amina Wadud's hermeneutics of the Qur'an: women rereading sacred texts', in Suha Taji-Farouki (ed.), *Modern Muslim Intellectuals and the Qur'an* (Oxford: Oxford University Press, 2006), pp. 97–123.
Barth, Karl, *Church Dogmatics* (Edinburgh: T. & T. Clark, 1956–75).
Bayat, Asaf, *Making Islam Democratic: Social Movements and the Post-Islamist Turn* (Stanford: Stanford University Press, 2007).
Bell, Richard, 'Muhammad's Visions 1', *Muslim Word*, 24(2), 1934, 145–54.
Bennett, Clinton, *Muslims and Modernity: An Introduction to the Issues and Debates* (London: Continuum, 2005).
Berry, Donald L. *Islam and Modernity through the Writings of Islamic Modernist Fazlur Rahman* (New York: The Edwin Mellon Press, 2003).
Black, Deborah L., 'Psychology: Soul and Intellect', in Peter Adamson and Richard C. Taylor (eds), *The Cambridge Companion to Arabic Philosophy* (Cambridge: Cambridge University Press, 2010), pp. 308–26.
Browers, Michaelle, 'Islam and Political Sinn: The Hermeneutics of Contemporary Islamic Reformists', in Michaelle Browers and Charles Kurzman (eds), *An Islamic Reformation* (Lanham: Lexington Books, 2004), pp. 54–78.
Bukhari, *Sahih al-Bukhari*, trans. Muhammad Muhsin Khan (New Delhi: Kitab Bhavan, 1984).
Burge, S. R., *Angels in Islam: Jalal al-Din al-Suyuti's al-Habāik fi akhbār al-malāik* (London: Routledge, 2012).

Campanini, Massimo, *The Qur'an: Modern Muslim Interpretations*, trans. Caroline Higgitt (London: Routledge, 2011).

Chejne, Anwar G., 'Arabic: Its Significance and Place in Arab-Muslim Society', *Middle East Journal*, 19(4), 1965, 447–70.

Chodkiewicz, Michel, *An Ocean without Shore*, trans. David Streight (Albany: State University of New York Press, 1993).

Cook, Michael, *The Koran: A Very Short Introduction* (Oxford: Oxford University Press, 2000).

Craig, Edward, 'Pluralism', in Edward Craig (ed.), *Routledge Encyclopedia of Philosophy*, Vol. 7 (London: Routledge, 1998).

Dabbagh, Soroush, *Ayīn dar Ayīneh: Moruri bar Ara-e Dīn-Shenāsāneh ʿAbdolkarim Soroush* [Religion in the Mirror: A Review of ʿAbdolkarim Soroush's Approach to Religion] (Tehran: Sirat, 2004).

Dahlen, Ashk, *Deciphering the Meaning of Revealed Law: The Surushian Paradigm in Shii Epistemology* (Stockholm: Elanders Gotab, 2001).

Dahlen, Ashk, *Islamic Law, Epistemology and Modernity: Legal Philosophy in Contemporary Iran* (New York: Routledge, 2003).

Dahlen, Ashk, 'Sirat al-mustaqim – One or Many? Religious Pluralism among Intellectuals in Iran', in Ibrahim M. Abu-Rabi (ed.), *The Blackwell Companion to Contemporary Islamic Thought* (Malden: Blackwell, 2006), pp. 425–48

Dashti, Ali, *Twenty Three Years: A Study of the Prophetic Career of Muhammad*, trans. F. R. C. (Bagely: Mazda Publishers, 1994).

Denny, Frederick Mathewson, 'Fazlur Rahman: Muslim Intellectual', *Muslim World*, 79(2), 1989, 91–101.

Duderija, Adis, *Constructing a Religiously Ideal 'Believer' and 'Woman' in Islam: Neo-traditional Salafis and Progressive Muslims' Method of Interpretation* (New York: Palgrave Macmillan, 2011).

Eck, Diana, *A New Religious America: How a Christian Country Has Now Become the World's Most Religiously Diverse Nation* (San Francisco: HarperSanFrancisco, 2001).

Edgar, Iain R., *The Dream in Islam: From Qur'anic Tradition to Jihadist Inspiration* (New York: Berghahn Books, 2011).

El-Desouky Ayman A., 'Between Hermeneutic Provenance and Textuality: The Qur'an and the Question of Method in Approaches to World Literarture', *Journal of Qur'anic Studies*, 16(3), 2014, 11–38.

El-Mesawi, Mihamed El-Tahir, 'Religion, Society and Culture in Malik Bennabi's Thought', in Ibrahim M. Abu-Rabi (ed.), *The Blackwell Companion to Contemporary Islamic Thought* (Malden: Blackwell, 2006), pp. 213–56.

Elmi, Muhammad Jafar, 'Word of God and Revelation: A Shia Perspective', in Anthony O'Mahony, Wulstan Peterburs and Mohammad A. Shomail (eds), *Catholics and Shia in Dialogue* (London: Melisende, 2004), pp. 278–89.

Ernst, Karl W., *How to read the Qur'an: A New Guide with Select Translations* (Chapel Hill: The University of North Carolina Press, 2011).

Esack, Farid, *Qur'an, Liberation and Pluralism: An Islamic Perspective of Interreligious Solidarity against Oppression* (Oxford: Oneworld, 1997).

Esack, Farid, *The Qur'an: A Short Introduction* (Oxford: Oneworld, 2002).

Fakhri, Majid, *A History of Islamic Philosophy* (New York: Columbia University Press, 1970).

Al-Farabi, *al-Siyāsa al-Madaniyya* [The Political Regime], ed. Fauzi M. Najjar (Beirut: Al-Zahra University Press, 1988).

Al-Farabi, *Fuṣūl al-Madanī* [Aphorisms of the Statesman], trans. D. M. Dunlop (Cambridge: Cambridge University Press, 1961).

Al-Farabi, *On the Perfect State*, trans. Richard Walzer (Oxford: Clarendon Press, 1985).

Firuzabadi, Majd al-Din Muhammad Ibn Ya'qub, *al-Qāmūs al-Mūhīt*, 2nd edn (Cairo: Mustafa al-Babi al-Hanbali, 1952).

Foody, Kathleen, 'Interiorizing Islam: Religious experience and state oversight in the Islamic Republic of Iran', *Journal of American Academy of Religion*, 83(3), 2015, 599–623.

Foody, Kathleen, 'The Limits of Religion: Liberalism and anti-liberalism in the Islamic Republic of Iran', *Culture and Religion*, 17(2), 2016, 183–99.

Fyzee, Asaf A. A., *A Modern Approach to Islam* (Bombay: Asia Publishing House, 1963).

Gadamer, Hans-Georg, *Truth and Method*, trans. Joel Weinsheimer and Donald G. Marshall (London and New York: Continuum Books, 1975).

Gadamer, Hans-Georg, *Philosophical Hermeneutics*, trans. David E. Linge (Berkeley: University of California Press, 1977).

Gatje, Helmut, *The Qur'ān and its Exegesis*, trans. Alford T. Welch (Berkeley: University of California Press, 1976).

Ghamari-Tabrizi, Behrooz, *Islam and Dissent in Post-revolutionary Iran: Abdolkarim Soroush, Religious Politics and Democratic Reform* (London: I. B. Tauris, 2008).

Ghazali, Abu Hamid, *Deliverance from Error: Five Key Texts Including His Spiritual Autobiography al-Munqidh min al-dalal*, trans. R. J. McCarthy (Louisville: Twayne Publishers, 1980).

Ghazali, Muhammad, *The Socio-Political Thought of Shah Wali Allah* (New Delhi: Adam Publishers, 2009).

Ghobadzadeh, Naser, *Religious Secularity: A Theological Challenge to the Islamic State* (Oxford: Oxford University Press, 2015).

Gleave, Robert, *Islam and Literalism: Literal Meaning and Interpretation in Islamic Legal Theory* (Edinburgh: Edinburgh University Press, 2012).

Goldberg, Ori, *Shi'i Theology in Iran: The Challenge of Religious Experience* (London: Routledge, 2012).

Graham, William A., *Divine Word and Prophetic Word in Early Islam: A Reconsideration of the Sources with Special Reference to the Divine Saying or Hadith Qudsi* (Paris: Mouton, 1977).

Grenz, Stanley J. and Roger E. Olson, *20th Century Theology: God and the World in a Transitional Age* (Downers Grove: InterVarsity Press, 1992).

Griffel, Frank, 'al-Ghazali's Concept of Prophecy: The Introduction of Avicennan Psychology into Asharite Theology', *Arabic Sciences and Philosophy*, 14(1), 2004, 101–44.

Griffel, Frank, 'Muslim philosophers' rationalist explanation of Muhammad's Prophecy', in Jonathan E. Brockopp (ed.), *The Cambridge Companion to Muhammad* (New York: Cambridge University Press, 2010), 158–79.

Halepota, A. J., *Philosophy of Shah Waliullah* (Lahore: Sind Sagar Academy, 1976).

Hallaq, Wael B., *A History of Islamic Legal Theories: An Introduction to Sunni Ususl al-Fiqh* (Cambridge: Cambridge University Press, 2005).

Hanafi, Hasan, *Qaḍāyā Mu'āṣirah* (Beirut: Dar al-Tanwir, 1981).

Hanafi, Hasan, 'Method of Thematic Interpretation of the Qur'an', in Stefan Wild (ed.), *The Qur'an as Text* (Leiden: Brill, 1996), pp. 195–211.

Hanafi, Hasan, *Islam in the Modern World*, Vol. 2 (Cairo: Dar ul-Kebaa, 2000).

Heemskerk, Margaretha E., 'Speech', in Jane Dammen McAuliffe (ed.), *Encyclopedia of the Qur'ān*, Vol. 5 (Leiden: Brill, 2006), pp. 108–112.

Hick, John, *An Interpretation of Religion: human responses to the transcendent* (London: Macmillan Press, 1989).

Hick, John, 'Christianity among the Religions of the World', *Discernment NS* 1(3), 1994, 11–24.

Hidayatullah, Aysha, 'Inspiration and Struggle: Muslim Feminist Theology and the Work of Elizabeth Schussler Fiorenza', *Journal of Feminist Studies in Religion*, 25(1), 2009, 162–70.

Hirsch, E. D., *Validity in Interpretation* (New Haven: Yale University Press, 1967).

Hirschkind, Charles, 'Heresy or Hermeneutics: The Case of Naṣr Hāmid Abu Zayd', *American Journal of Islamic Social Sciences*, 12(4), 1995, 463–77.

Husayn, Taha, *Fi al-shi'r al-jahilī* [on Jahili poems] (Cairo: Al-Nahr lil-nashr wal-tawiz, 1996).

Hussain, Amir, 'Muslims, Pluralism, and Interfaith Dialogue', in Omid Safi (ed.), *Progressive Muslims on Justice, Gender and Pluralism* (Oxford: Oneworld, 2003), 251–69.

Ibn Khaldun, *The Muqaddimah: An Introduction to History*, trans. Franz Rosental, abridged and ed. N. J. Dawood (London: Routledge & Kegan Paul, 1987).

Ibn Sina, *Treatise on Psychology*, ed. Mahmud Shahabi (Tehran: Khayam, 1315 H.S.).

Ibn Sina, *Ṭabī'īāt-e Dāneshnāmeh 'Alāeī*, ed. Muhammad Meshkat (Tehran: Melli, 1331 H.S.).

Ibn Sina, 'On the Proof of Prophecies', in Ralph Lerner and Muhsin Mahdi (eds), *Medieval Political Philosophy: A Sourcebook* (New York: Cornell University Press, 1963), pp. 113–33.

Ibn Sina, *al-Mabda' va al-Ma'ād* [The Origin and The Return], ed. Abdullah Nurani (Tehran: Mutaleat-e Eslami, 1985).

Ibn Sina, 'On the Soul', in *Medieval Islamic Philosophical Writings*, trans. Muhammad Ali Khalidi (Cambridge: Cambridge University Press, 2005), pp. 27–58.

Iqbal, Muhammad, *The Reconstruction of Religious Thought in Islam* (Lahore: Ashraf Press, 1958).

Izutsu, Toshihiko, *God and Man in the Qur'an: Semantics of the Qur'anic Weltanschauung*, reprint edn (Kuala Lumpur: Islamic Book Trust, 2008).

Jahanbakhsh, Forough, 'Introduction: Abdolkarim Soroush's Neo-Rationalist Approach to Islam', in Abdolkarim Soroush, *The Expansion of Prophetic Experience: Essays on Historicity, Contingency and Plurality in Religion*, trans. Nilou Mobasser (Leiden: Brill, 2009), pp. xv–xlix.

Jahanshahrad, Houri, 'A Genuine Civil Society and Its Implications for the Iranian Women's Movement', *Women's History Review*, 21(2), 2012, 233–52.

Jakobson, Roman, 'Linguistics and Poetics', in Thomas Sebeok (ed.), *Style in Language* (Cambridge, MA: MIT Press, 1960), pp. 350–77.

James, William, *Varieties of Religious Experience* (New York: Collier Books, 1968).

Javadi Amoli, Abdullah, 'Ayatollah 'Allameh Javadi Amoli va Pluralism-e Dīnī' [Ayatollah 'Allameh Javadi Amoli and Religious Pluralism], *Ketab-e Naqd*, 4, 1997, pp. 352–3.

Kamrava, Mehran, *Iran's Intellectual Revolution* (Cambridge: Cambridge University Press, 2008).

Kassab, Elizabeth Suzanne, *Contemporary Arab Thought: Cultural Critique in Comparative Perspective* (New York: Columbia University Press, 2010).

Katz, Steven, 'Language, Epistemology and Mysticism', in Steven Katz (ed.), *Mysticism and Philosophical Analysis* (New York: Oxford University Press, 1978), pp. 22–74.

Kermani, Navid, 'From Revelation to Interpretation: Naṣr Hāmid Abu Zayd and the Literary Study of the Qur'an', in Suha Taji-Farouki (ed.), *Modern Muslim Intellectuals and the Qur'an* (Oxford: Oxford University Press, 2006), pp. 169–92.

Kersten, Carool, *Cosmopolitans and Heretics: New Muslim Intellectuals and the Study of Islam* (New York: Colombia University Press, 2011).

Khalidi, Tarif, *Images of Muhammad: Narratives of the Prophet in Islam across the Centuries* (New York: Crown Publishing Group, 2009).

Kurzman, Charles, 'Introduction: Liberal Islam and Its Islamic Context', in Charles Kurzman (ed.), *Liberal Islam: A Sourcebook* (Oxford: Oxford University Press, 1998), pp. 3–26.

Lahoud, Nelly, *Political Thought in Islam: A Study in Intellectual Boundaries* (New York: Taylor & Francis, 2005).

Leaman, Oliver, *A Brief Introduction to Islamic Philosophy* (Cambridge: Polity Press, 2007).

Leirvik, Oddbjørn, 'Waḥy and Tanzīl', *Studia Theologica*, 69(2), 2015, 101–25.

Lotman, Yuri, *The Structure of the Artistic Text*, trans. Gail Lenhoff and Ronald Vroon (Ann Arbor: University of Michigan Press, 1977).

Lowry, Joseph E., *Early Islamic Legal Theory: The Risāla of Muhammad ibn Idris al-Shāfiʿi* (Leiden: Brill, 2007).

Madaninejad, Banafsheh, 'New Theology in the Islamic Republic of Iran: A Comparative Study between Abdolkarim Soroush and Mohsen Kadivar', PhD thesis (Austin: The University of Texas at Austin, 2011).

Madigan, Daniel A., 'The Search for Islam's True Scholasticism', in Jose Ignacio Cabezon (ed.), *Scholasticism: Cross-Cultural and Comparative Perspectives* (New York: State University of New York Press, 1998), pp. 35–63.

Madigan, Daniel A., *The Qurʾan's Self-Image: Writing and Authority in Islam's Scripture* (Princeton: Princeton University Press, 2001).

Madigan, Daniel A., 'Book', *Encyclopedia of the Qurʾān*, Jane Dammen McAuliffe (ed.), Vol. 1 (Leiden: Brill, 2006), pp. 242–51.

Madigan, Daniel A., 'Revelation and Inspiration', *Encyclopedia of the Qurʾān*, Jane Dammen McAuliffe (ed.), Vol. 4 (Leiden: Brill, 2006), pp. 437–48.

Mahdi, Muhsin S., *al-Farabi and the Foundation of Islamic Political Philosophy* (Chicago: University of Chicago Press, 2001).

Managheb, Sayyed Mostafa and Abdullah Mehrabi, 'Philosophical hermeneutic and its interaction with principles of Qurʾān apprehension', *International Research Journal of Applied and Basic Sciences*, 7(4), 2013, 232–42.

Mansour, Iskandar, 'The Unpredictability of the Past: Turāth and Hermeneutics', PhD thesis (University of California Press, 2000).

Martin, Richard, Mark R. Woodward and Dwi S. Atmaja, *Defenders of Reason in Islam: Mutazilism from Medieval School to Modern Symbol* (Oxford: Oneworld, 1997).

Mayer, Ann Elizabeth, *Islam and Human Rights* (Boulder: Westview Press, 2013).

McGrath, Alister, *Historical Theology: An Introduction to the History of Christian Thought* (Oxford: Blackwell, 1998).

Mernissi, Fatima, *Islam and Democracy: Fear of the Modern World* (Reading, MA: Addison-Wesley Publishing, 1992).

Miraj, Muhammad, 'Shah Wali Allah's Concept of the Shariʿa', in Khurshid Ahmad and Zafar Ishaq Ansari (eds), *Islamic Perspectives: Studies in Honour of Mawlana Sayyid Abul Ala Mawdudi* (London: Saudi Publishing House, 1979), pp. 343–58.

Mir-Hosseini, Ziba, *Islam and Gender: The Religious Debate in Contemporary Iran* (Princeton: Princeton University Press, 1999).

Moosa, Ebrahim, 'Introduction', in Fazlur Rahman, *Revival and Reform in Islam: A Study of Islamic Fundamentalism* (Oxford: Oneworld, 2000), pp. 1–29.

Moosa, Ebrahim, 'The Debts and Burdens of Critical Islam', in Omid Safi (ed.), *Progressive Muslims on Justice, Gender and Pluralism* (Oxford: Oneworld, 2003), pp. 111–27.

Moosa, Ebrahim, 'The Human Person in Iqbal's Thought', in H. C. Hillier and Basit Bilal Koshul (eds), *Muhammad Iqbal: Essays on the Reconstruction of Modern Muslim Thought* (Edinburgh: Edinburgh University Press, 2015), pp. 12–32.

Mulla Sadra, *Asfār* [The Journeys], Vol. 3, ed. R. Lutfi et al. (Tehran and Qum: Shirkat Dar al-Ma'arif al-Islamiyyah, 1958–69).

Mulla Sadra, *Tafsīr al-Qur'ān al-Karīm* [The Interpretation of the Qur'ān], Vol. 1 (Qum, 1966).

Mulla Sadra, *al-Mabda' va al-Ma'ād* [The Origin and The Return], ed. Jalal al-din Ashtiyani and Seyyed Hossein Nasr (Tehran: Hikmat va Falsafeh, 1976).

Nahidi, Shahram, 'Toward a New Qur'ānic Hermeneutics Based on Historio-Critical and Inter-textual Approaches: The Case of the Crucifixion of Jesus in the Tafasir of Eight Muslim Exegetes', PhD thesis (Montreal: Montreal University, 2013).

Natour, Manalal, 'The Role of Women in the Egyptian Revolution of 25 January 2011', in Muhammad S. Olimat (ed.), *Arab Spring and Arab Women: Challenges and Opportunities* (New York: Routledge, 2014), pp. 70–85.

Nettler, Ronald L., *Past Trials and Present Tribulations: A Muslim Fundamentalist's View of the Jews* (Oxford: Pergamon Press, 1987).

Ohlander, Erik, 'Modern Qur'anic Hermeneutics', *Religion Compass*, 3(4), 2009, 620–39.

Okumus, Mesut, 'The Influence of Ibn Sīnā on al-Ghazzālī in Qur'anic Hermeneutics', *Muslim World*, 102(2), 2012, 390–411.

Ormiston, Gayle L. and Alan D. Schrift, *The Hermeneutic Tradition: From Ast to Ricoeur* (Albany: State University of New York Press, 1990).

Ormsby, Eric, 'Poor Man's Prophecy: al-Ghazali on Dreams', in Louise Marlow (ed.), *Dreaming across Boundaries: The Interpretation of Dreams Islamic Lands* (Cambridge, MA: Harvard University Press, 2008), pp. 142–52.

Panikkar, Raimon, 'The Crosscultural Dialogue', in Joseph Prabhu (ed.), *The Crosscultural Challenge of Raimon Panikkar* (New York: Orbis Books, 1996), pp. 243–71.

Peters, J. R. T. M., *God's Created Speech: A Study in the Speculative Theology of the Mu'tazili Qadi l-Qudat Abu l-Hasan Abd al-Jabbar bn Ahmad al-Hamadani* (Leiden: Brill, 1976).

Pink, Johanna, 'Striving for a new Exegesis of the Qur'ān', in Sabine Schmidtke (ed.), *The Oxford Handbook of Islamic Theology* (Oxford: Oxford University Press, 2016), pp. 765–92.

Plantinga, Alvin and Nicholas Wolterstorff, *Faith and Rationality: Reason and Belief in God* (Notre Dame: University of Notre Dame Press, 1983).

Proudfoot, Wayne, *Religious Experience* (Berkeley: University of California Press, 1985).

Qadir, C. A., *Philosophy and Science in the Islamic World* (London: Routledge, 1990).

Rahman, Yusuf, 'The Hermeneutical Theory of Nasr Hamid Abu Zayd: An Analytical Study of His Method of Interpreting the Qur'an', PhD thesis (McGill University, 2001).

Rahman, Yusuf, 'The Qur'ān in Egypt: Naṣr Abū Zayd's Literary Approach', in Khaleel Mohammed, Andrew Rippin and North Haledon (eds), *Coming to Terms with the Qur'an: A Volume in Honor of Professor Issa Boullata* (North Haledon: Islamic Publications International, 2010), pp. 227–65.

Rajaee, Farhang, *Islamism and modernism: The changing discourse in Iran* (Austin: University of Texas Press, 2007).

Riis, Ole, 'Modes of Religious Pluralism under Conditions of Globalization', *International Journal of Multicultural Societies*, 1(1), 1999, 20–34.

Rodinson, Maxime, *Muhammad*, trans. Anne Carter (New York: The Penguin Press, 1980).

Sachedina, Abdulaziz, *The Islamic Roots of Democratic Pluralism* (Oxford: Oxford University Press, 2001).

Sadri, Ahmad, 'The Iran Situation', interviewed by Foaad Khosmood, www.zmag.org.

Sadri, Mahmoud, 'Sacral defense of secularism: The political theologies of Soroush, Shabestari and Kadivar', *International Journal of Politics, Culture and Society*, 15(2), 2001, 257–70.

Saeed, Abdullah, 'Qur'ān: Tradition of Scholarship and Interpretation', in Lindsay Jones and Charles J. Adams (eds), *Encyclopedia of Religion*, Vol. 11 (Detroit: Macmillan, 2005), pp.7561–70.

Saeed, Abdullah, 'Fazlur Rahman: a Framework for Interpreting the Ethico-legal Content of the Qur'an', in Suha Taji-Farouki (ed.), *Modern Muslim Intellectuals and the Qur'an* (Oxford: Oxford University Press, 2006), pp. 37–66.

Saeed, Abdullah, *Interpreting the Qur'an: Towards a Contemporary Approach* (New York: Routledge, 2006).

Saeed, Abdullah, 'Some Reflections on the Contextualist Approach to ethico-legal texts of the Qur'ān', *Bulletin of School of Oriental and African Studies*, 71(2), 2008, 221 37.

Saeed, Abdullah, 'Reading the Qur'ān', in Amyn B. Sajoo (ed.), *A Companion to the Muslim World* (London: I. B. Tauris, 2009), pp. 55–85.

Saeed, Abdullah, *Reading the Qur'an in the Twenty-First Century: A Contextualist Approach* (New York: Routledge, 2014).

Safi, Omid, 'Between Ijtihad of the Presupposition and Gender Equality: Cross-Pollination between Progressive Islam and Iranian Reform', in Carl W. Ernst and Richard Martin (eds), *Rethinking Islamic Studies: From Orientalism to Cosmopolitanism* (Columbia: The University of South Carolina Press, 2010), pp. 72–96.

Said, A. A. and M. S. Funk, 'Dynamism of Cultural Diversity and Tolerance in Islam', in A. A. Said and M. S. Funk (eds), *Cultural Diversity and Islam* (Lanham: University Press of America, 2003), pp. 17–29.

Schleiermacher, Friedrich D. E., *Hermeneutics: The Hand-written Manuscripts*, trans. James Duke and Jack Forstman (Atlanta: Scholars Press, 1986).

Schwerin, Ulrich Von, *The Dissident Mullah: Ayatollah Montazeri and the Struggle for Reform in Revolutionary Iran* (London: I. B. Tauris, 2015).

Sharf, Robert H., 'Experience', in M. C. Taylor (ed.), *Critical Terms for Religious Studies* (Chicago: University of Chicago Press, 1998), pp. 94–116.

Sharif, Muhammad Miyan, *A History of Muslim Philosophy with Short Accounts of Other Disciplines and the Modern Renaissance in Muslim Lands* (Harrassowitz: Pakistan Philosophical Congress, 1961).

Shirazi, Sam, 'Pineapples in Paradise: Why Islam Does not Necessarily Support Human Rights and Why That Is a Good Thing', *Religion and Human Rights*, 10(1), 2015, 24–44.

Sid, Muhammad Ata, 'The Hermeneutical Problem of the Qur'ān in Islamic History', PhD thesis (Temple University, 1975).

Sirry, Munim, *Scriptural Polemics: The Qur'ān and Other Religions* (Oxford: Oxford University Press, 2014).

Smart, Ninian, *The Religious Experience of Mankind* (New York: Charles Scribner's Sons, 1969).

Smith, Jonathan Z., 'Religion, Religions, Religious', in Mark C. Taylor, *Critical Terms for Religious Studies* (Chicago: University of Chicago Press, 1998), pp. 269–84.

Smith, Wilfred Cantwell, *Islam in Modern History* (New York: Princeton University Press, 1959).

Soage, Ana Belen, 'Shūra and Democracy: Two Sides of the Same Coin?', *Religion Compass*, 8(3), 2014, 90–103.

Soltani, Ebrahim, 'Dīnshenāsī-e Abdolkarim Soroush' [Abdulkarim Soroush's Approach to Religious Studies], *Aftab*, l, 2000, 50–9.

Sonn, Tamara, 'Fazlur Rahman's Islamic Methodology', *The Muslim World*, 81(3–4), 1991, 212–30.

Sonn, Tamara, 'Fazlur Rahman and Islamic Feminism', in Earle H. Waugh and Frederick M. Denny (eds), *The Shaping of An American Islamic Discourse: A Memorial to Fazlur Rahman* (Atlanta: Scholars Press for the University of South Florida, 1998), pp. 123–45.

Stenger, Mary Ann, 'Faith and Religion', in Russell Re Manning (ed.), *Cambridge Companion to Paul Tillich* (Cambridge: Cambridge University Press, 2009), pp. 91–104.

Sukidi, 'Naṣr Hāmid Abū Zayd and the Quest for a Humanistic Hermeneutics of the Qur'ān', *Die Welt des Islams*, 49(2), 2009, 181–211.

Sviri, Sara, 'Dreaming Analysed and Recorded', in David Shulman and Guy G. Stroumsa (eds), *Dream Culture* (London: Routledge, 1999), pp. 252–73.

Tavassoli, Sasan, *Christian Encounters with Iran* (London: I. B. Tauris, 2011).

Troll, Christian W., *Sayyid Aḥmad Khān: A reinterpretation of Muslim Theology* (New Delhi: Vikas Publishing House, 1978).

Vahdat, Farzin, 'Post-Revolutionary Islamic Discourses on Modernity in Iran: Expansion and Contraction of Human Subjectivity', *International Journal of Middle East Studies*, 35(4), 2003, 599–631.

Vakili, Valla, 'Abdolkarim Soroush and Critical Discourse in Iran', in John Esposito (ed.), *Makers of Contemporary Islam* (Oxford: Oxford University Press, 2001), pp. 150–76.

Vishanoff, David R., *The Formation of Islamic Hermeneutics: How Sunni Legal Theories Imagined a Revealed Law* (New Haven: American Oriental Society, 2011).

Völker, Katharina, 'Qur'an and Reform: Rahman, Arkoun, Abu Zayd', PhD thesis (University of Otago, 2011).

Völker, Katharina, 'Two Accounts of Qur'anic Revelation', *Islam and Christian–Muslim Relations*, 26(3), 2015, 271–86.

Wahyudi, Yudian, 'Hasan Hanafi on Salafism and Secularism', in Ibrahim M. Abu-Rabi (ed.), *Blackwell Companion to Contemporary Islamic Thought* (Oxford: Blackwell, 2006), pp. 257–70.

Walbridge, John, *God and Logic in Islam: The Caliphate of Reason* (Cambridge: Cambridge University Press, 2011).

Wali Allah, Shah, *Al-Khayr al-Kathir* [the Great Benefit] (Akora Khatak, 1959).

Wali Allah, Shah, *Sufism and the Islamic Tradition: The Lamahat and Sataat of Shah Waliullah*, trans. G. N. Jalbani and D. B. Fry (London: The Octagon Press, 1980).

Wansbrough, John, *Qur'anic Studies: Sources and Methods of Scriptural Interpretation* (New York: Prometheus Books, 2004).

Ward, Graham, 'In the Daylight Forever? Language and Silence', in Oliver Davies and Denys Turner (eds), *Silence and the Word* (Cambridge: Cambridge University Press, 2002), pp. 159–84.

Watt, William Montgomery, *Muhammad at Mecca* (Oxford: Oxford University Press, 1953).

Watt, William Montgomery, *Islamic Revelation in the Modern World* (Edinburgh: Edinburgh University Press, 1969).

Watt, William Montgomery and Richard Bell, *Introduction to the Qur'an* (Edinburgh: Edinburgh University Press, 1970).

Watt, William Montgomery, *Islam and Christianity Today: A Contribution to Dialogue* (London: Routledge, 1983).

Waugh, Earle H., 'The Legacies of Fazlur Rahman for Islam in America', *The American Journal of Islamic Social Sciences*, 16(3), 1999, 27–44.

Webb, Gisela, 'Gabriel', in Jane Dammen McAuliffe (ed.), *Encyclopedia of the Qur'ān*, Vol. 2 (Washington: Georgetown University, 2005), pp. 278–80.

Wensinck, A. J., *Muslim Creed* (Cambridge: Cambridge University Press, 1932).

Wensinck, A. J. and Andrew Rippin, 'Waḥy', in Paul Bearman, et al. (eds), *Encyclopædia of Islam*, 2nd edn, Vol. 11 (Leiden: Brill, 2002), pp. 53–6.

Wild, Stefan, 'We have Sent Down to Thee the Book with the Truth: spatial and temporal implications of the Qur'ānic concepts of nuzul, tanzīl and inzal', in Stefan Wild (ed.), *The Qur'an as Text* (Leiden: Brill, 1996), pp. 137–53.

Wolfson, Harry Austryn, *The Philosophy of Kalam* (Cambridge, MA: Harvard University Press, 1976).

Zarkashi, Muhammad Ibn Bahadur, *al-Burhān fī 'Ulūm al-Qur'ān* [the Proof in the Sciences of the Qur'ān] (Beirut: Dar al- M'arifah, 1957).

Index